Fading From Memory: Abandoned Buildings and Spaces in Britain and Ireland

Tim Sandle

ISBN: 9798852537379

DEDICATION

This book is dedicated to by Mother for teaching me the value of the understanding past, whatever the context.

CONTENTS

FOREWORD

Why photograph abandoned buildings and their associated spaces? Simply, if these places and spaces are not captured need to be captured then, one day, they are simply gone. Faded from memory.

With these urban landscapes and buildings there's a keenness on my part to preserve aspects of the past. These are places in varying states of decay; some symbolize happiness, others sadness; some are haunting, others are hopeful. Some look beautiful; others are less pleasing to the eye, yet all of them trigger an emotive response. What was the building used for? Who lived or worked there? (or, in more than one case, incarcerated) Could such a building be erected today?

Should these buildings be preserved? This isn't for me to say. Not everything from the past can be kept. Some of the buildings are dangerous, structurally or relating to the materials used in a less safety conscious time. Some will be converted into more aesthetically pleasing and functional structures while preserving aspects of their former glories. Others will be knocked down and the land redeveloped. Some may still be standing fifty years from now.

The buildings have different forms and relate to different circumstances. Some are near to where I live, others are further afield. I've attempted to capture different features with each image. There's also some commentary. You can read this if you like.

The images were taken over a ten year period (2012 to 2022). I didn't set out to create a book, but having amassed many images, it just happened.

Were there any criteria for selection? No really. It had to be a building or a space close to a building that perhaps had some connection with a building (a bit of a loose definition, but it's my book). I have restricted the selection to Britain and Ireland. If there's a follow-up, the geographical reach might be expanded.

Can the buildings be visited? Most are generally accessible. Some are clearly visible, others are hidden, requiring a meander. Even those that are visible can often be hurried past. Although some, like castle ruins, will be purposefully visited. Most you probably wouldn't want to go and see anyway. Enjoy the pictures instead.

Why use black and white? A personal preference for monochrome. I like variations of light and dark. I like the aspects that can be seen under conditions of better contrast. Perhaps it is also befitting of the abandoned nature of the buildings and their surrounds.

I also think black and white images affect the mood and can conjure different emotions. Mood influences perspective, as do the patterns of shadow and light. I'm also of the view that texture is more apparent, sometimes. Certainly shapes are, especially contours.

Is black and white sufficiently realistic? We see in color; hence black and white images are not 'reality' yet they show different aspects of our reality. These are different forms of expression.

That's enough questions.

Tim Sandle
St Albans, UK

1 **ASYLUM**

During the 20th Century the U.K. had far more psychiatric institutions for holding its subjects than it does today. More enlightened approaches to 'mental illness' have led to alternative care options. In Hertfordshire, three hospitals were situated in close proximity to each other: Middlesex County Asylum, Harperbury Hospital and Shenley Hospital. The Middlesex County Asylum was later renamed Napsbury Hospital and it was located in London Colney (or 'near London Colney' as many of the current residents of the area are wont to describe it).

In 1988 the Thatcher government reduced the scope of National Health Service (NHS) care with the transfer of responsibility for the long term care of the mentally ill to local authorities. This led to the closure and sell off of the large mental hospitals, along with their often spacious grounds, as mental patients were transferred to 'care in the community'. This succeeded in creating many more societal problems than it solved.

The big Hertfordshire sites were redeveloped as housing estates, and in the case of Napsbury, an estate of expensive housing and apartments. It is now called Napsbury Park.

The transition process was, however, relatively slow and I had the opportunity to 'visit' the main hospital building before it was demolished in 2014. The asylum was designed by Rowland Plumbe in 1900 to serve the county of Middlesex, and the four images here were from the main hospital building before it was demolished.

The four images I've taken capture the hospital in different perspectives and there are some interesting variations of light.

Image 1 looks like the scene from a horror movie or macabre video game. Will something emerge from the shadows? *Image 2* captures the contrast of the darkness inside the building, and the piles of rubble, and the afternoon glow of the summer sun.

Image 3 makes me think of a resident desperate to escape ,although it is more likely teenagers using the building for smoking and drinking sprayed the message, in red paint, onto the white wall. Whatever the origin, the message is perhaps a suitable symbolic indictment on the mental health policy of the twentieth century.

The final image (*image 4*) has some interesting light and dark effects. However, the focal point is the door. Would you venture through it?

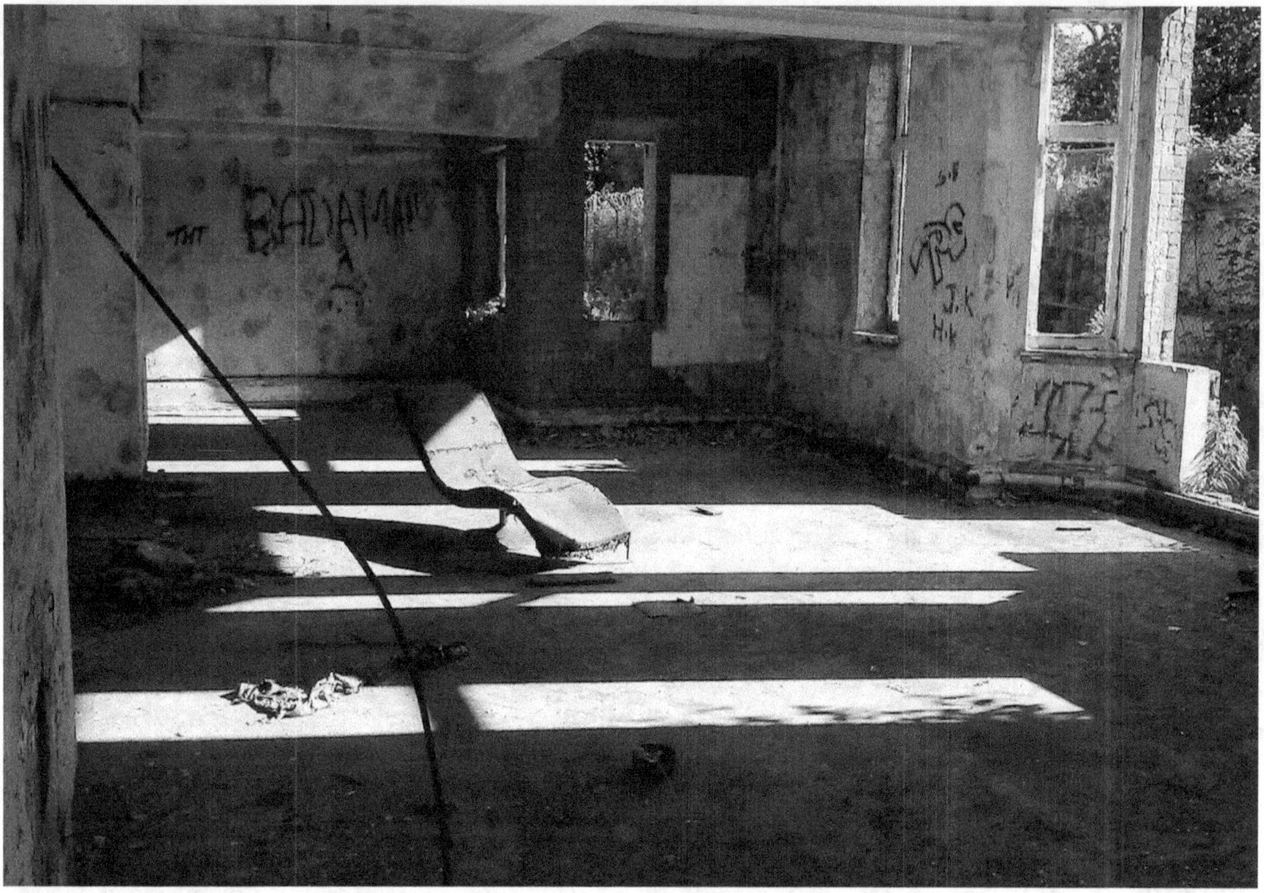

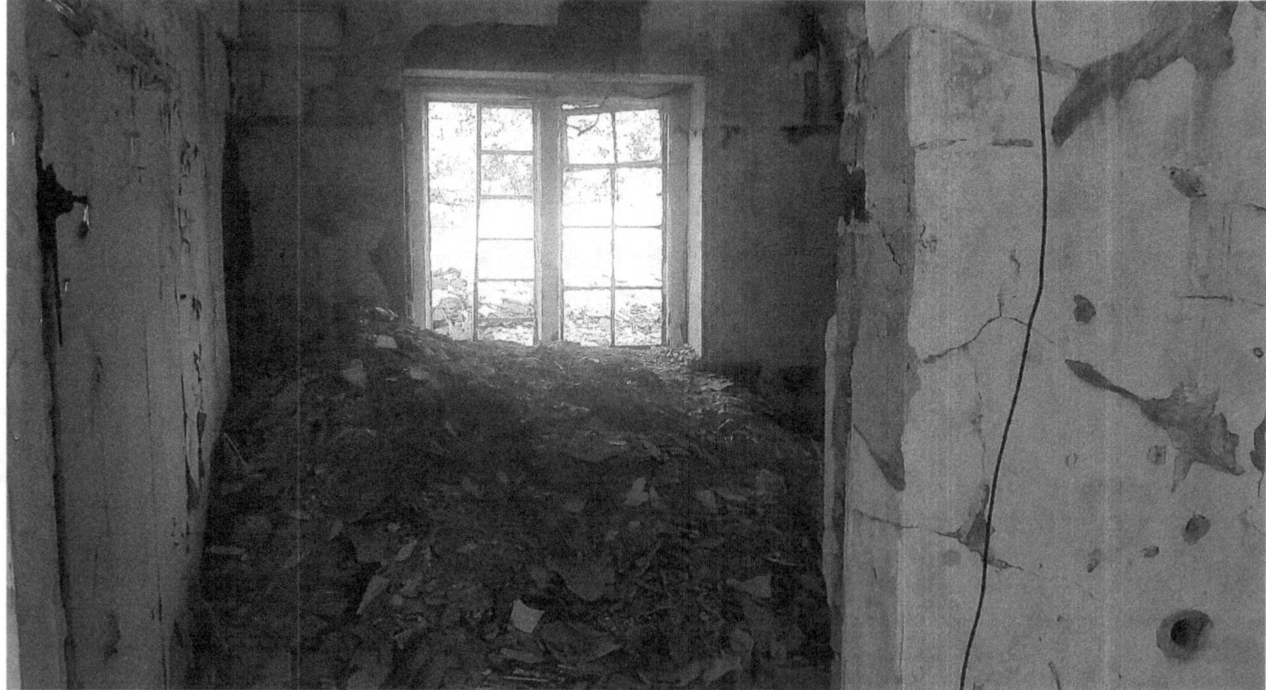

Image 1:   Inside the abandoned hospital on a summer's afternoon

Image 2: Dark and light

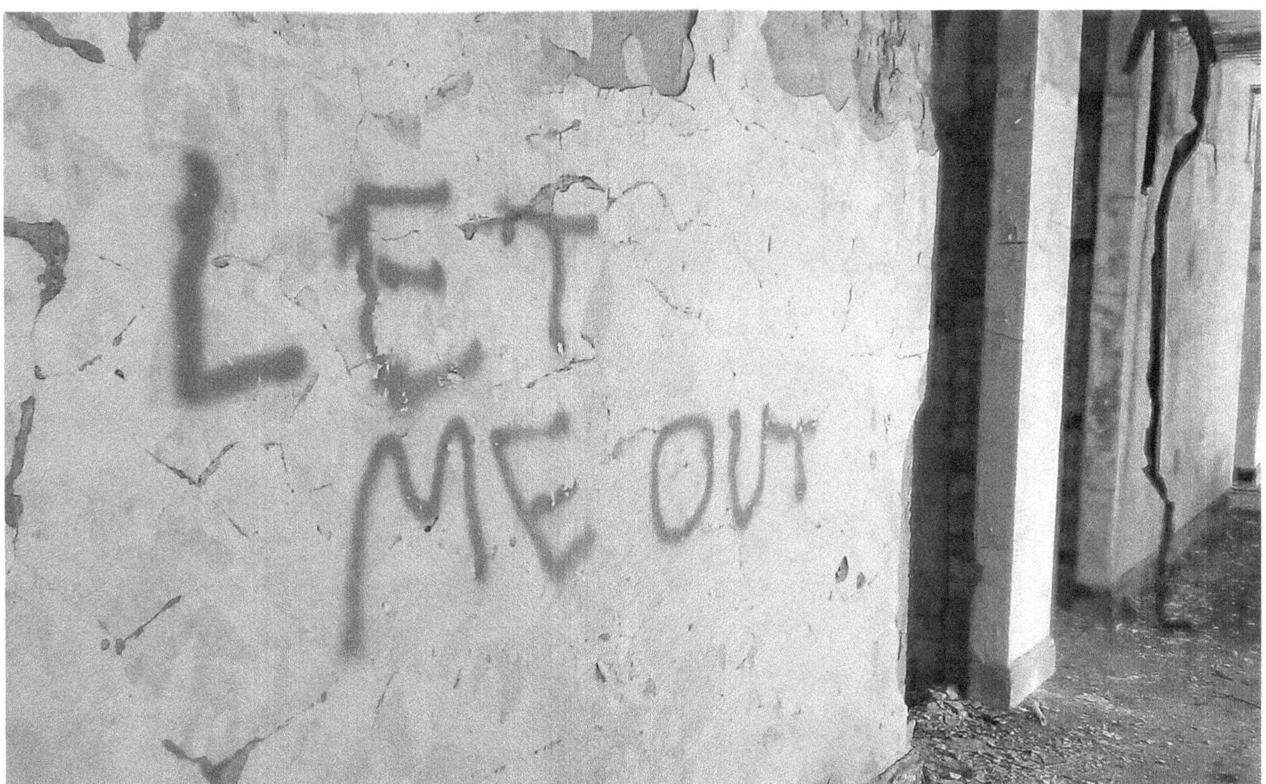

Image 3: Why leave?

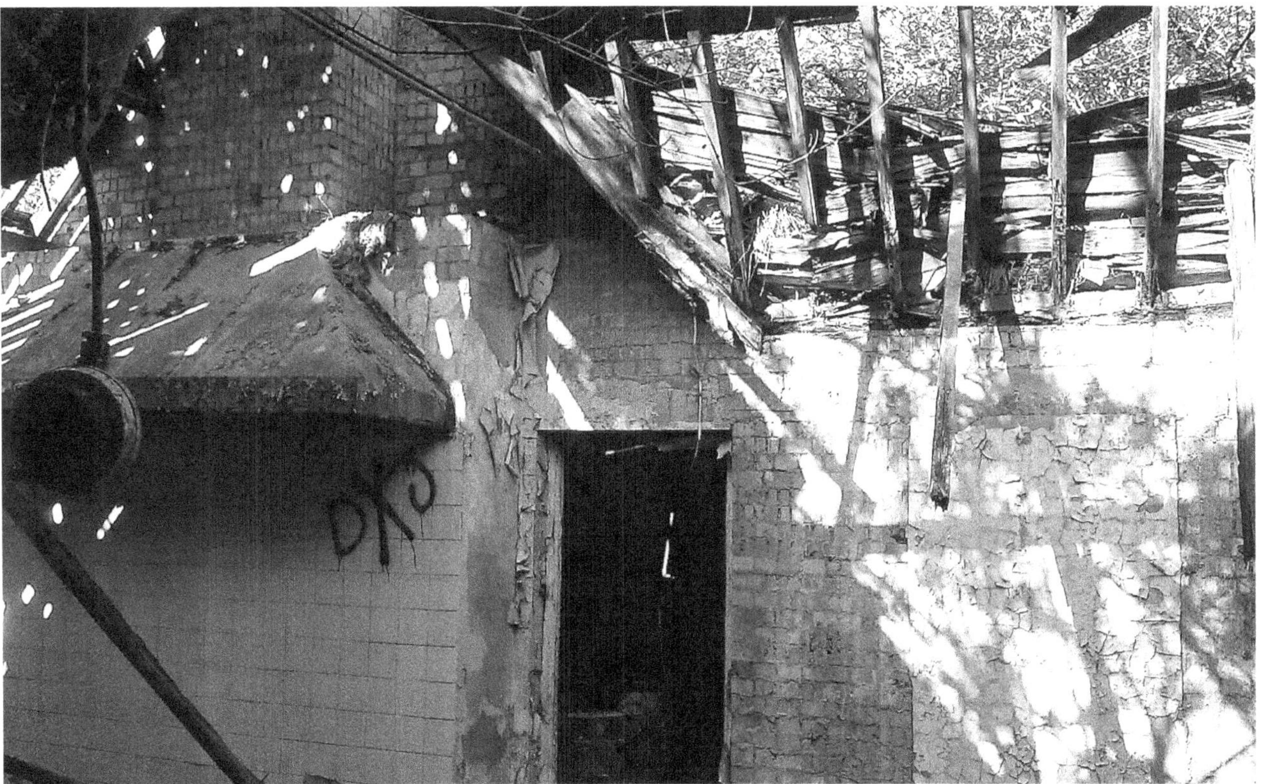

Image 4: Someone's at the door

Originally the site was dedicated to agricultural use - Napsbury Manor Farm . I think *image 4* partly captures this, providing a touch of a 'farmhouse' feel although it is an image of inside a derelict hospital (as the tiling indicates).

The grounds of the hospital were designed by William Goldring and included a fernery. Among the splendor of today's luxury buildings, the grounds retain much of their old charm (the grounds were designated by English Heritage as a Grade II historic park in 2001). Sadly, none of the original hospital buildings were retained.

<h1 style="text-align:center">2 LISTER</h1>

The Lister Institute of Preventative Medicine was founded in 1893 as the British Institute and then the Jenner Institute before adopting the name of its main benefactor, Lord Lister – the father of antiseptic surgery. The Institute had bases in Chelsea, London, and Aldenham in Hertfordshire (which became the Elstree Laboratories). Today the Elstree laboratories are home to Bio Products Laboratory (BPL) , an organization that grew out of Lister.

The Elstree laboratories were originally the site of a farm – Queensbury Lodge Farm – and many of the farm buildings were either re-supposed as laboratories or they continued to be used to house animals, since the early work of the Institute involved developing sera grown in sheep, horses and cows.

Some of the original buildings remain, although many are being knocked down or they are falling into disrepair. Access to the site is limited, so these images provide a rare opportunity to capture a largely forgotten aspect of British scientific excellence.

Image 5 depicts Queensbury Lodge, the original farmhouse which became a working laboratory for plague research before its final years were reserved as an administrative building. Closed in 2017, the building is slowly crumbling. It should be listed, but it isn't; it should be preserved, and maybe it will. The image was taken on a particularly sunny day, with the sun at full burst, in June 2023 using a wide-angle shot. The front of building is surrounded by fencing, but rules are there to be broken.

Images 6 and *7* are taken inside the abandoned Queensbury Lodge. Here there is a cellar, used for housing records. The cellar has flooded a few times. It reminds me of a war room, from the Second World War, where secret files were kept and battle plans drawn up by generals. In reality, the cellar house personnel files.

With the shot of the stairs, I like the sense of foreboding and the dangerous looking electrical boxes. Would you go down? Down in the cellar, I've used a softer lighting. I like the reflective tones.

Image 9 is of a brick-encased building, probably once used for electrical supply to the farmhouse. It looks isolated.

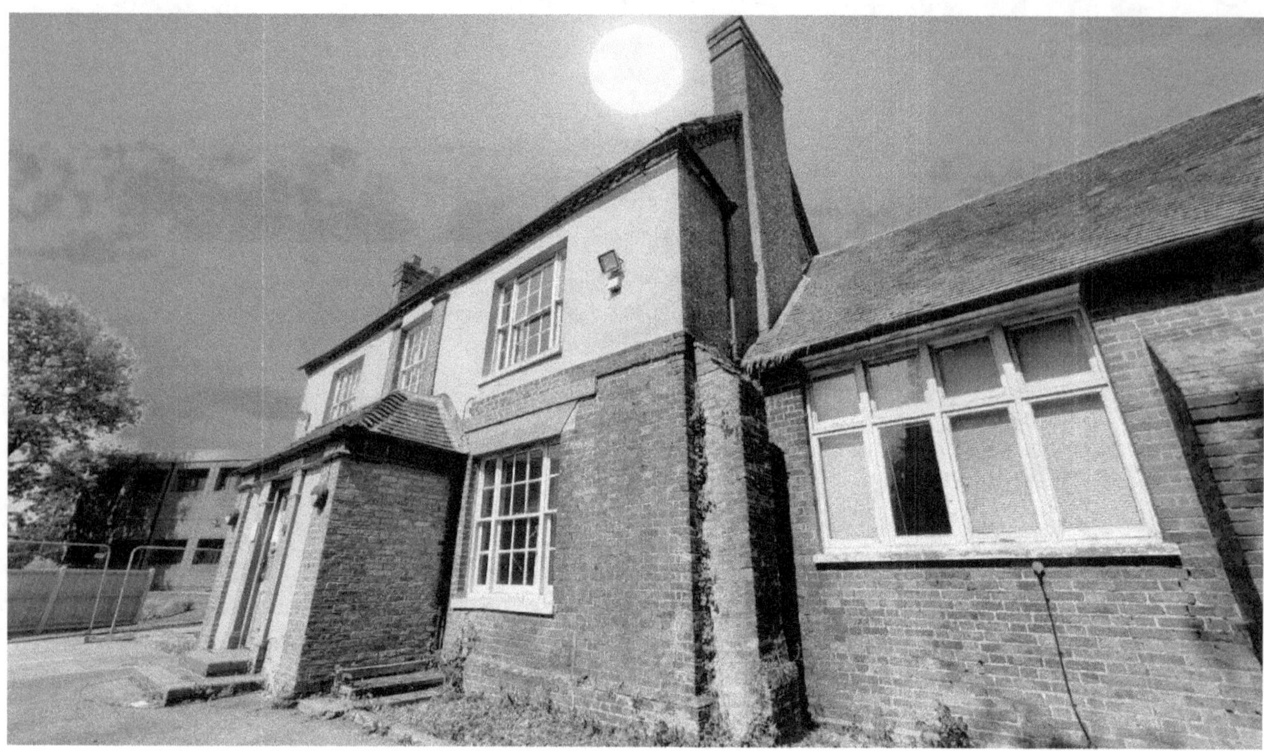

Image 5: Queensbury Lodge

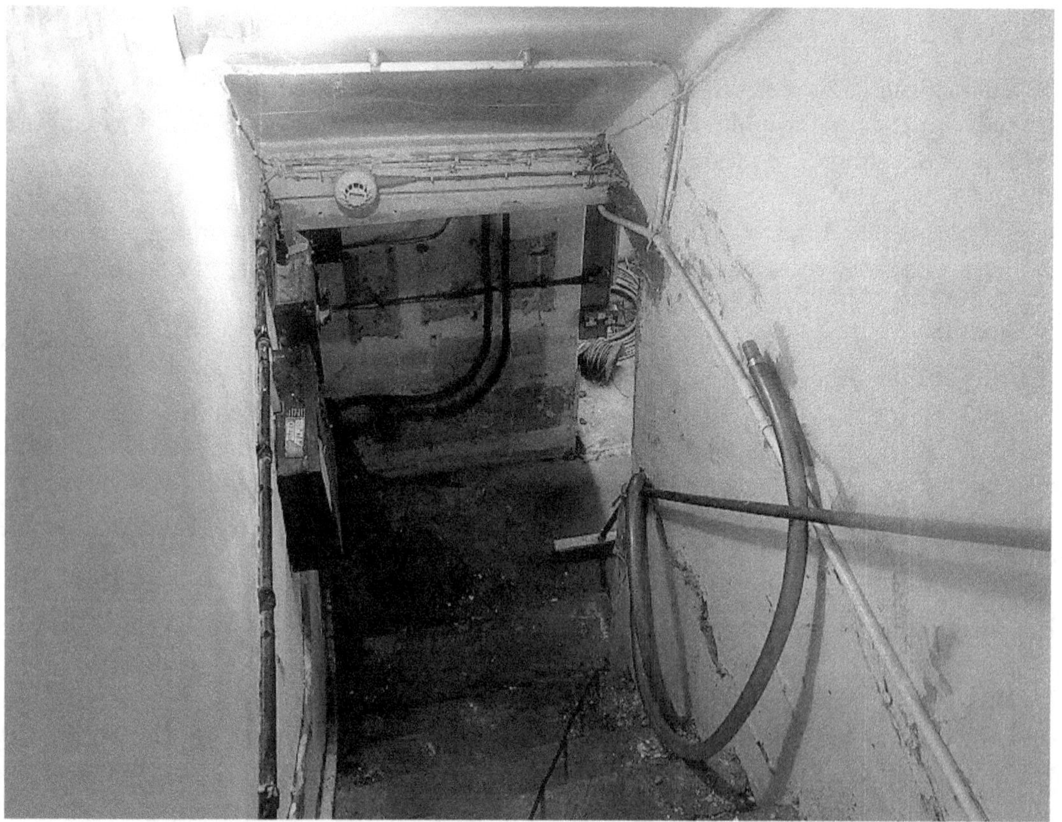

Image 6: Down the stairs we go

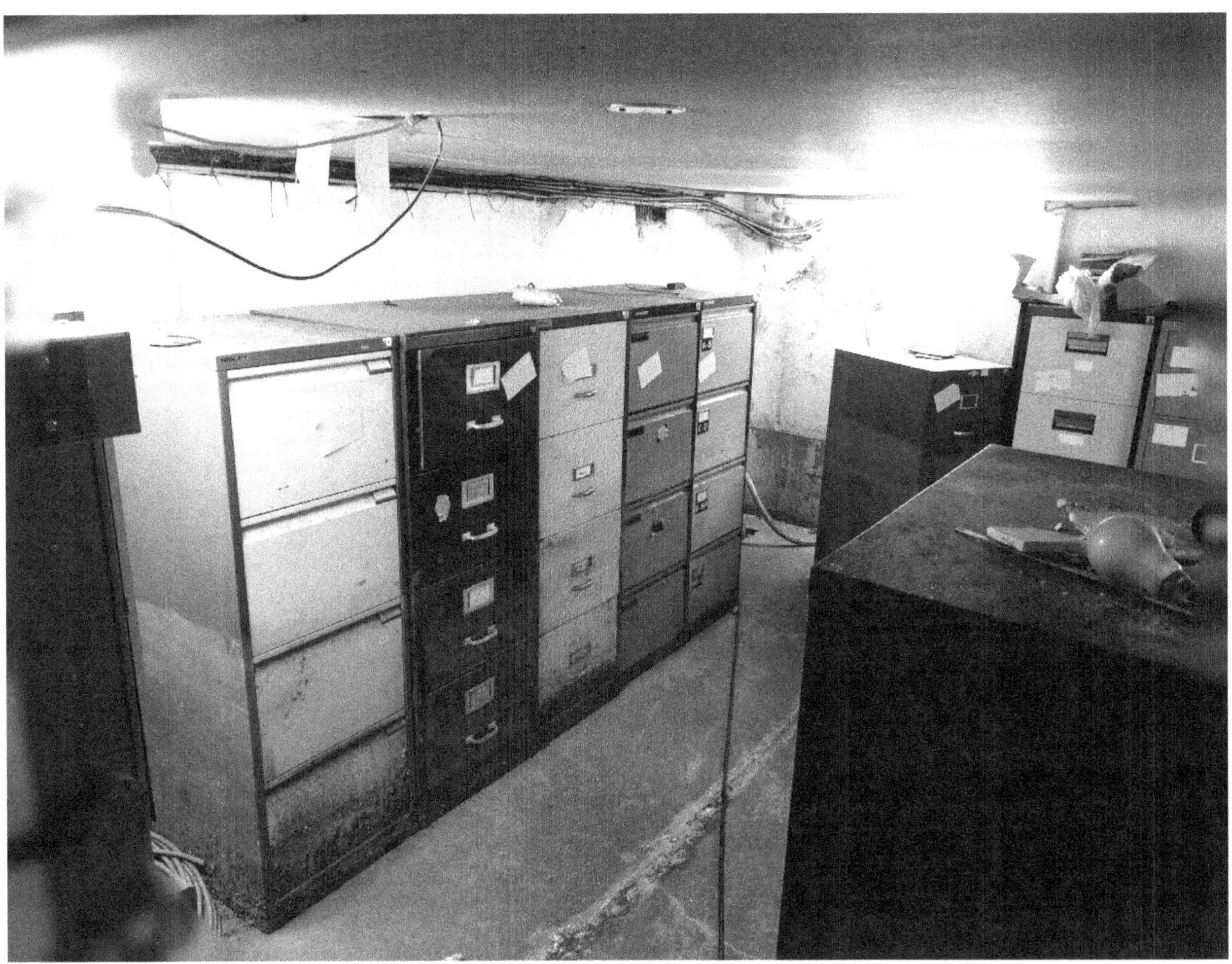

Image 7: Dank cellar

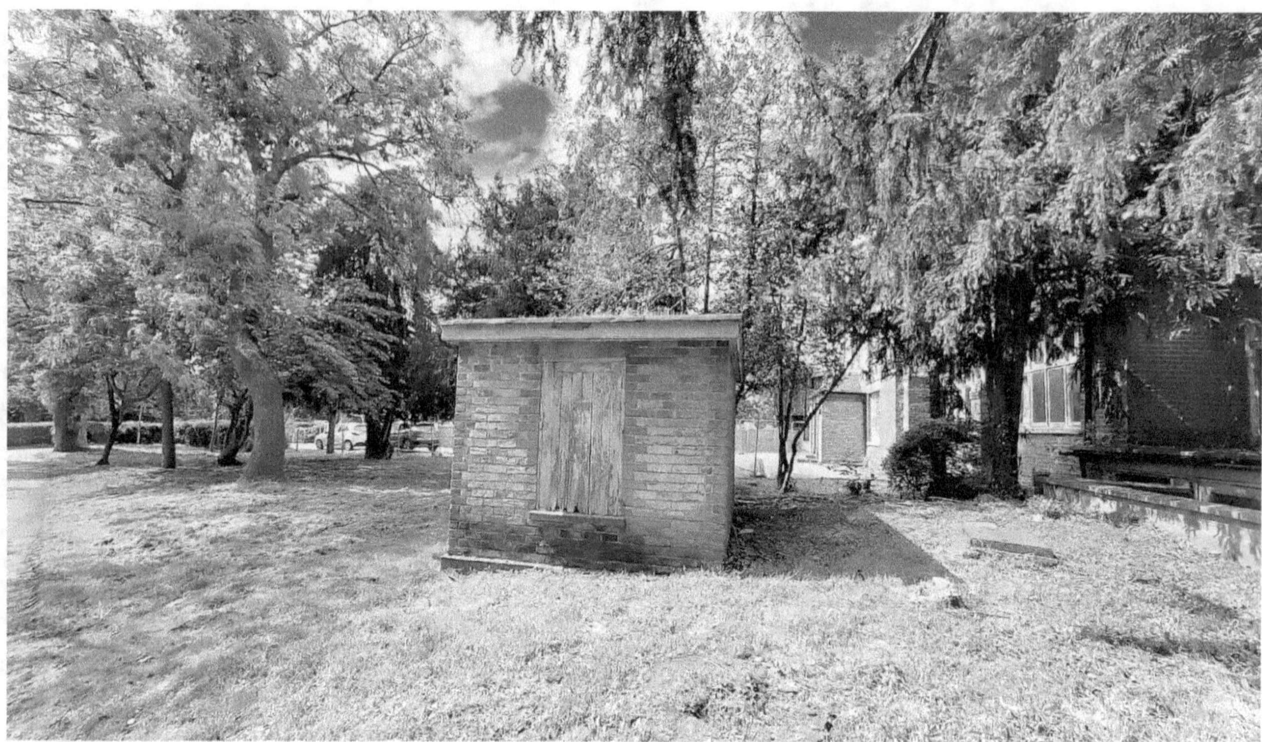

Image 9: Knock-knock

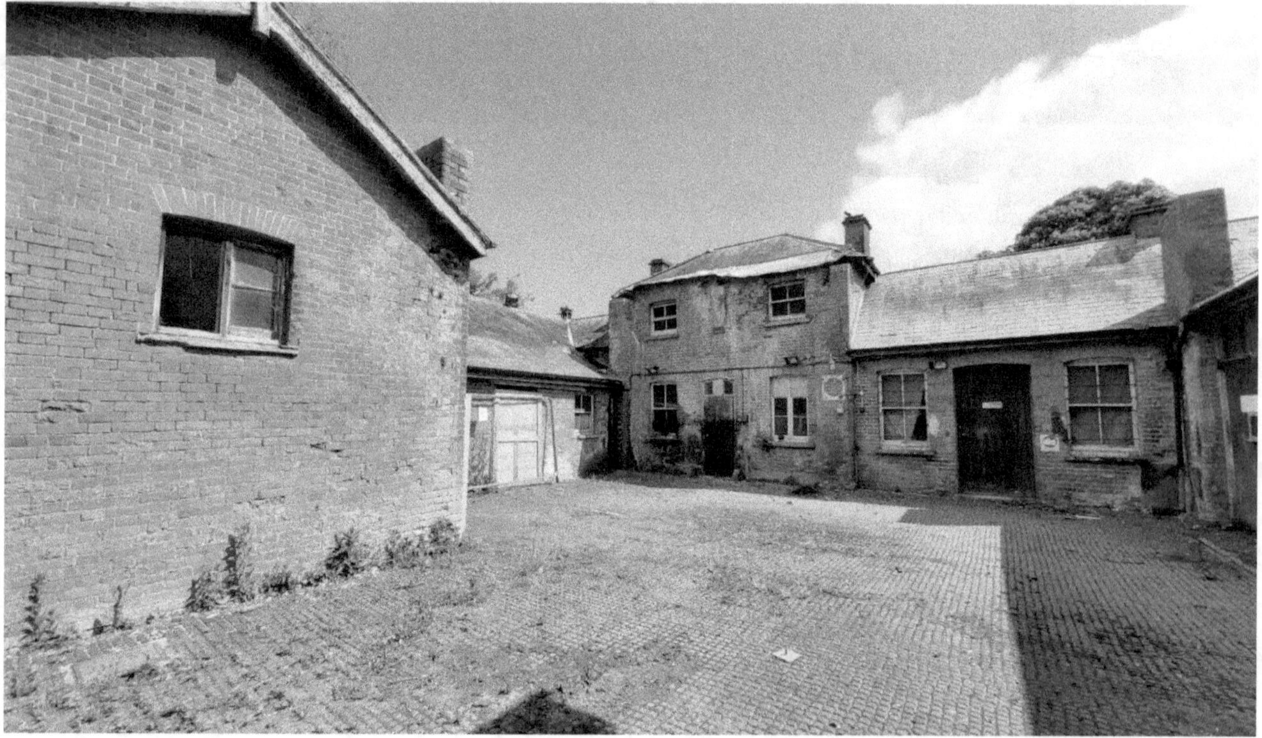

Image 10: Stable stables

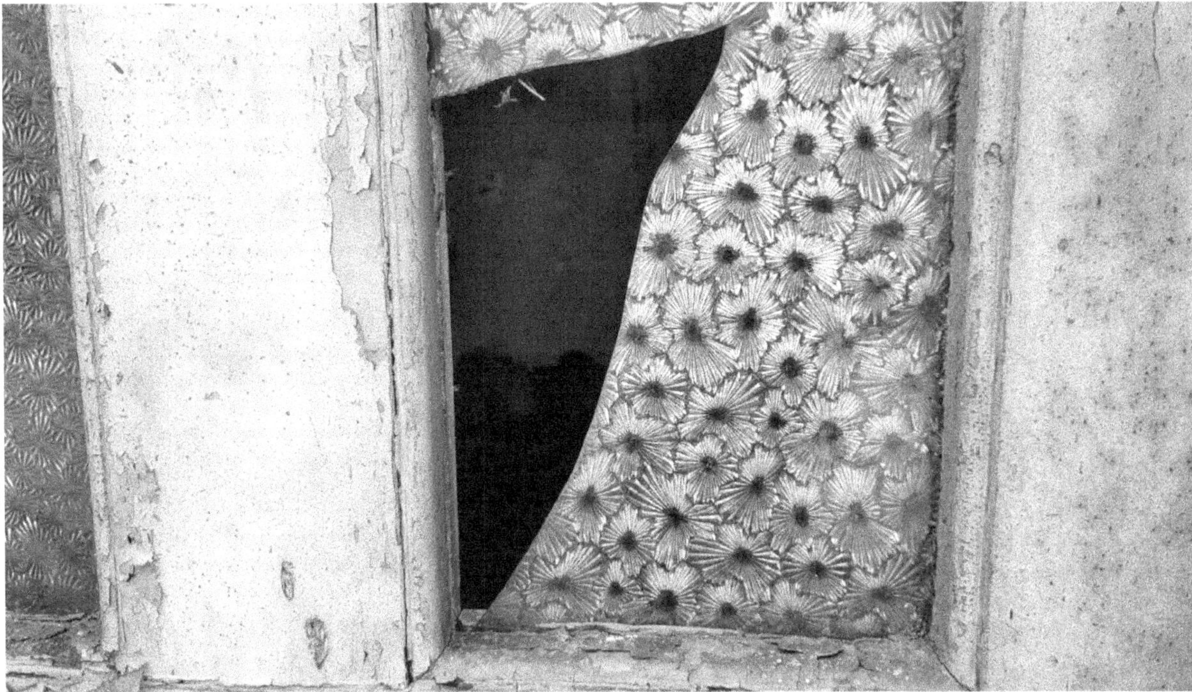

Image 11: Sound of breaking glass

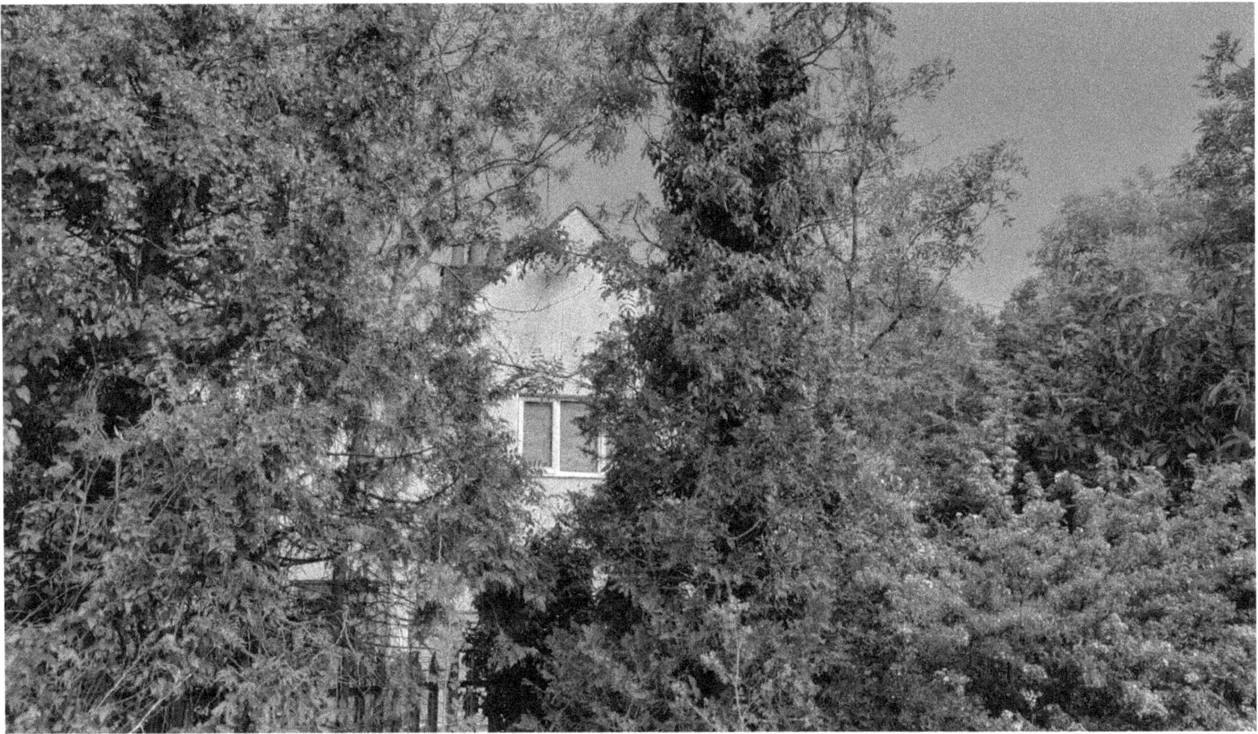

Image 12: Someone lived here once

Image 10 shows the stable block, where the farm animals were kept on the working farm and subsequently for the Lister Institute research. On passing to BPL it became a site services facility for many years. Today most of it is derelict. Yet it remains an attractive looking Victorian (mostly) brick structure, functional yet also aesthetically pleasing to the eye. A place once a center of activity, now mostly untouched.

The recently untouched nature of the stables is reflected in *Image 11*. This picture is simply a broken window on part of the front to one of the rooms that forms the old stables. I like the way the glass is patterned and how the person who installed it had some eye for detail. The flower-lie patterns on the glass contrast to the concrete surrounds. It seems appropriate that the concrete is darker and the glass lighter, which was another advantage of taking these pictures during the summer.

Image 12 is of the Lister Cottages. These were built to house medical workers and students, given the rural location. The first four cottages were built in 1914 and today they could be turned into attractive period cottages. Instead, they are boarded up and set to be demolished. Rather than photograph the cottage directly, I wanted to capture the idea of peeking through the tall trees that have grown up around the house. The eye of the interloper.

3 RUINS

Berkhamsted Castle is a Norman motte-and-bailey castle. The remains are located in the leafy, sleepy town of Berkhamsted, Hertfordshire. The site is maintained by English Heritage, free to enter and to clamber around. I had the opportunity to visit the castle as the sun was setting, during late September. There are various vantage points to take different images. I've selected two.

The castle is an oft photographed site, so I tried to present two sections of the battlements from a different perspective and seeking to capture the sunsetting through the ruins.

The castle's history saw it in use through the 11th century through to the late 15th century, after which the castle fell into decline. There was a risk that the construction of the London and Birmingham Railway during the 1830s would see the complete demolition; however, this was avoided through an act of Parliament.

Dimensionally, the central feature is the Berkhamsted motte mound. This is some 14 meters high (45.9 feet) and 55 meters (180.4 feet) in diameter. The motte stands on a shell keep of about 18 meters wide (59 feet), and the bailey occupies around 1.3 hectares (13,000 square meters). The original castle was built from stone and it once had two complete moats.

Motte is a reference to the specific form of motte-and-bailey castle, a European fortification featuring a wooden or stone keep situated on a raised area of ground called a motte, accompanied by a walled courtyard, or bailey, surrounded by a protective ditch and palisade.

There is an abundance of flint (the sedimentary cryptocrystalline form of the mineral quartz), which I always find attractive looking and varied in form. In the south of England there are many buildings put together using flintstone, during the early-to-mid portion of the Middle Ages. It was most common where no good building stone was available locally and prior to brick-making.

With the images (*Image 13* and *Image 14*) there is little to add other than to the feel and mood. I think there is a peacefulness to both images, a stillness. Perhaps the second image is slightly haunting?

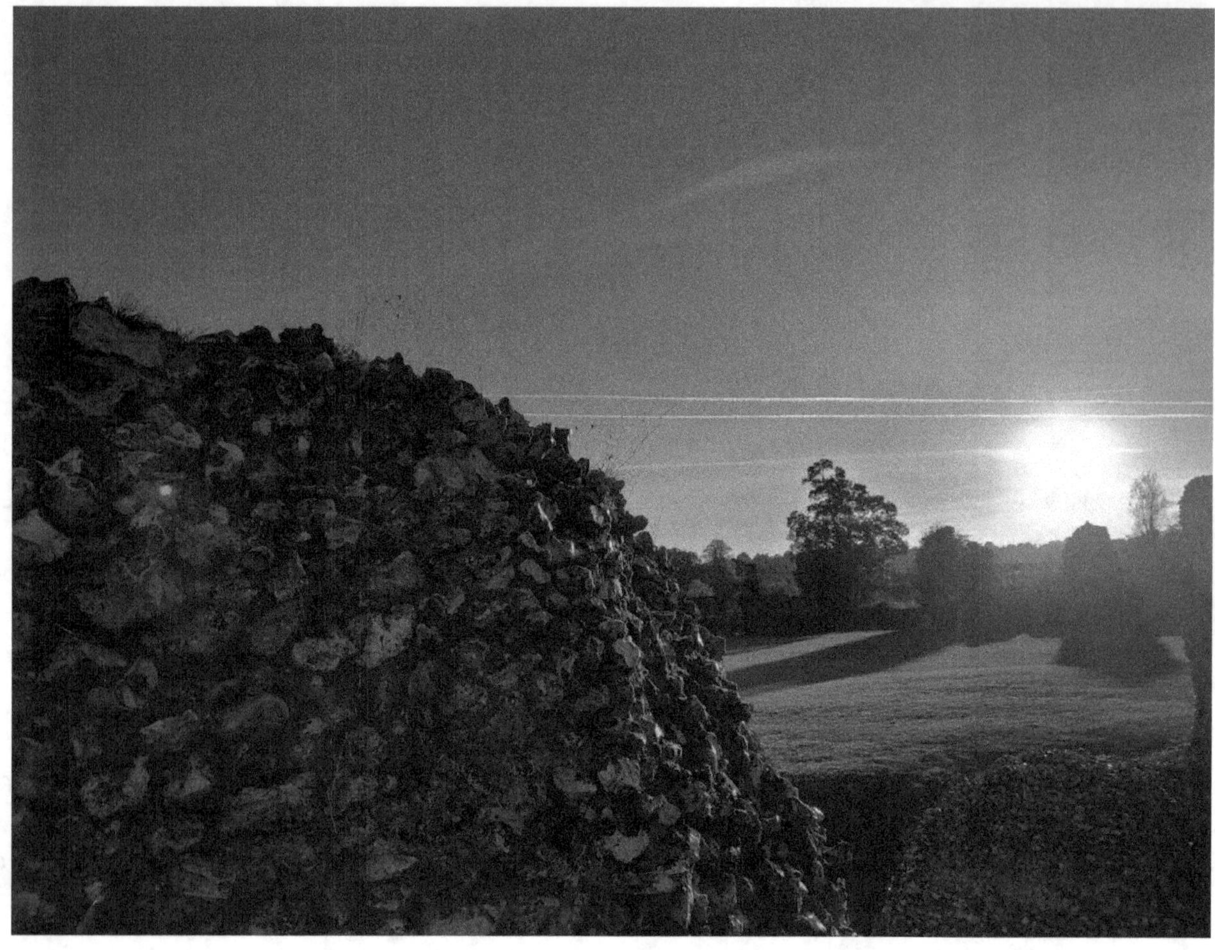

Image 13: Flit wall of Berkhampstead Castle as the sun sets on a later September's day.

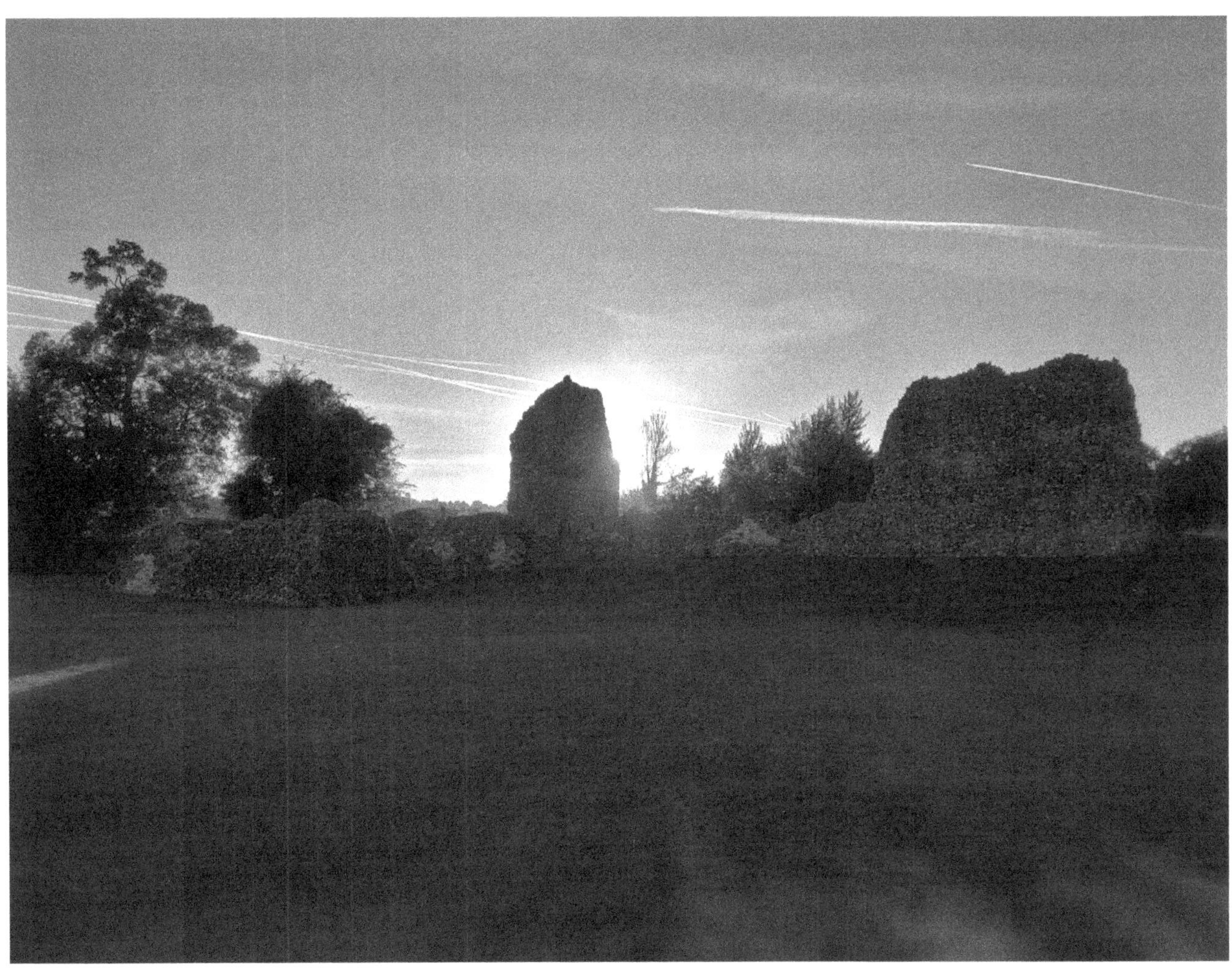

Image 14: Tower at Berkhampstead Castle, with the fading sun behind it. Haunting?

York has many interesting buildings and a host of abandoned ones. There is just one image here, keeping with the Norman-built castle theme. Other images will appear in another place, another space.

The picture is of Clifford's Tower, another site maintained by English Heritage. The picture was taken during December, during the afternoon.

Clifford's Tower has been a royal mint, a medieval stronghold and a Civil War garrison. Today, many people climb to the roof deck to cast their eyes across York's historic skyline.

With *Image 15* I like the way the sky almost wraps around the castle. I'm also pleased with the way the tree veers into view. Also notice how the grooves in the earth of the mound almost become the continuation of the rays of light shining downwards. At least it seems thar way to me.

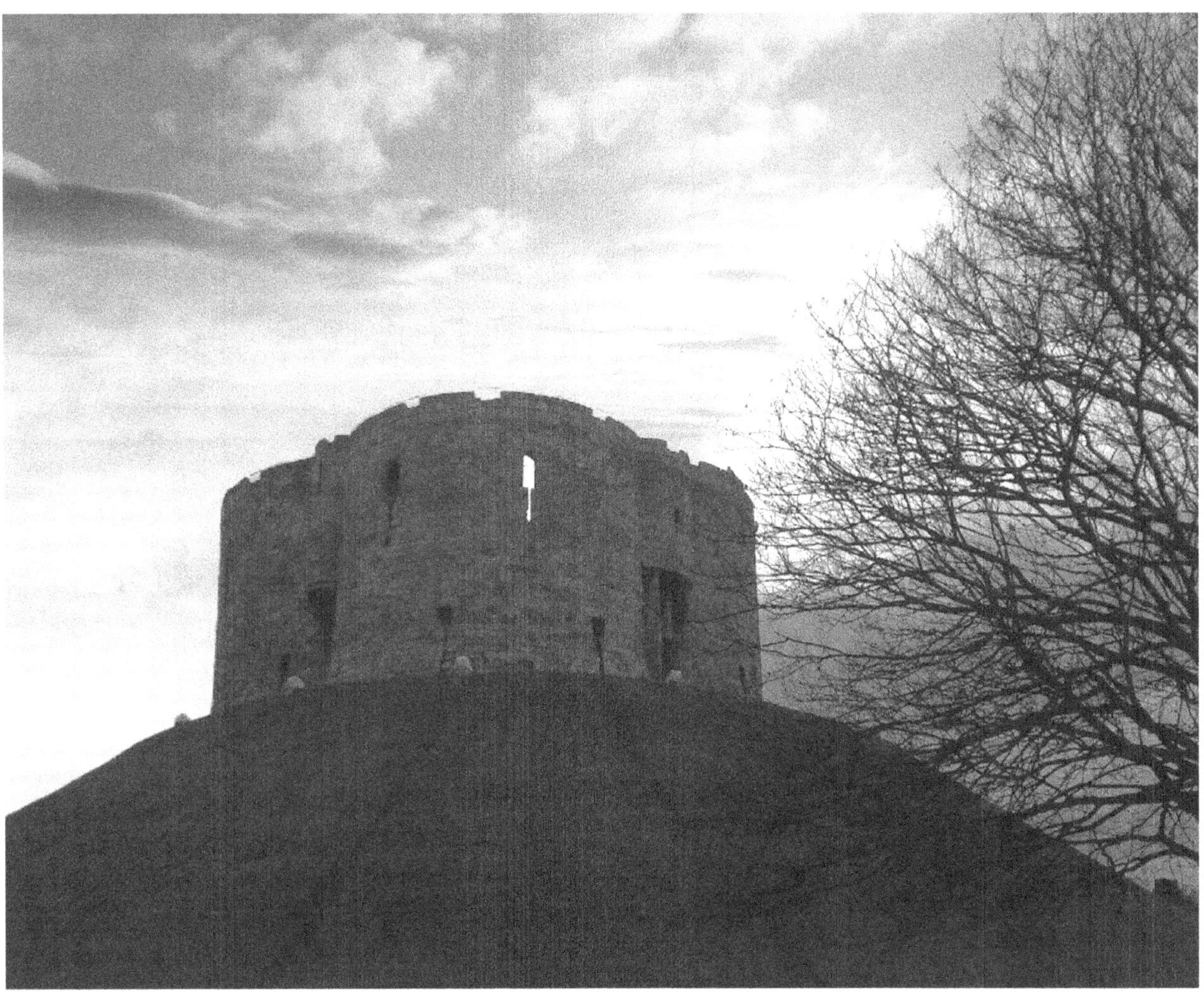

Image 15: Lighting up York

The following tree images are of what is commonly known as Sopwell Nunnery, ruins that are located on the edge of the city of St. Albans. However, the ruins are not actually those of the original nunnery. The crumbling façade is of a building called Lee Hall.

Sopwell Nunnery was founded on this site in 1140. The atmospheric ruins are the remains of a mansion belonging to an adviser of Henry VIII. In 1540, after the Dissolution of the Monasteries, Henry VIII granted the land to Sir Richard Lee, a member of the king's court. Lee demolished the nunnery and built a house on its foundations.

The romantic ruins are the remains of Sir Richard Lee's Tudor mansion.

Both *Images 16* and *17* capture the remains of the Tudor building. Both have used a filter, which varies the monochrome slightly. I think there is a haunting beauty to these images. I prefer to think of the remains as the nunnery, but only because there could be something spookier about this.

Image 18 is a closeup of the stone of the Lee building. In many places there is an amass of cobwebs, which can add to the somewhat ghostly nature of the buildings. This image shows a spider inching along the silk, creating a fine tangled-web in preparation for the next flying prey to be captured.

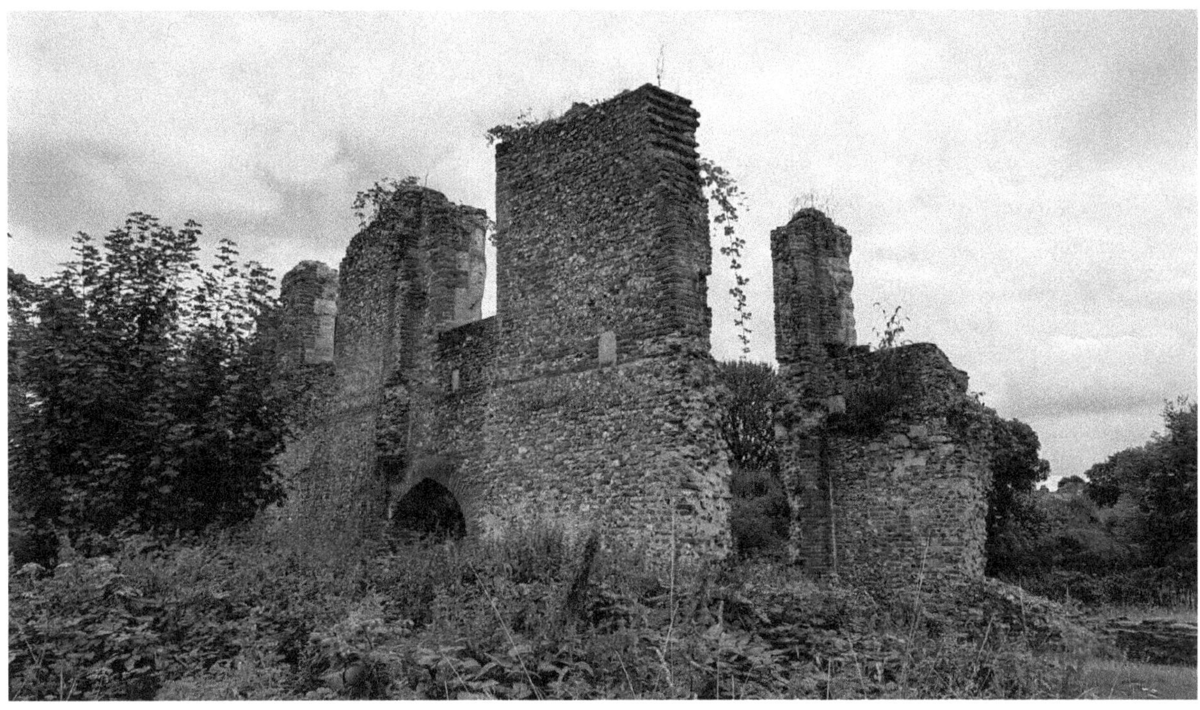

Image 16: Get thee to a nunnery

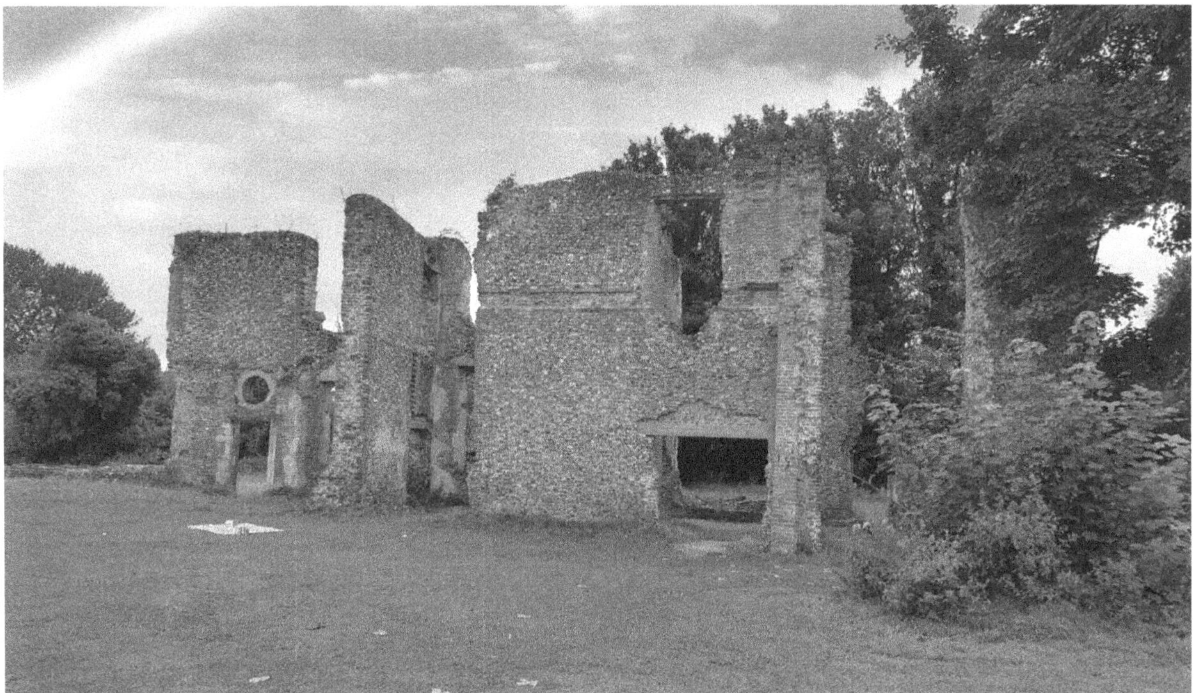

Image 17: The crumbling remains of the Lee building

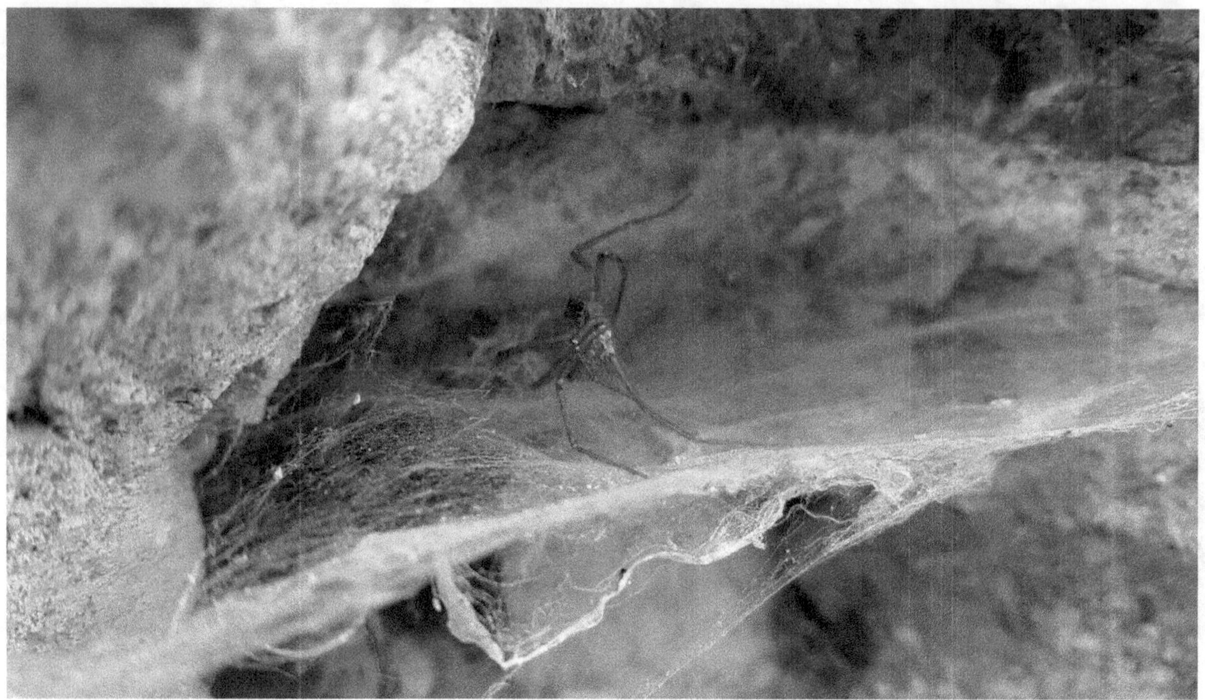

Image 18: A home among the ruins

4 CITIES

There is an image here, from Bristol. This is a wall of a building that shows damage from World War II. It has been left unrepaired, I think, as reminder of the impact of the conflict upon the area.

During the time of the Second World War, Bristol had an important harbor and shipyards. The Bristol Aeroplane Company factory made Blenheim and Beaufort bombers, and the Beaufighter combat plane for the Royal Air Force. These made it an obvious target for air raids.

The city was bombed heavily between June 1940 and May 1944. The longest period of regular bombing, known as the 'Bristol Blitz' began in autumn 1940 and ended the following spring. The first bombs of the Bristol Blitz fell at around 6 pm on Sunday 24 November 1940. A further six bombing raids took place until the last major attack in April 1941.

The wall (along Baldwin Street), in *Image 19*, captures the frailty of structures and as a continuing reminder of the damage that conflict causes.

Image 20 is the former naval boat HMS Wilton., located in a dry dock in Leigh-on-Sea in Essex. HMS Wilton was a former world war two coastal minesweeper. It is set to be converted into a club house as part of a private yacht club. She was the first warship in the world to be constructed from glass-reinforced plastic (GRP).

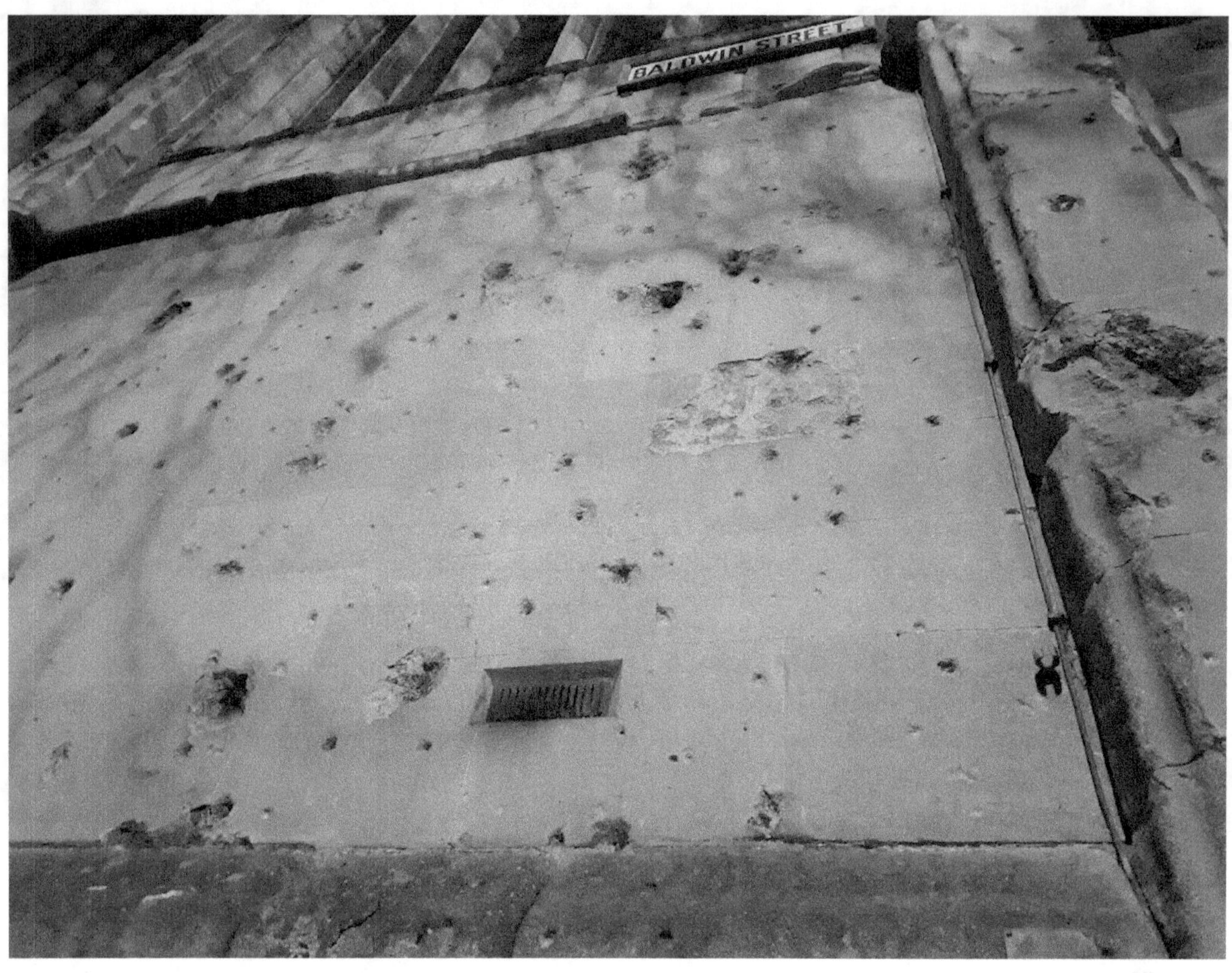

Image 19: Wartime wall damage on a wall in Bristol. Conflict(ing) patterns?

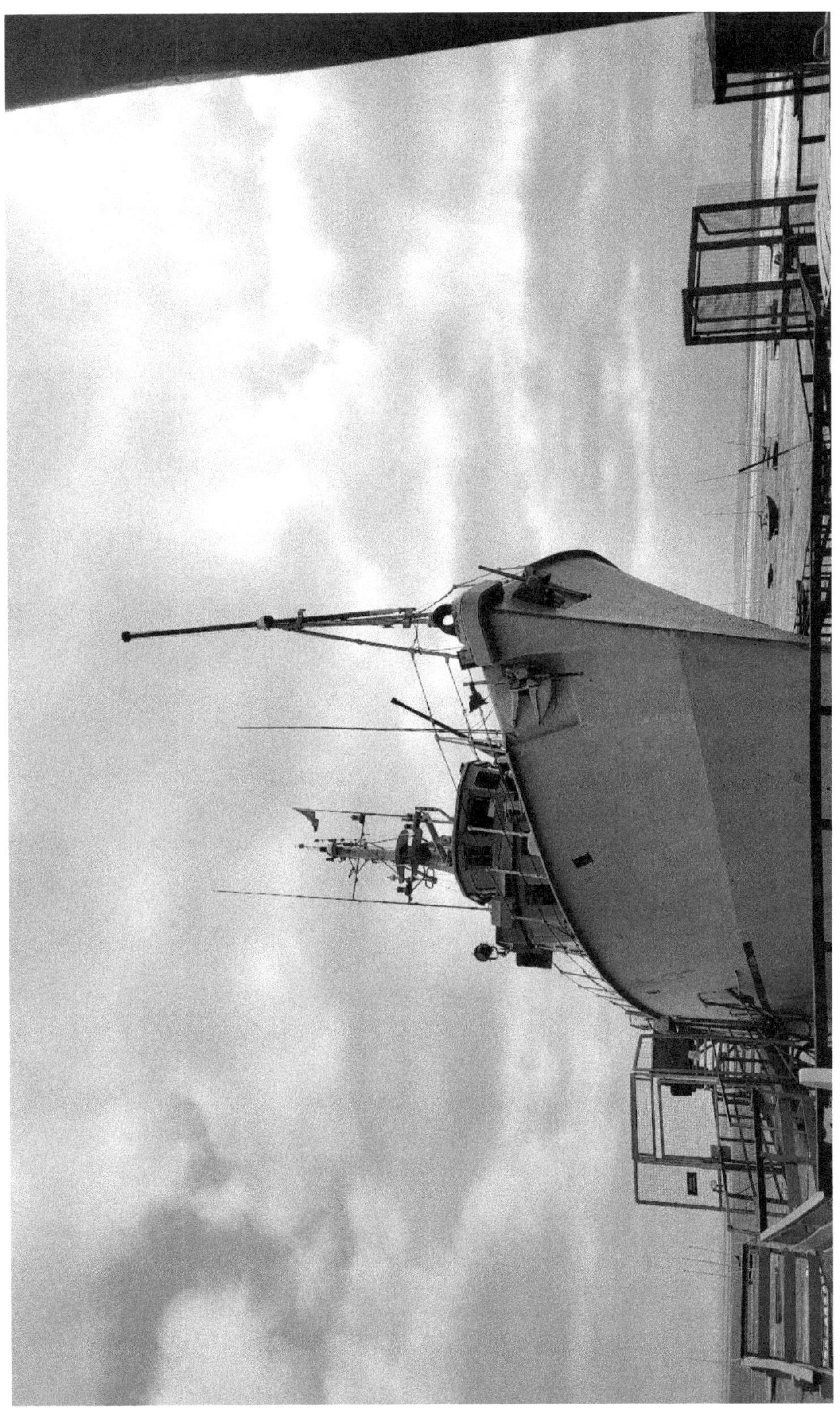

Image 20: Warship

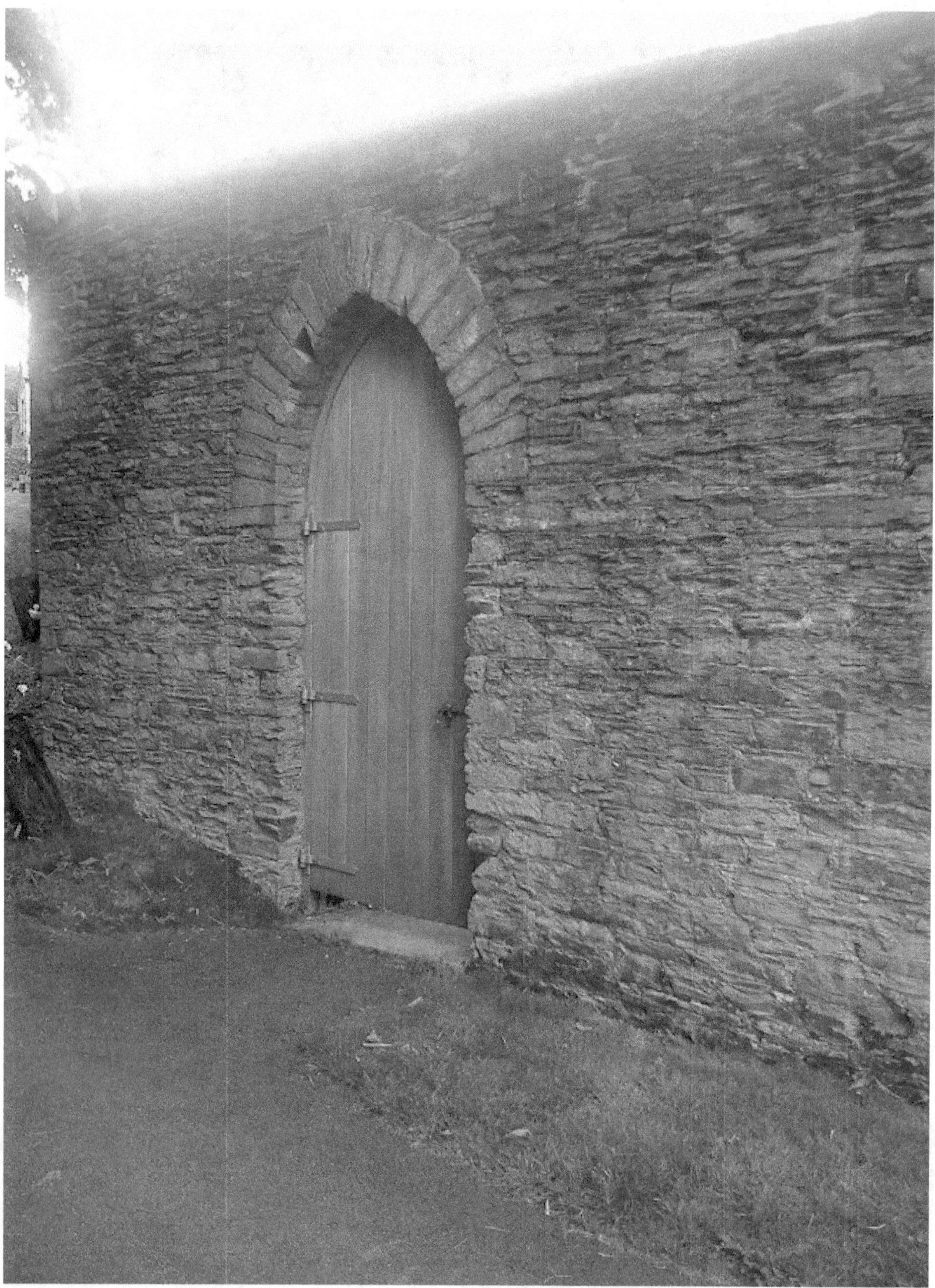

Image 21: Someone's at the door

Image 21 is of St. Albans, close to the Abbey where there is a walled garden. Behind the door is a pleasant garden. However, for me, the door looks less inviting. The picture was taken during the summer and there is a nice glow of light above the wall.

Image 22 is of an advertising sign, marketing a service from yesteryear. It remains daubed, albeit fading slightly, on the side of a takeaway establishment along London Road in St. Albans.

Image 23 is slightly different from others captured so far. The wall is old, the boarded up shopfront has been in this condition for many years and I've walked past it regularly. The graffiti, is however, new. The idea of the old meets new is intriguing. Does the graffiti enhance what was an ugly looking board or detract from the character? In this case, I'd side with the former.

Nathan Bowen is a self-styled guerrilla street artist who actively works as an art vigilante. By this, Bowen seeks out his definition of dull, lifeless spaces around London and seeks to enliven them. Bowen seeks to transform old walls and create new works of art.

Bowen's style is fast, dynamic and unpredictable, his signature characters known as 'The Demons' invade many building site hoardings.

St. Alban's, in the city center, has many alleyways and passageways. Many of these twist and turn and help to connect the many pubs and shops together. With *Image 24* I was keen to capture the grain of the brickwork and the narrowness of the passageway. I like the way there is a clink of light diffusing through, adding to the sense of claustrophobia.

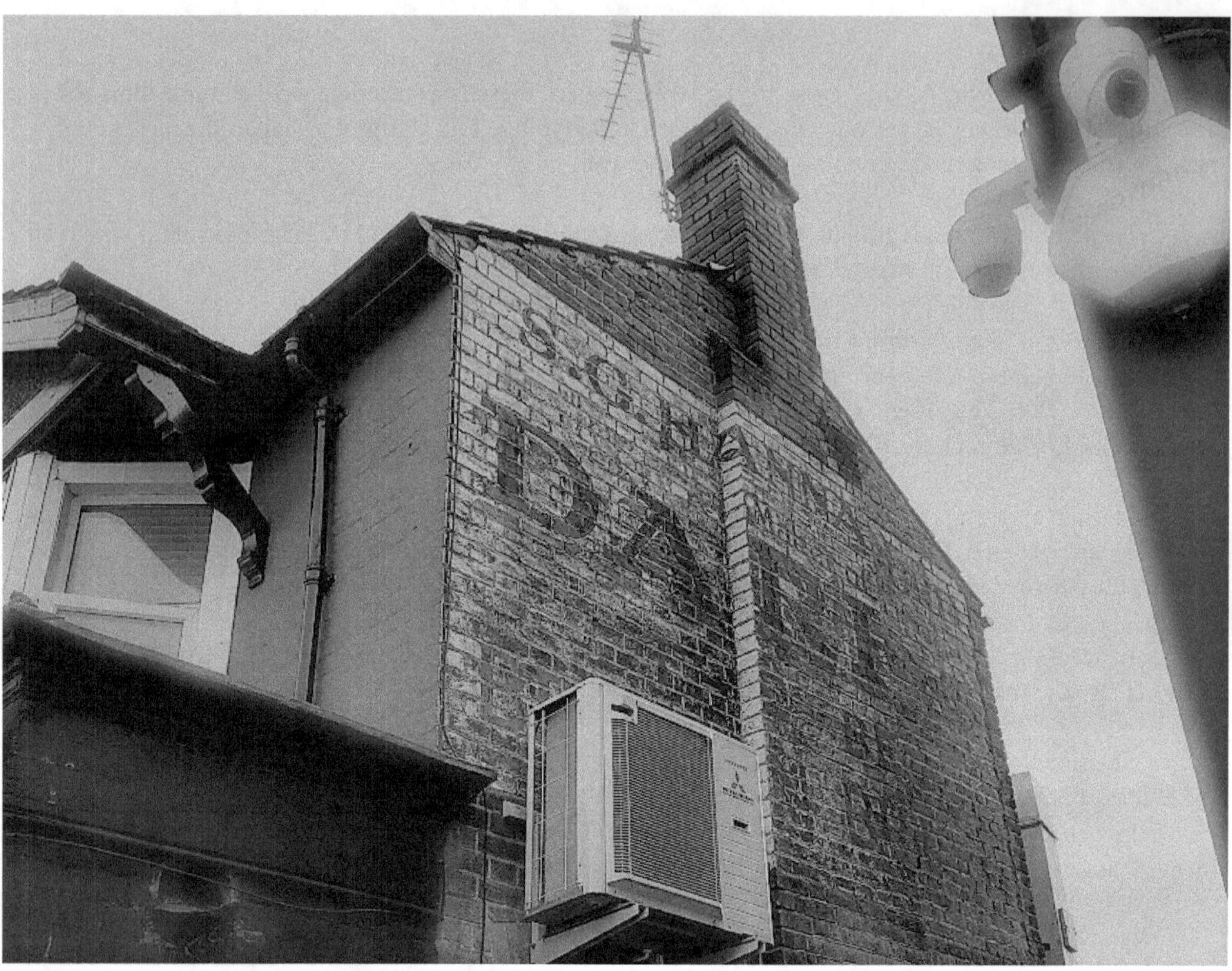

Image 22: Old advertising sign

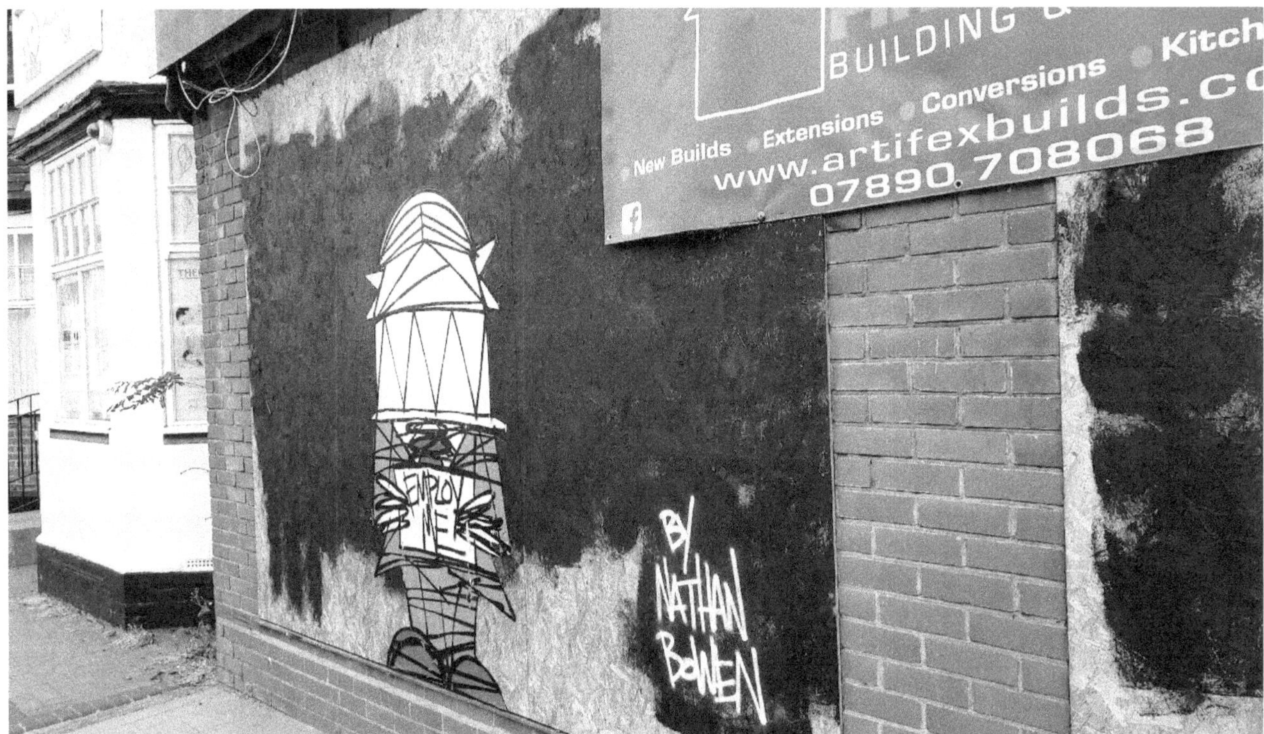

Image 23: Graffiti by Nathan Bowen

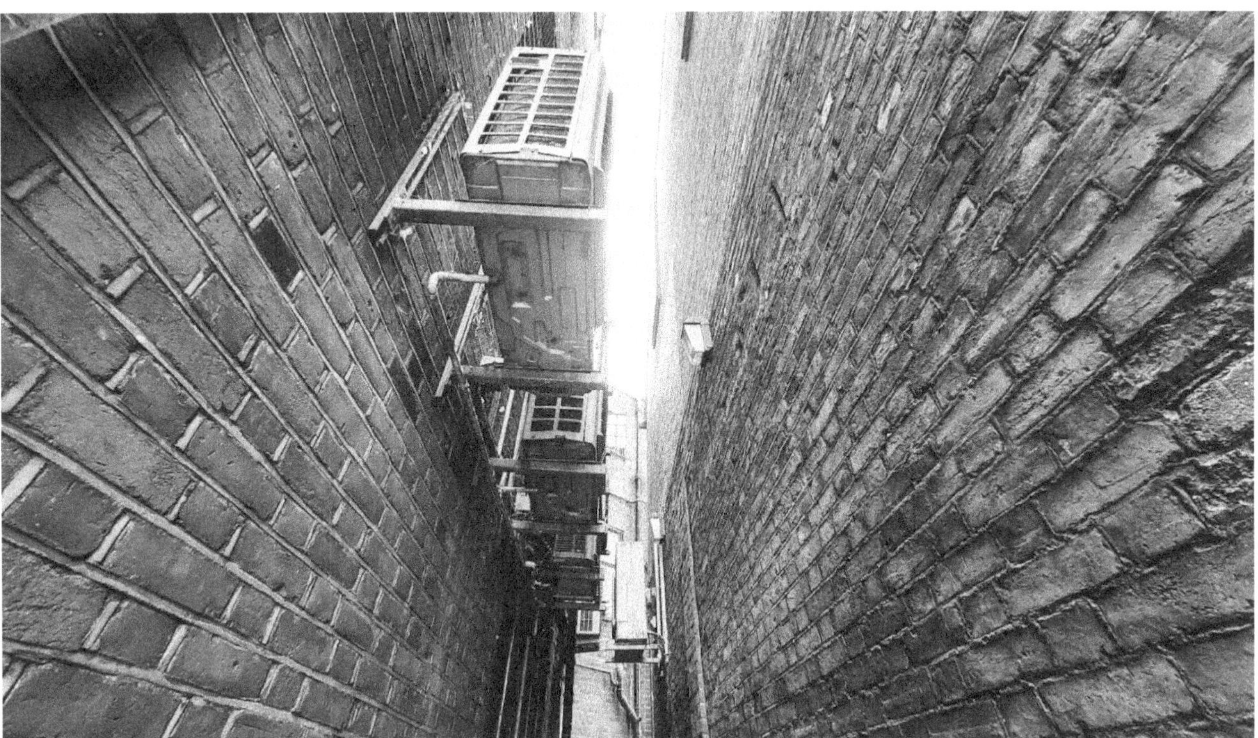

Image 24: Through the alleyway

5 **URBAN**

Towns, villages, suburbs. Ordinary places. I live in an ordinary British town. But some of the structures are old, with many buildings dating back to the 1920s and 1930s. Most of these are standing, intact structures. But not all.

Even the seemingly ordinary can be interesting. Even the seemingly bland can actually be beautiful. Or at least intriguing.

Image 25 is a disused telecommunications hub, once part of the Post Office in the U.K., then transferred to privatized British Telecommunications. Totally wired.

Image 26 is simply a large pile of bricks in a driveway near to where I live. These were from something that had been demolished, all higgledy-piggledy, rather than being set aside to build a new construct.

A trolley in the road in the rain forms *Image 27*.It's from a local Sainsbury's, in a road as the rain comes down. It is sort of symbolic of a throw away culture.

Images 28 and *29* are of an old garden shed. The concrete, asbestos lined building was slowly crumbling apart. It is now long gone. The garden theme extends with *Image 30*, which is of an unkempt garden. One pat is earth, worn down; the other a little wild, with grasses.

The pictures that form *Images 31* and *32* are of a storage container in London Colney. It has been there for years, with no sign of ever being opened. What could be inside?

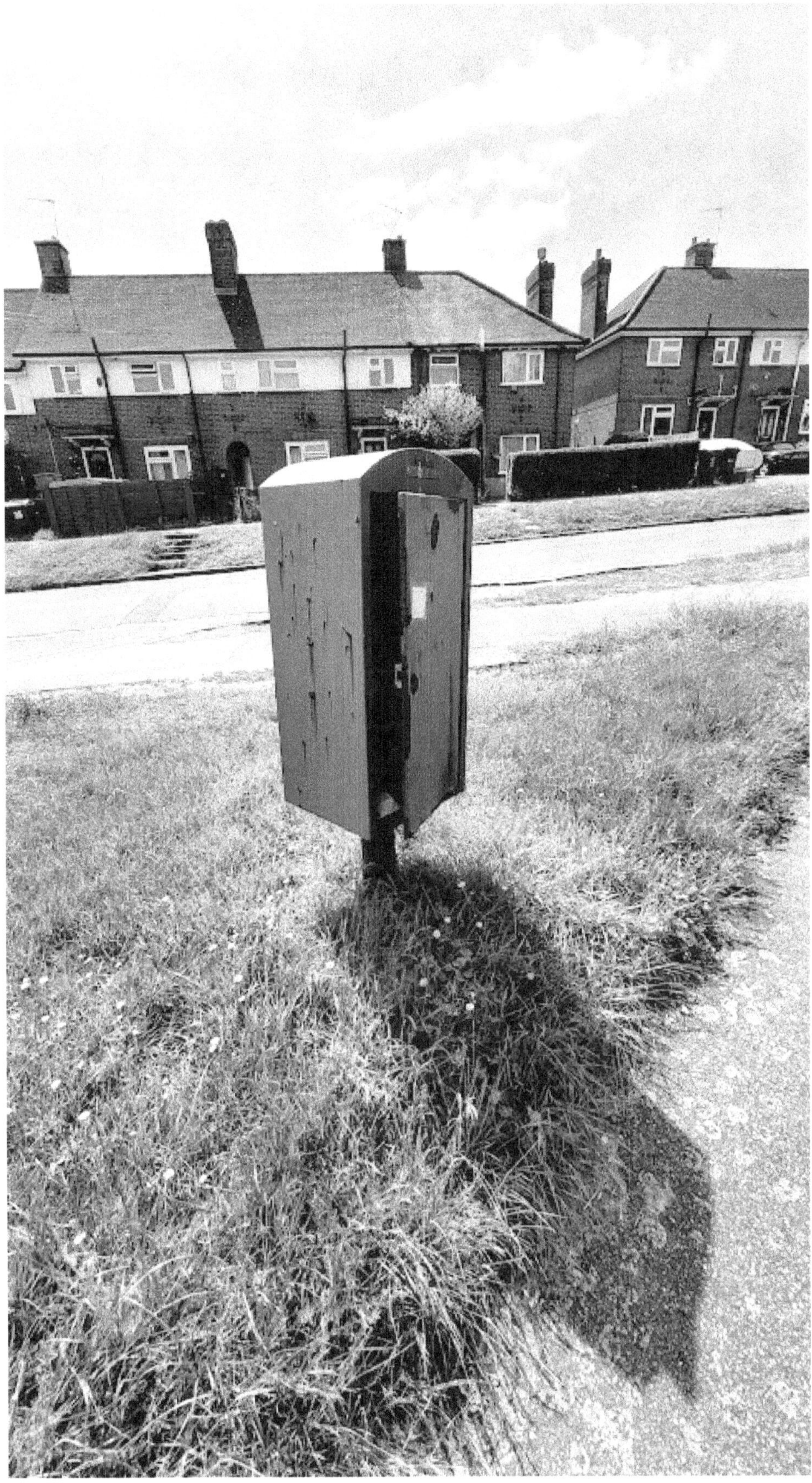

Image 25: Send me a message

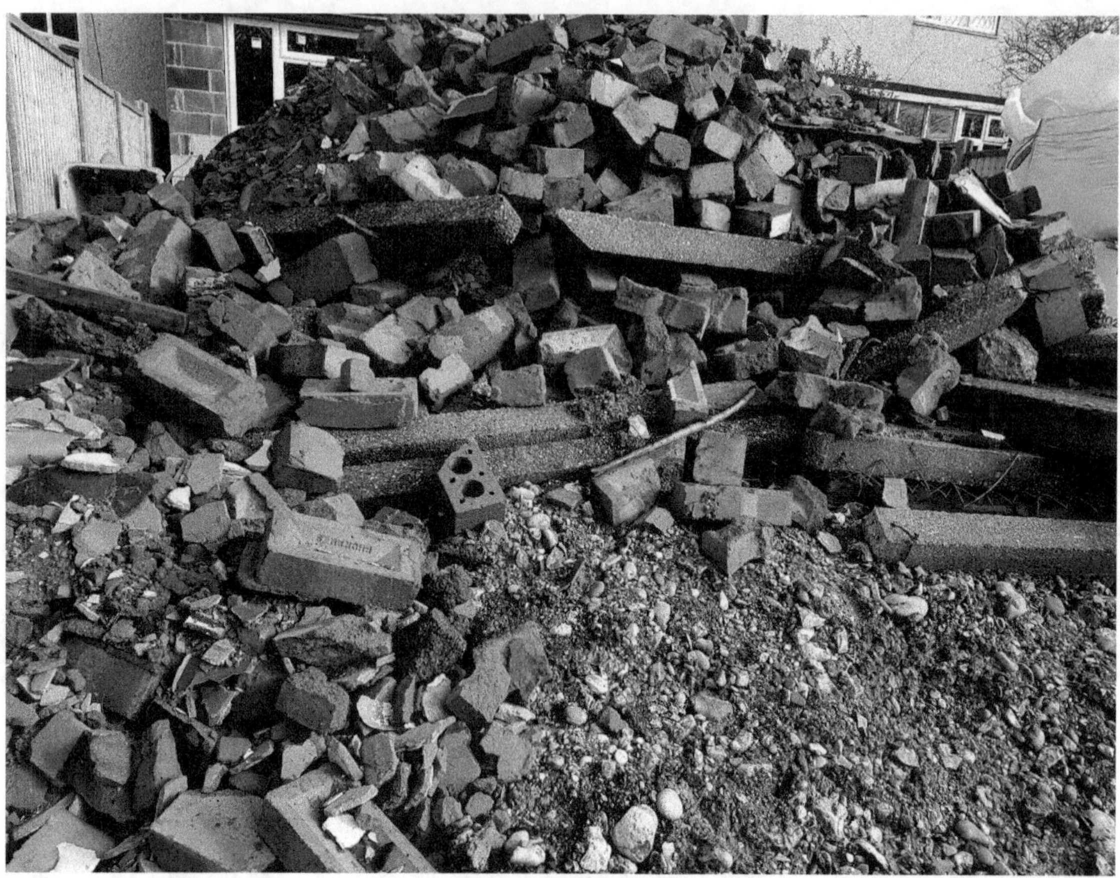

Image 26: Bricked.

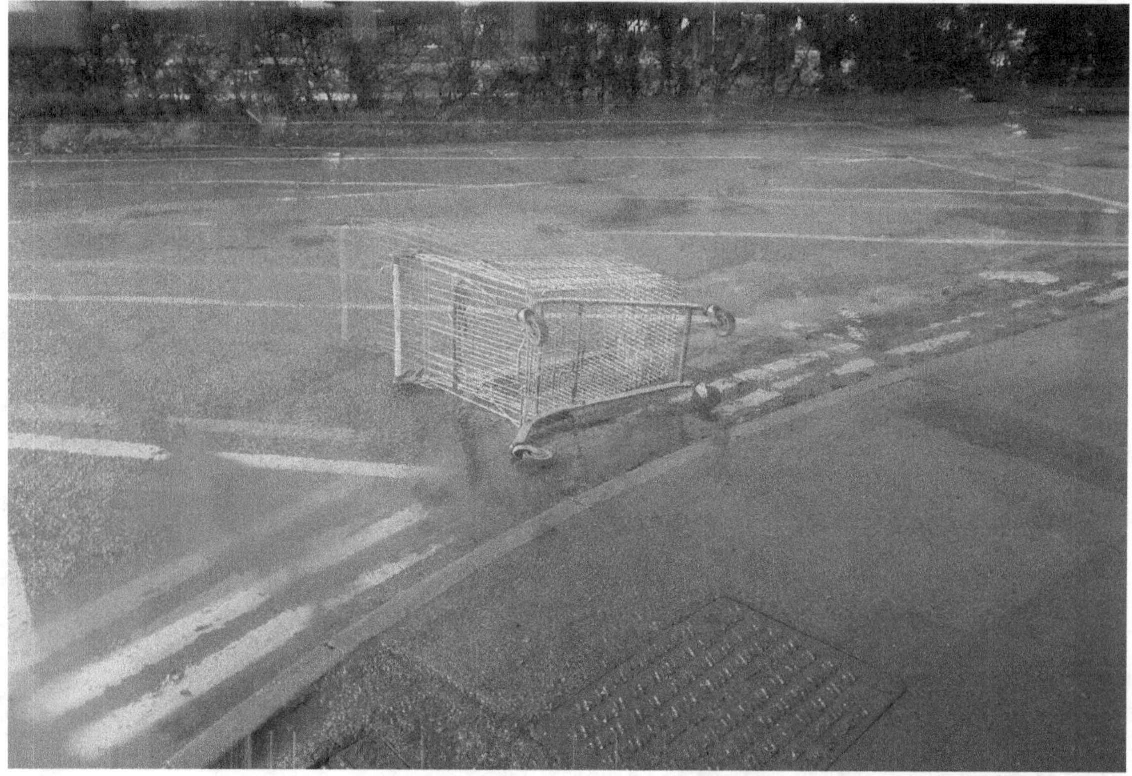

Image 27: Trollied.

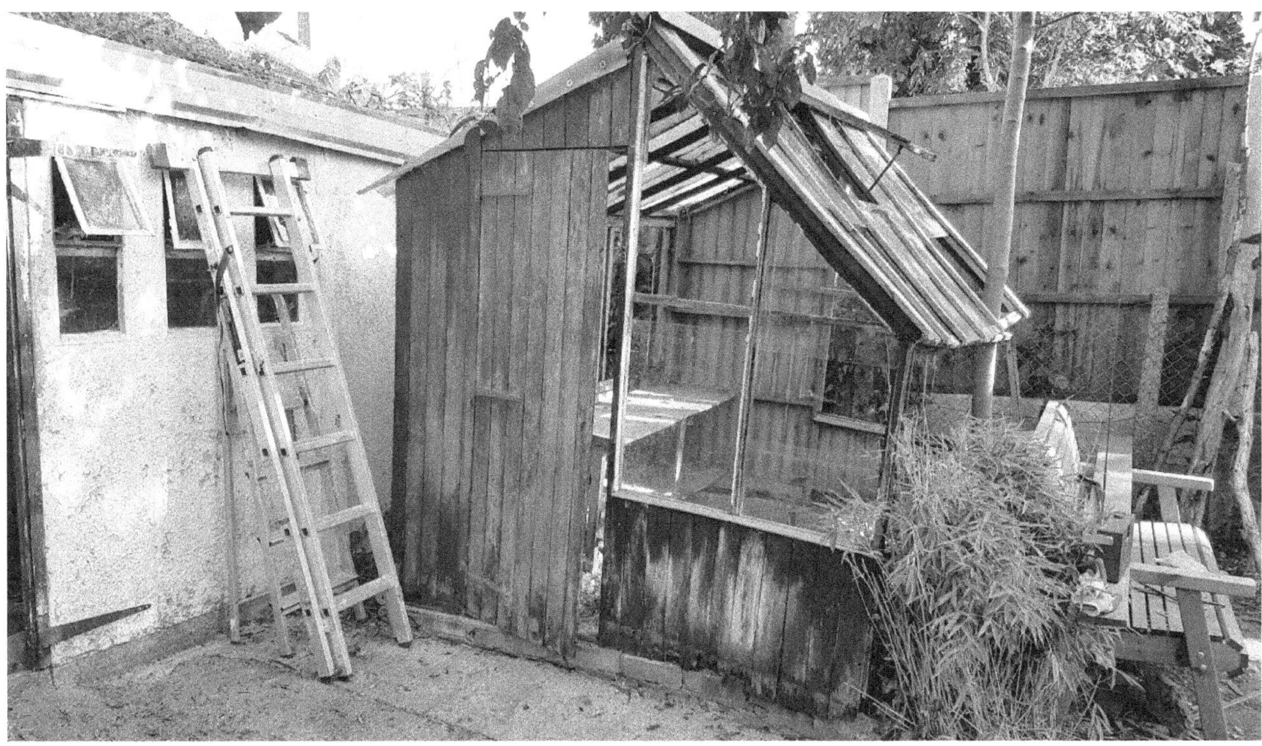

Image 28: Crumbling garden buildings

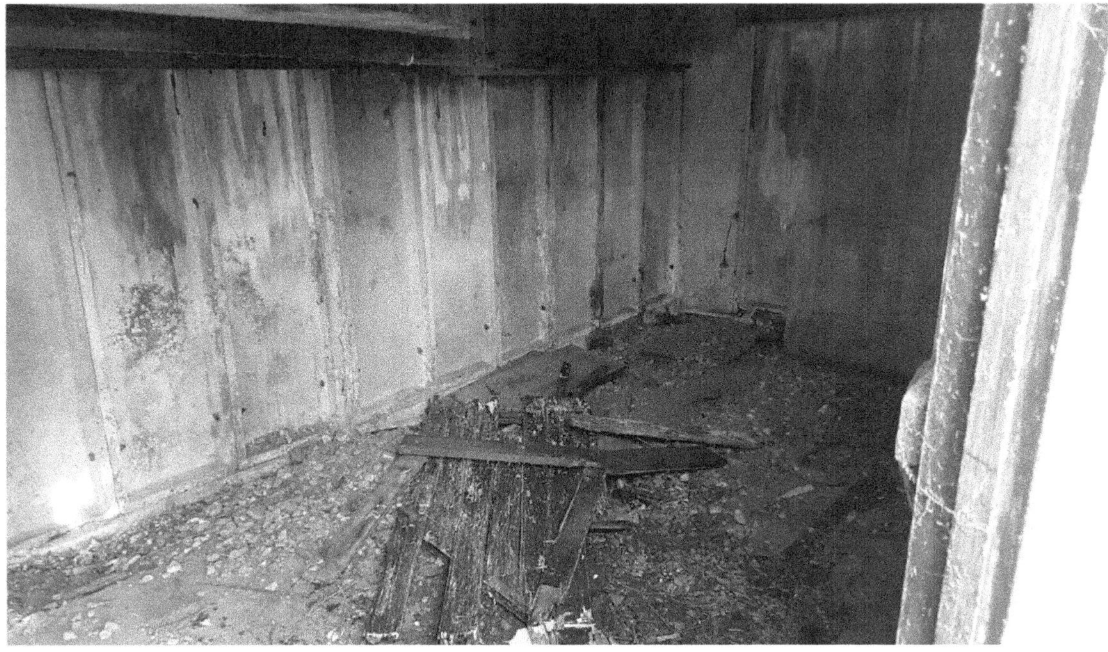

Image 29: Earthy

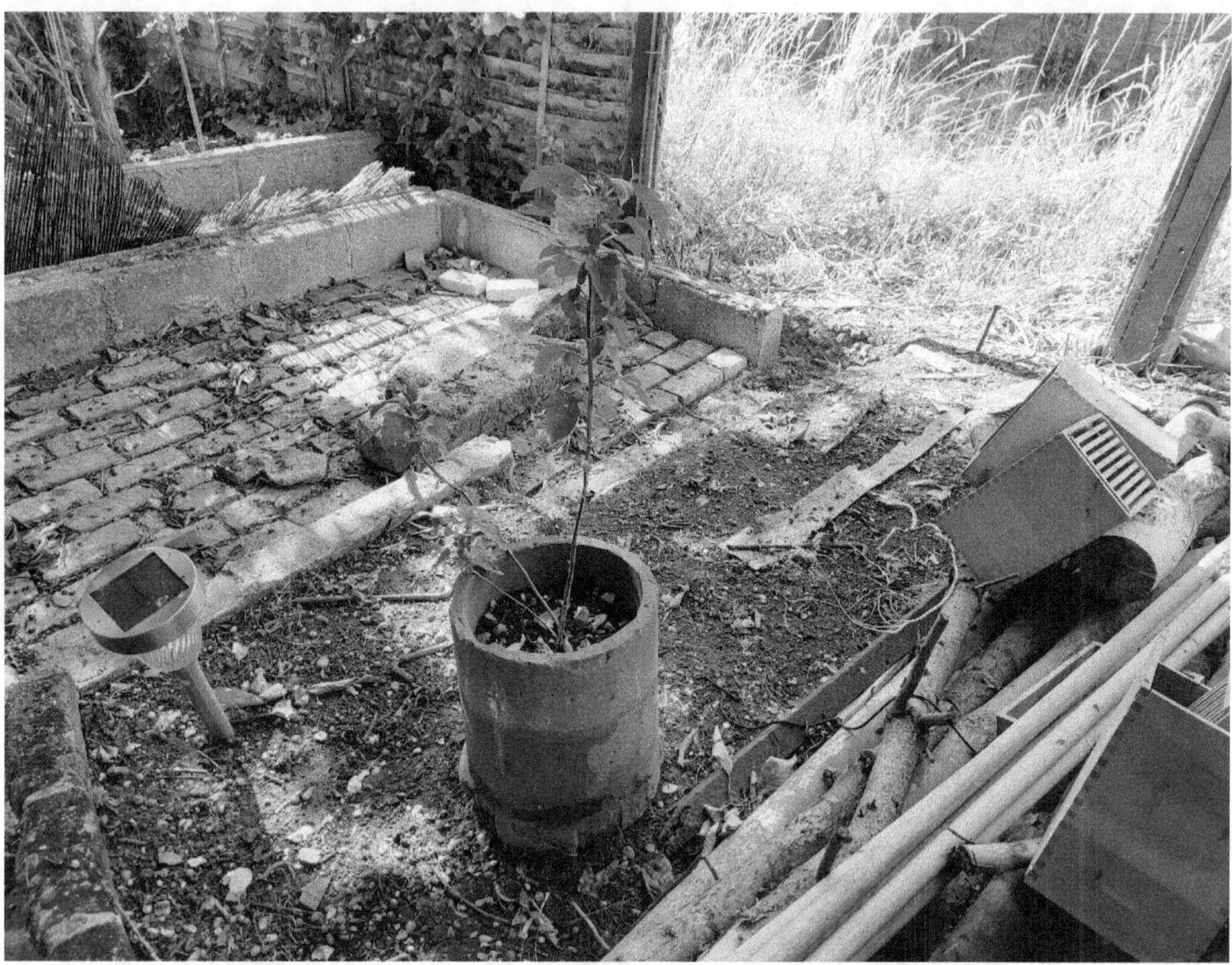

Image 30: Grow your own

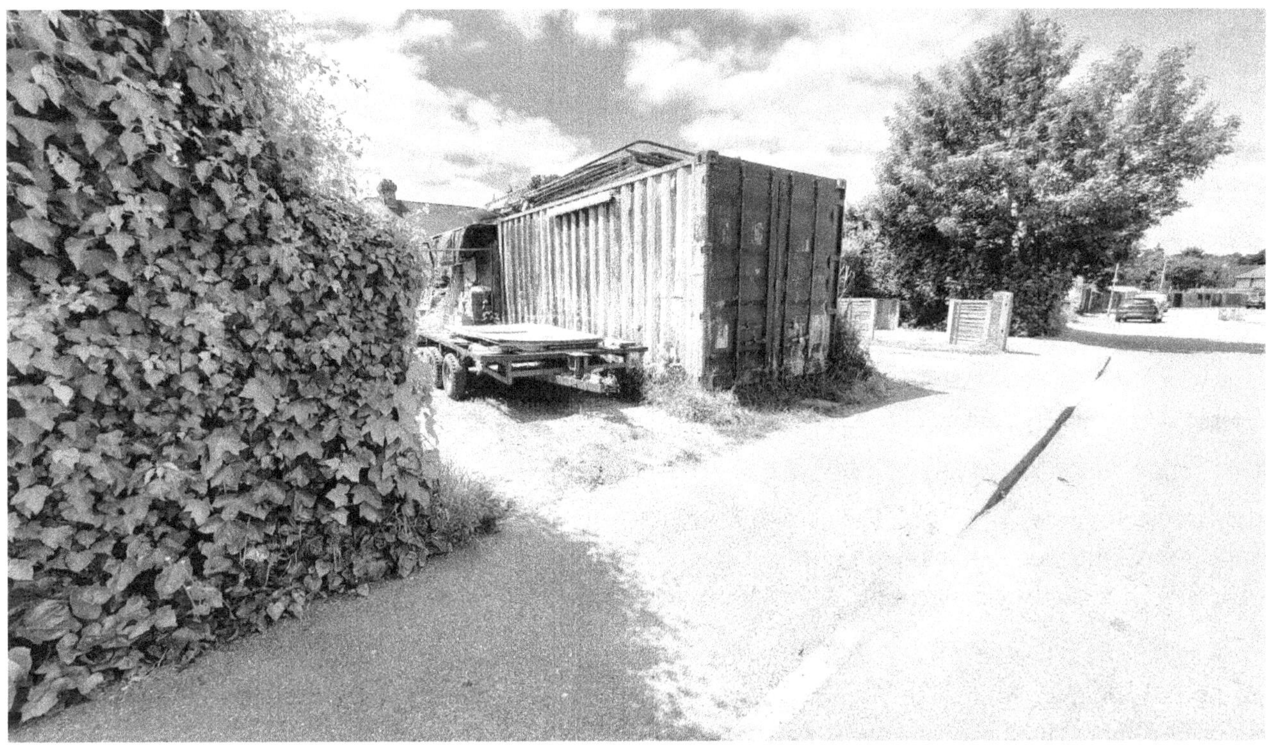

Image 31: What's inside?

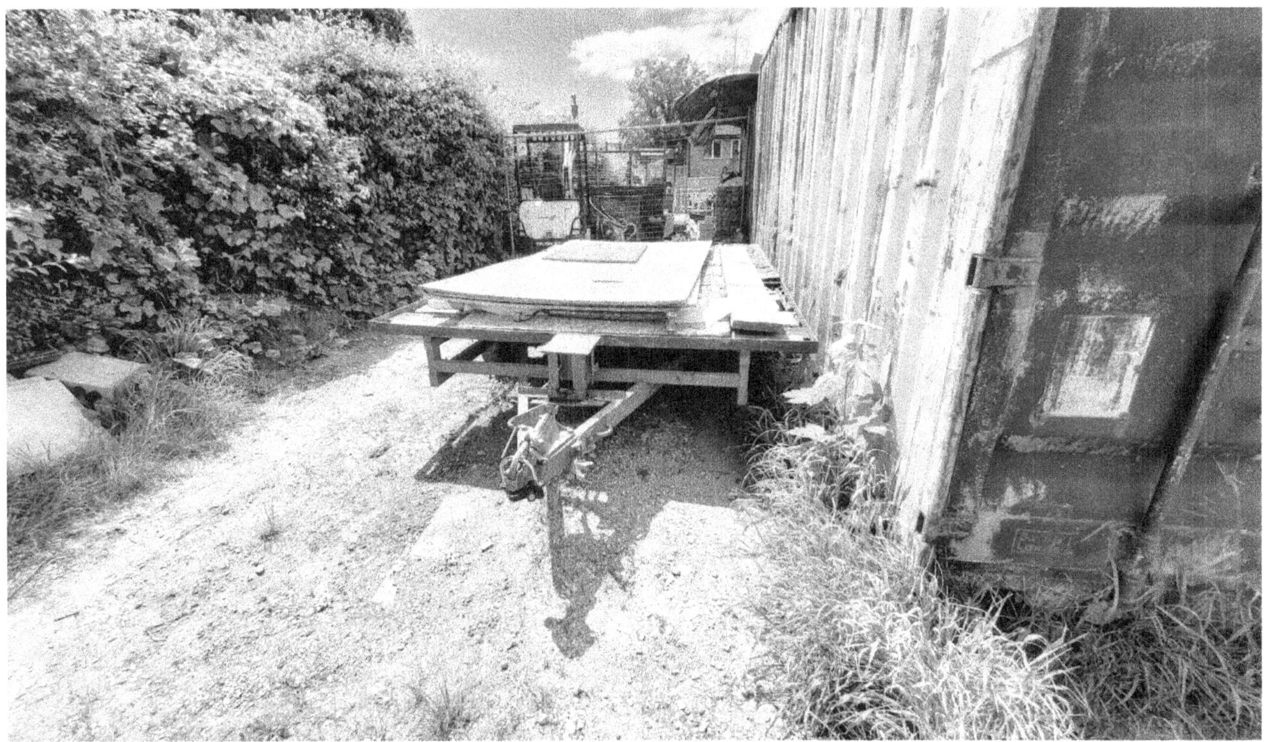

Image 32: Old materials

Images 33 and *34* are of streets in London Colney, a town that is now a suburb of the city of St. Albans. It takes its name from the River Colne, first recorded in 1555, referred to "Colney on the road to London". There's no river in sight here. Just discarded junk, probably the result of fly-tipping from a passing van; and another communications box alongside a seemingly random bollard.

Image 35 is of a garden in London Colney, where a barrow sits motionless. It is perhaps sometimes used, although it has remained in the same spot for many years. I've taken the image as if I was peeking through, spying on the garden as an interloper. Which of course, I was.

A discussed hard drive from a laptop forms the next image. It was on the side of the road and I took it home to photograph. Does it contain state secrets or is it wiped? Or perhaps *Image 36*, should it ever be reconnected, contains of nothing of interest at all.

The church in *Image 37* looks like it should be from somewhere in the U.S. It isn't, despite the architectural resemblances. The church never sees any activity and it therefore qualifies as 'abandoned', housed behind heavy iron gates. It is an independent free evangelical church, build in 1958. A motto on a nearby board reads "Where Jesus is the same Yesterday, Today and Forever".

The bridge in *Image 38* is located in Boreham Wood, a town that was once the hunting ground of Elstree Manor. The bridge is unkept, enlivened by a little spray painting courtesy of local youths. It hangs over a railway line.

Elsewhere in Boreham Wood is Red Road and the street connects to an area of open fields and woodland. *Image 39* is located on a path through the wood. Discarded ironwork, a little too big to be of domestic use, so probably from a farmer.

A wall in the winter, with the tantalizing beauty of ice crystals embedded with moss forms *Image 40*. Fragile and precious.

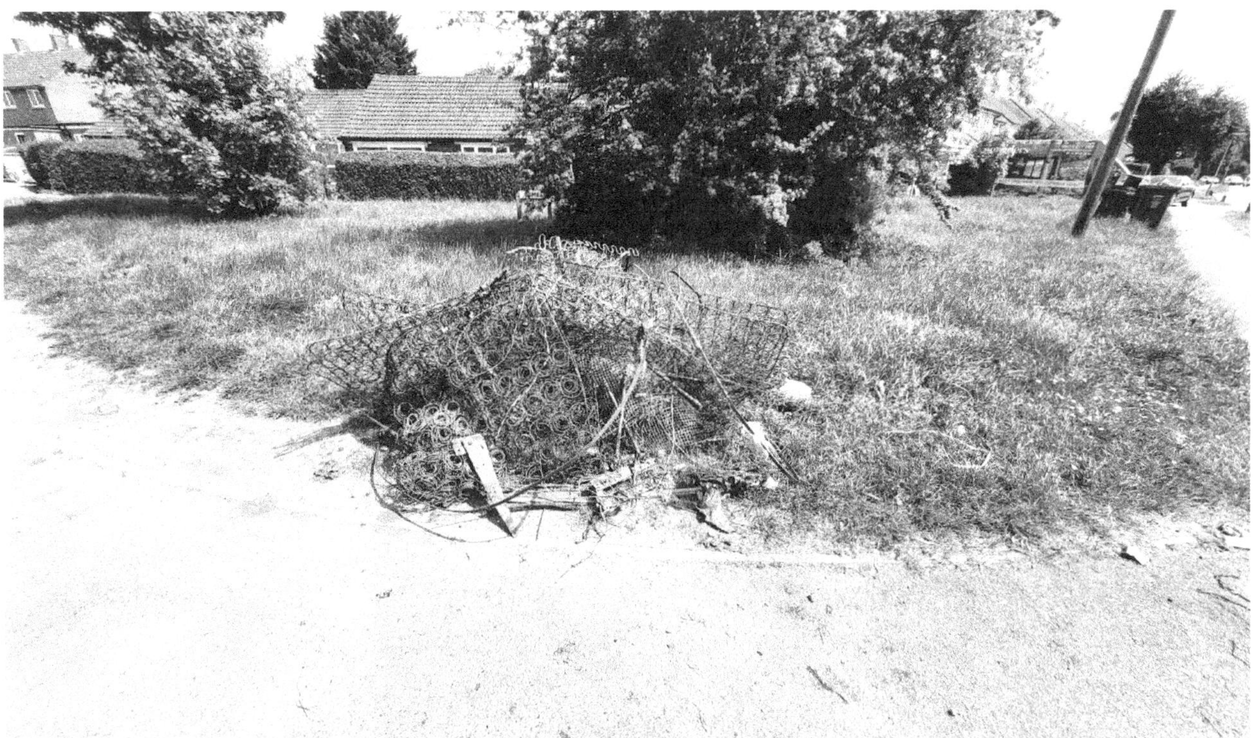

Image 33: Old ideas

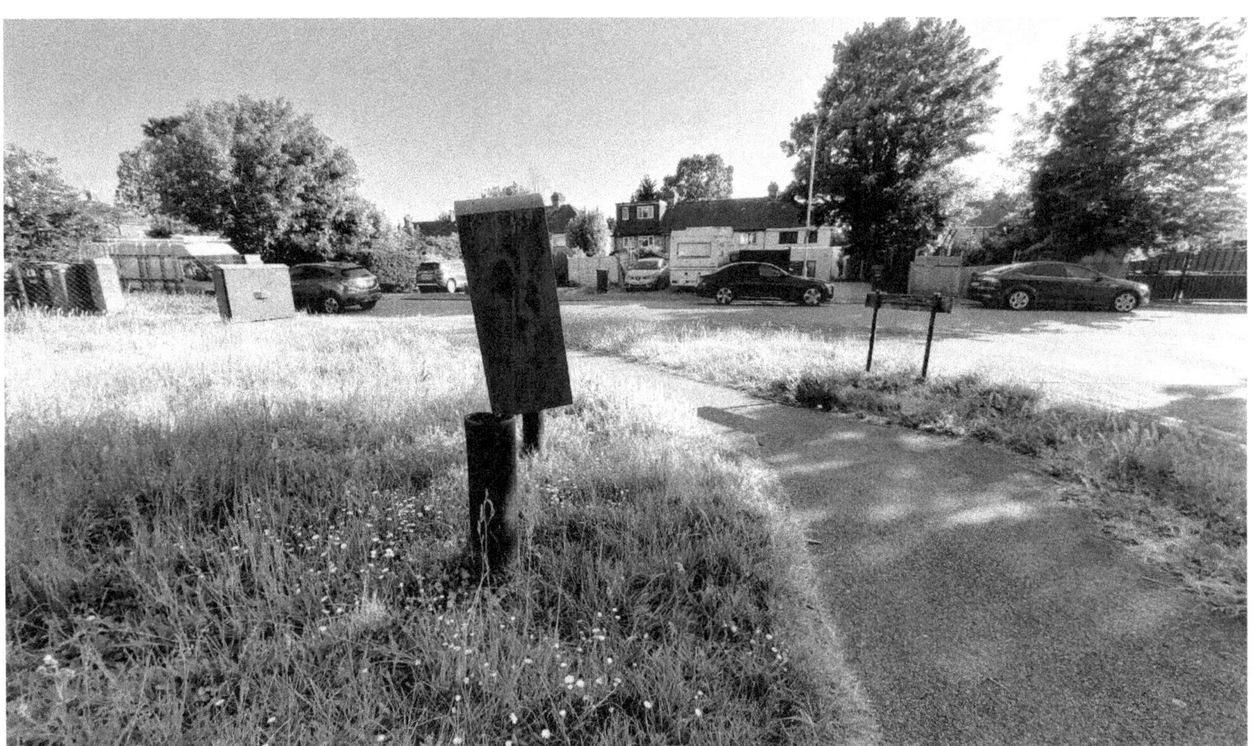

Image 34: Street lights

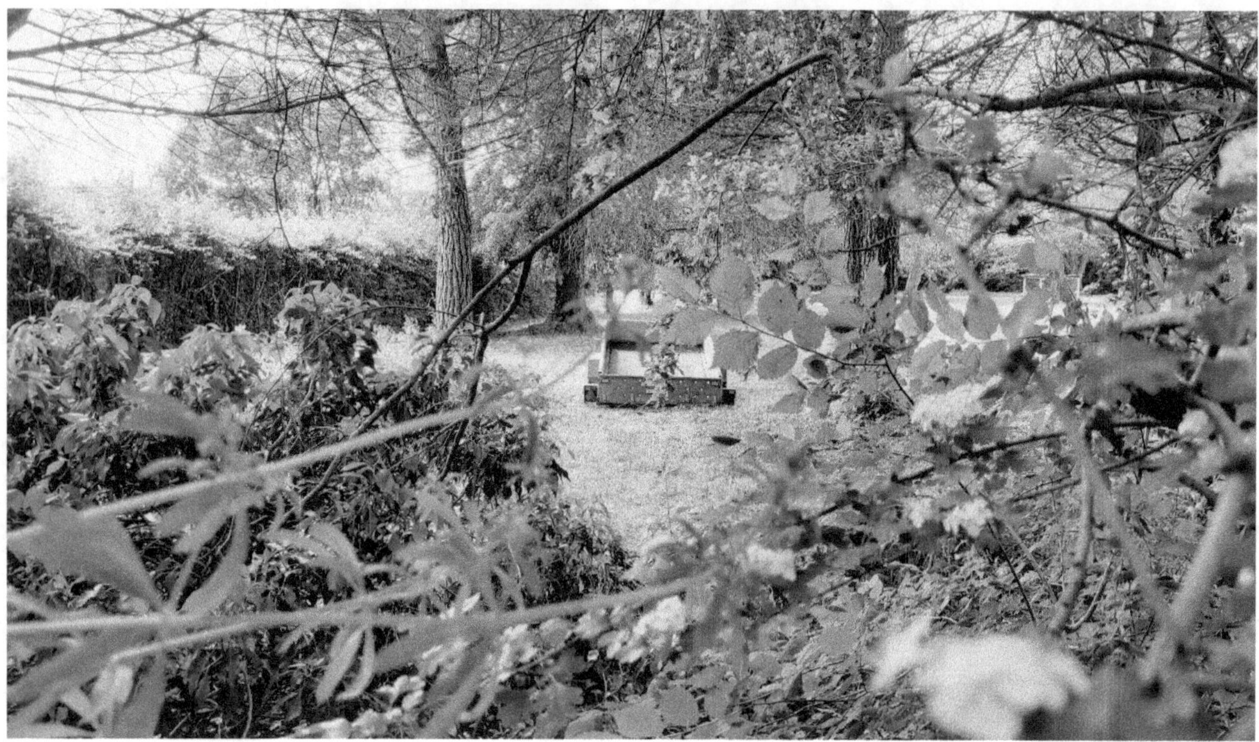

Image 35: Peeking

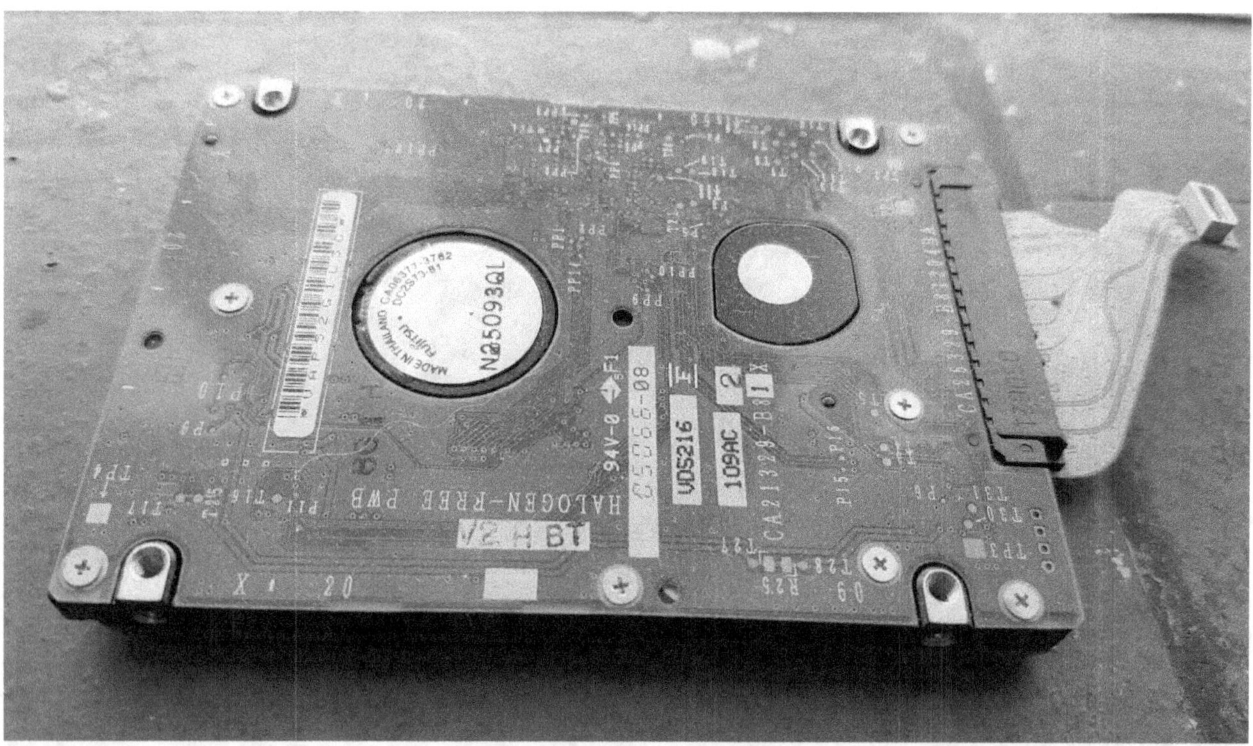

Image 36: Short circuit

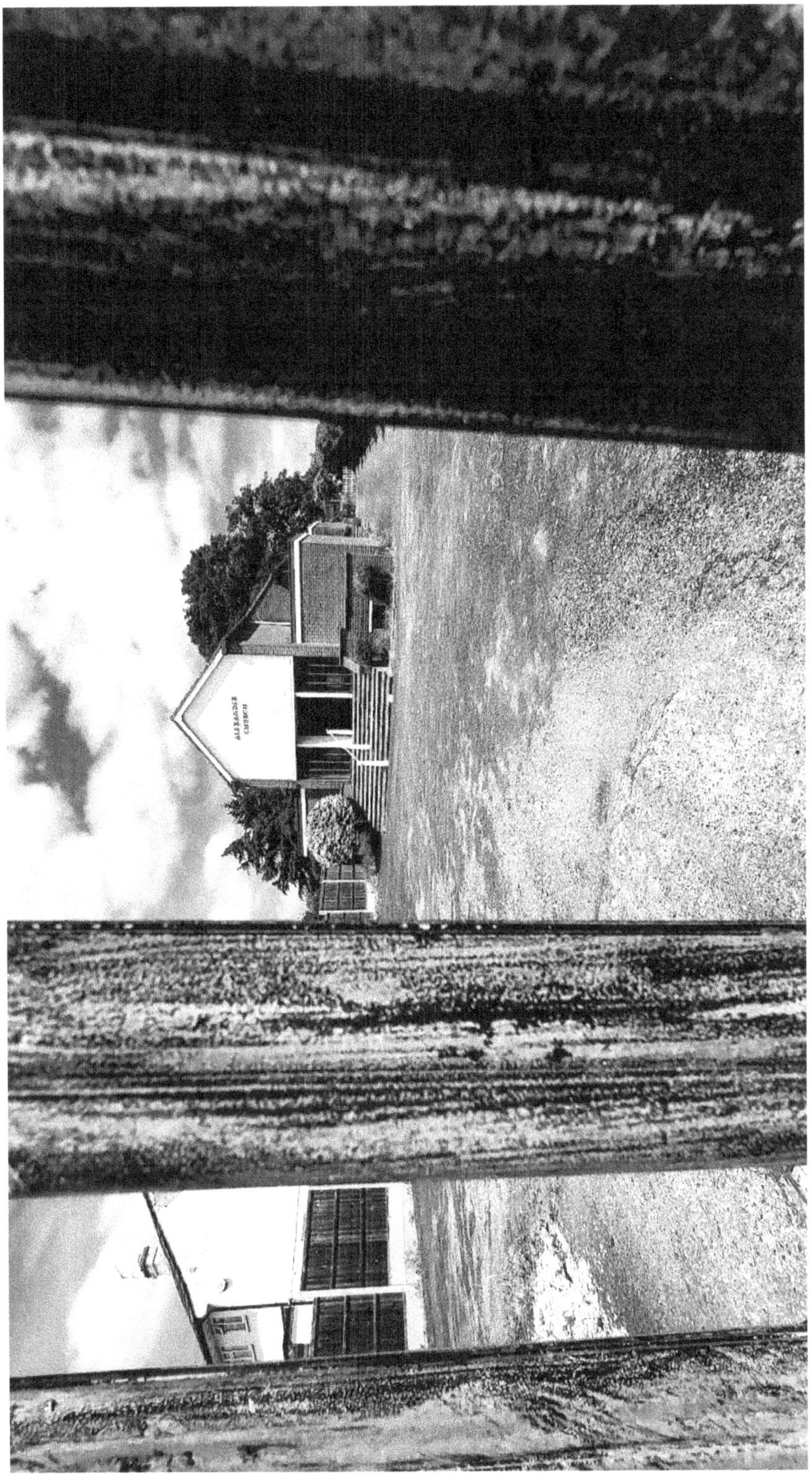

Image 37: Get to the church on time

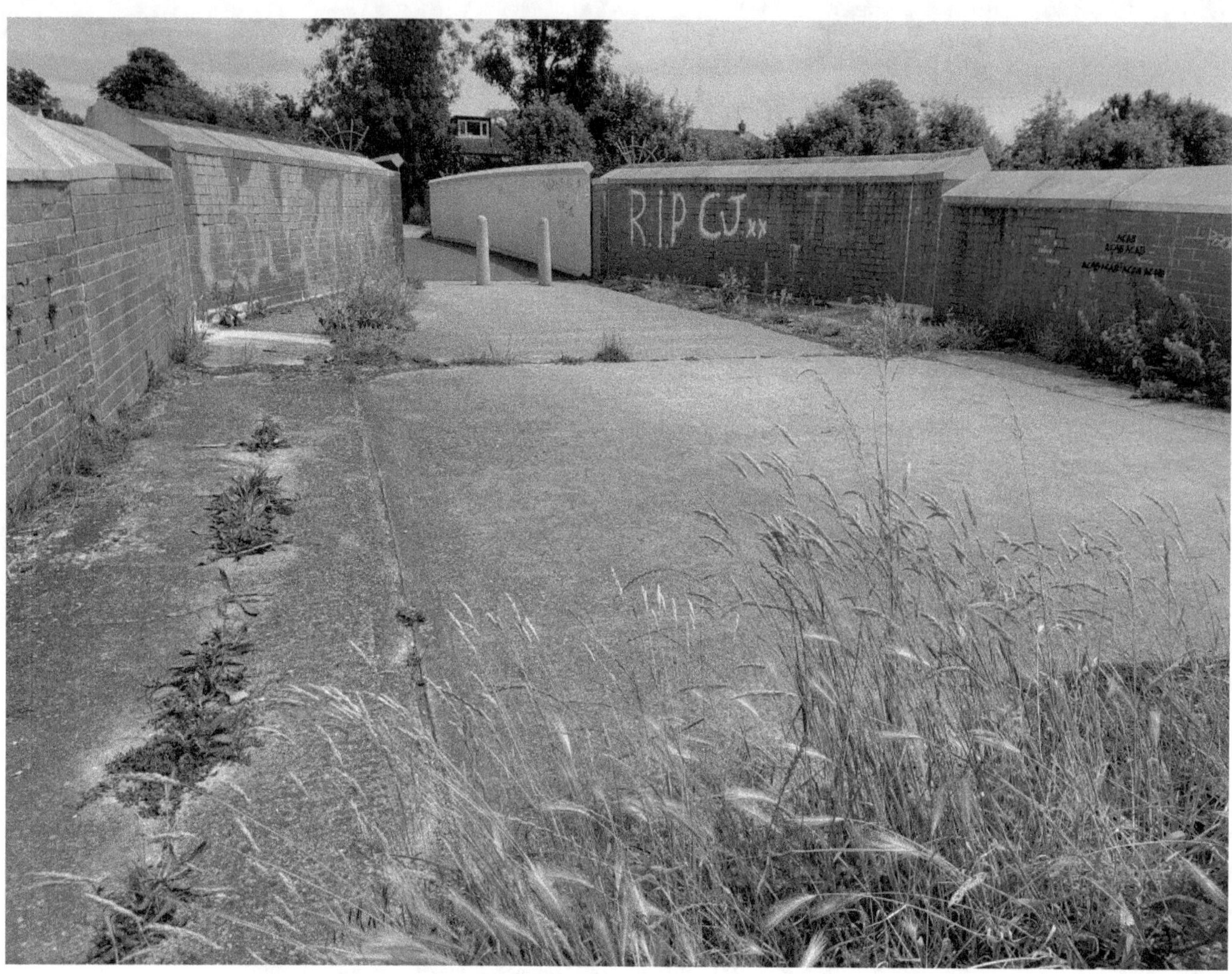

Image 38: Bridge too far

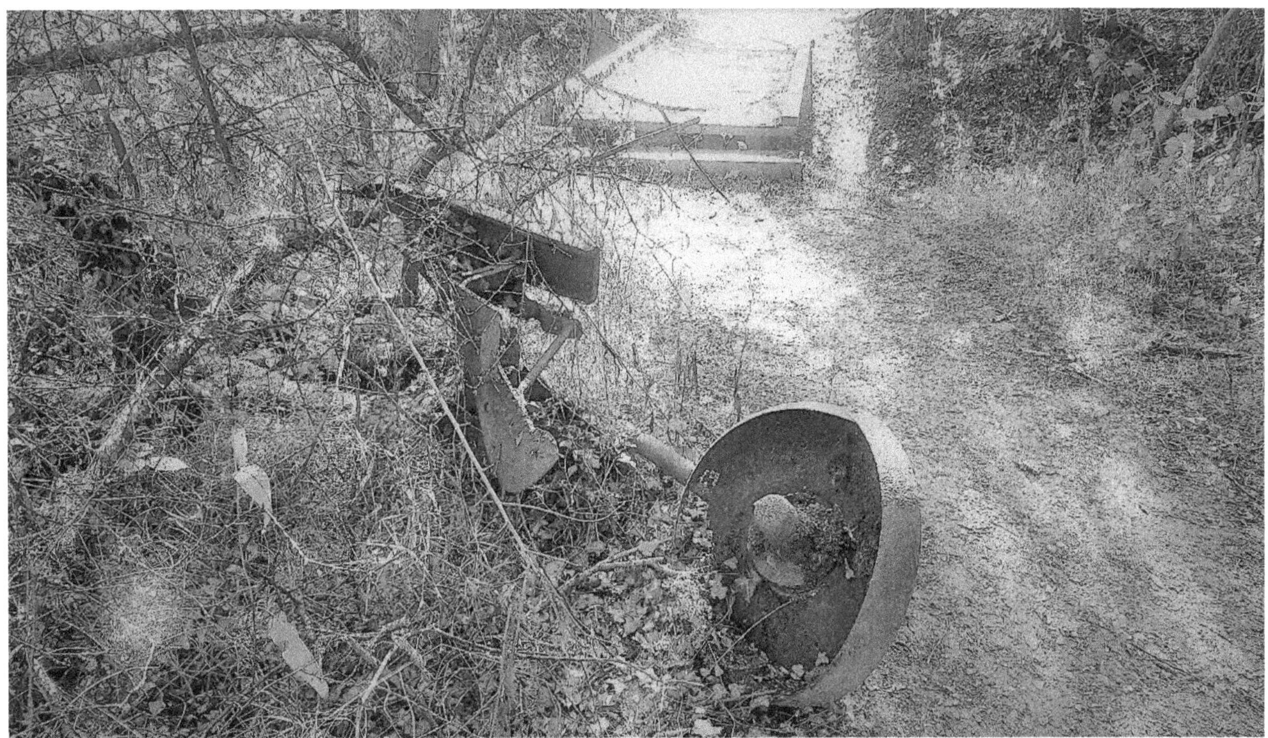

Image 39: Red Road

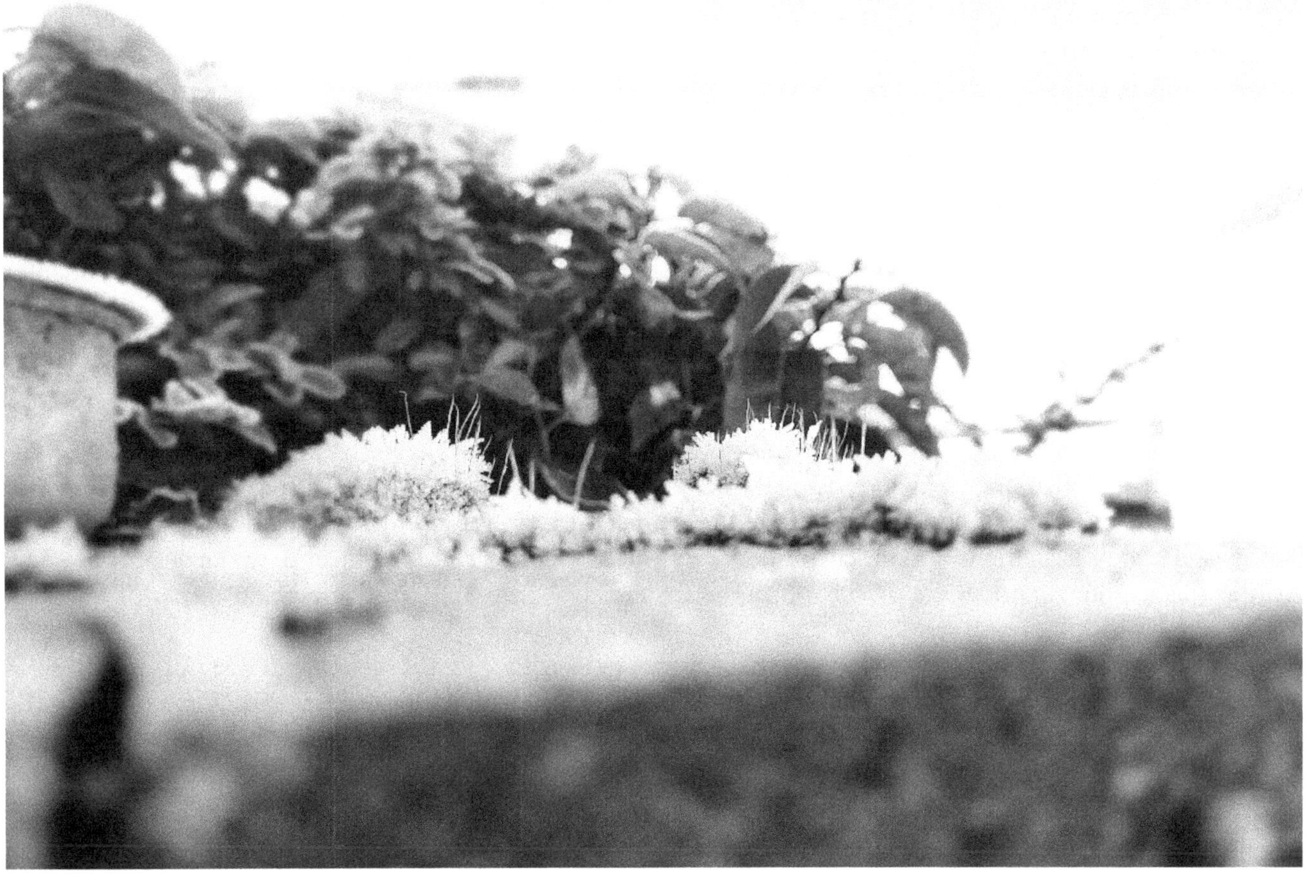

Image 40: Iced

6 VILLAGE

Villages contain many interesting buildings and objects. The selection of village buildings here are drawn from the English counties of Hertfordshire, Kent, Bedfordshire, and Essex.

A charming out building is presented in *Image 41*, constructed from timber and a naturally occurring aggregate of minerals and mineraloid matter. It is found in a placed called Patchetts Green, a hamlet of several historic houses, including the Three Compasses public house, Little Patchetts Green Farm, and Patchetts Farm. These are contained in the parish of Aldenham.

Discarded metal or a work of art? *Image 42* is a sculpture, found in the village of Shenley. Shenley is a village and civil parish in Hertfordshire, England, between Barnet and St Albans. The sculpture is found in Shenley Park. Once a private Estate known as Porters Park, then a site of a Mental Hospital, Shenley Park is now a unique self-funded Park, open for the public.

Image 43 is a concrete base for a pillar, surrounded by grass. A discarded object, yet one that retains a usefulness and its original beauty.

Located in a Regency and Victorian layered garden, the section of brick wall that forms the backdrop to *Image 44* was once a well-maintained floral garden. It now represents an abandoned section of the Swiss Garden near the Old Warden Aerodrome, Old Warden in Bedfordshire. Between 1135 and 1537, the village grew up under the protection of the Cistercian Wardon (a Catholic religious order of monks).

Image 45 is from a section of an old hangar maintained by the Shuttleworth Trust, an organization committed to the preservation of transport artefacts, which is also located in Old Warden. I like the combination of the polish of the metal, the V-formation and the scattering of clouds.

The 46th picture is of an old building located somewhere in Essex. I found the image but to my shame I can't recall where it is from. Perhaps the anonymity adds to the mystery? It's a fine looking brick and timber structure, nonetheless.

Image 47 is of some discarded farm equipment in Essex, close to a village called Battelesbridge. The village is known for its interesting collection of antique shops and so-called 'vintage' ware. The pretty village straddles the River Crouch. As to the name of the village the origins are unclear, although some historians link it to the Battle of Assandune, fought between the Saxons and the Danes.

With the image, Britain's agricultural history is important, sustaining life and wellbeing for centuries. Here is equipment used to plough fields gathering rust. Important once, of little practical value now, but important, nevertheless.

Image 48 is from the same area. The building is being converted into an antiques emporium. By the late 19th century, there were mills, farms, coal yards, lime kilns and maltings in the village. Wharves on both sides of the river enabled boats to be loaded with flour and hay for animal bedding, with incoming cargoes of coal. Malt, lime and chalk were also traded, while the river provided good catches of fish. The image depicts the former maltings. The building would have housed the process of process of steeping, germinating and drying grain to convert it into malt. As to wat can be done with malt? Malted grain is used to make beer, whisky, malted milk, malt vinegar, confections such as Maltesers and Whoppers, flavored drinks such as Horlicks, Ovaltine, and Milo, and some baked goods, such as malt loaf, bagels, and Rich Tea biscuits.

Image 49 begs the question 'where does this door lead to?' This is the wooden door with the glimpse of a garden. The garden is private, the door is public. The door looked locked shut, probably not used very often, there being other forms of access. This means it meets the category of being 'abandoned' as I loosely define it. The door, the wall, and the garden are from Kent, a wonderous little village that will remain nameless.

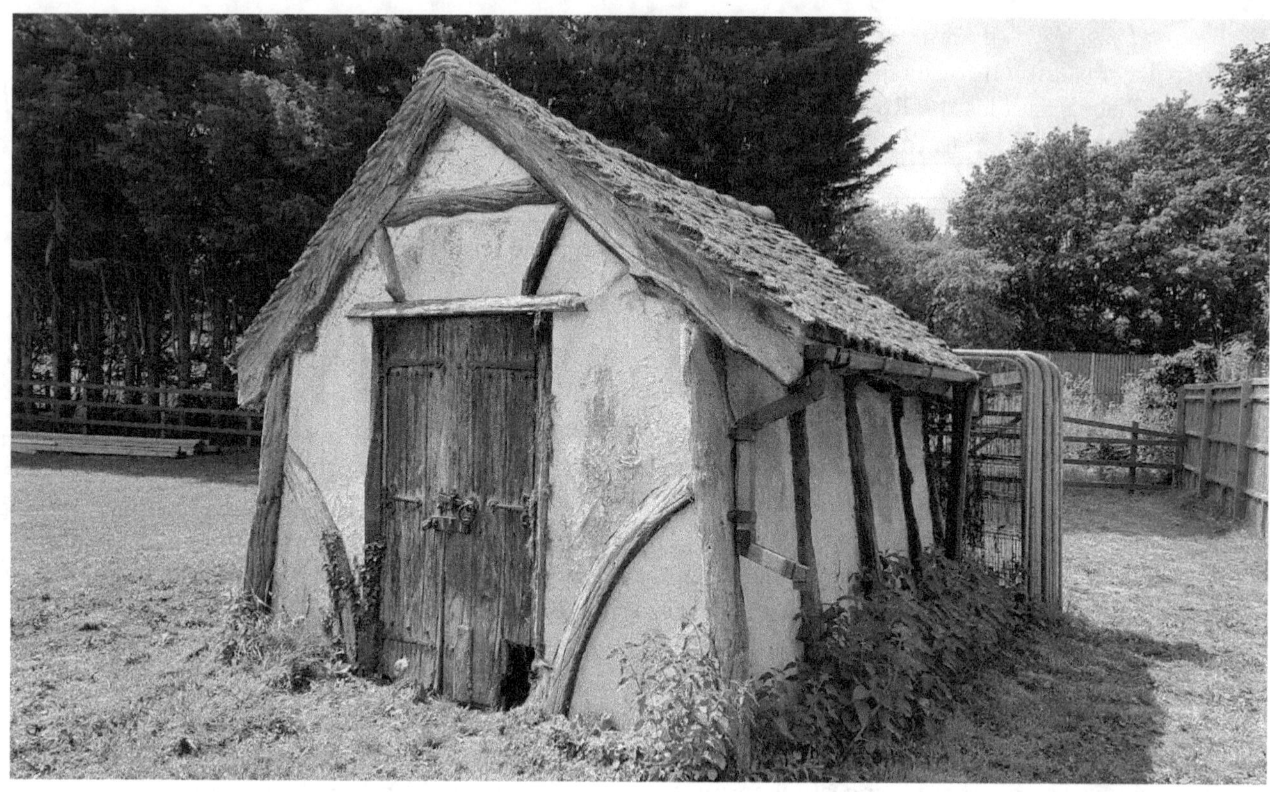

Image 41: Latitude 51°39'52"North and longitude 0°20'56"West

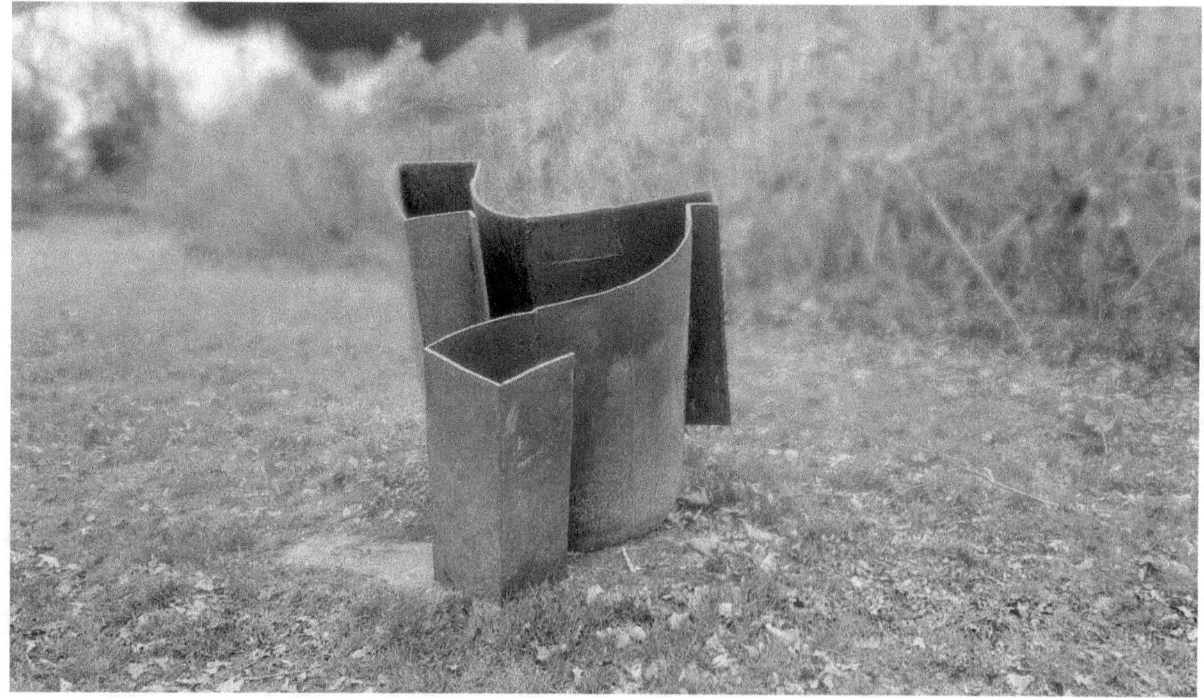

Image 42: Metal sculpture, Shenley

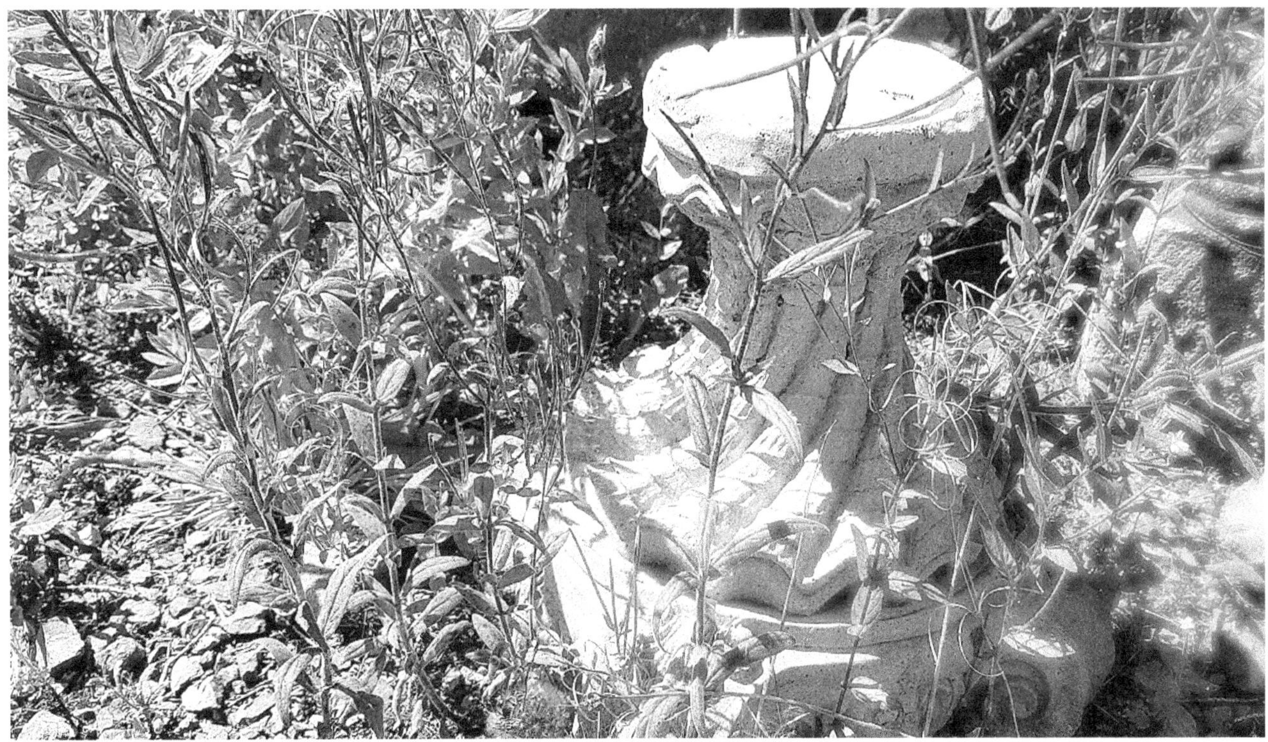

Image 43: Structural awakening

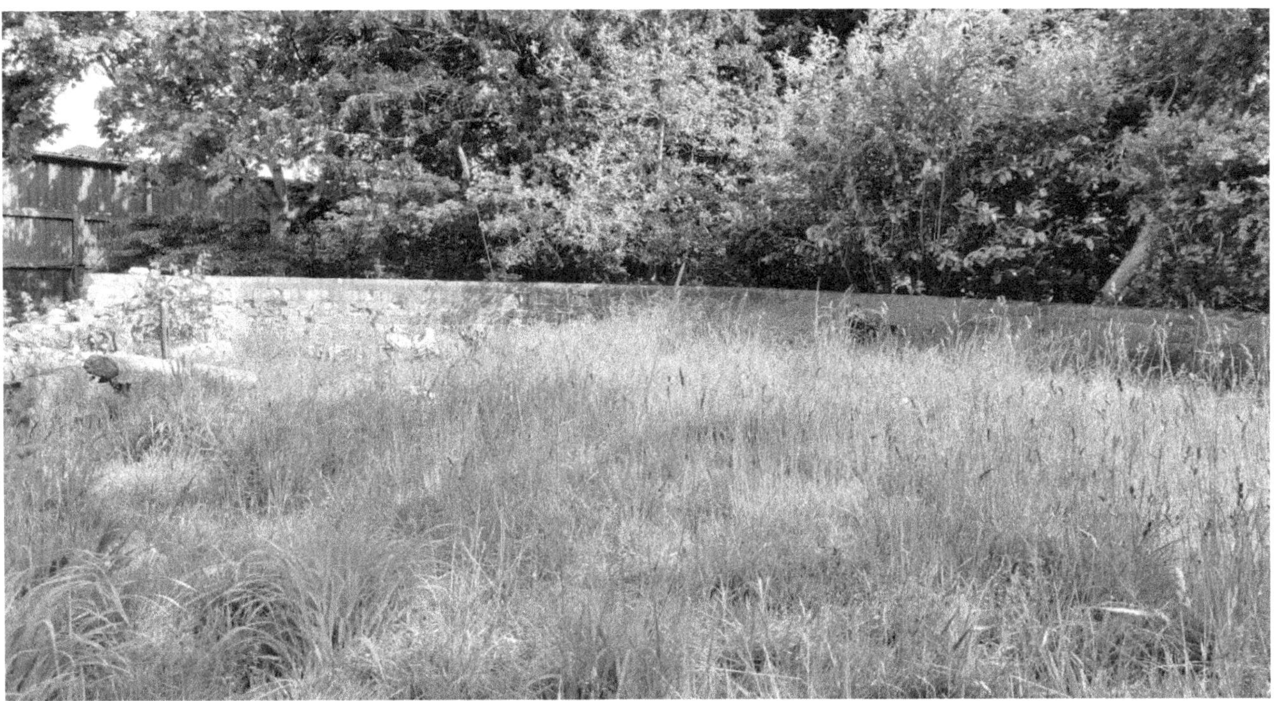

Image 44: Old wall of a once walled garden

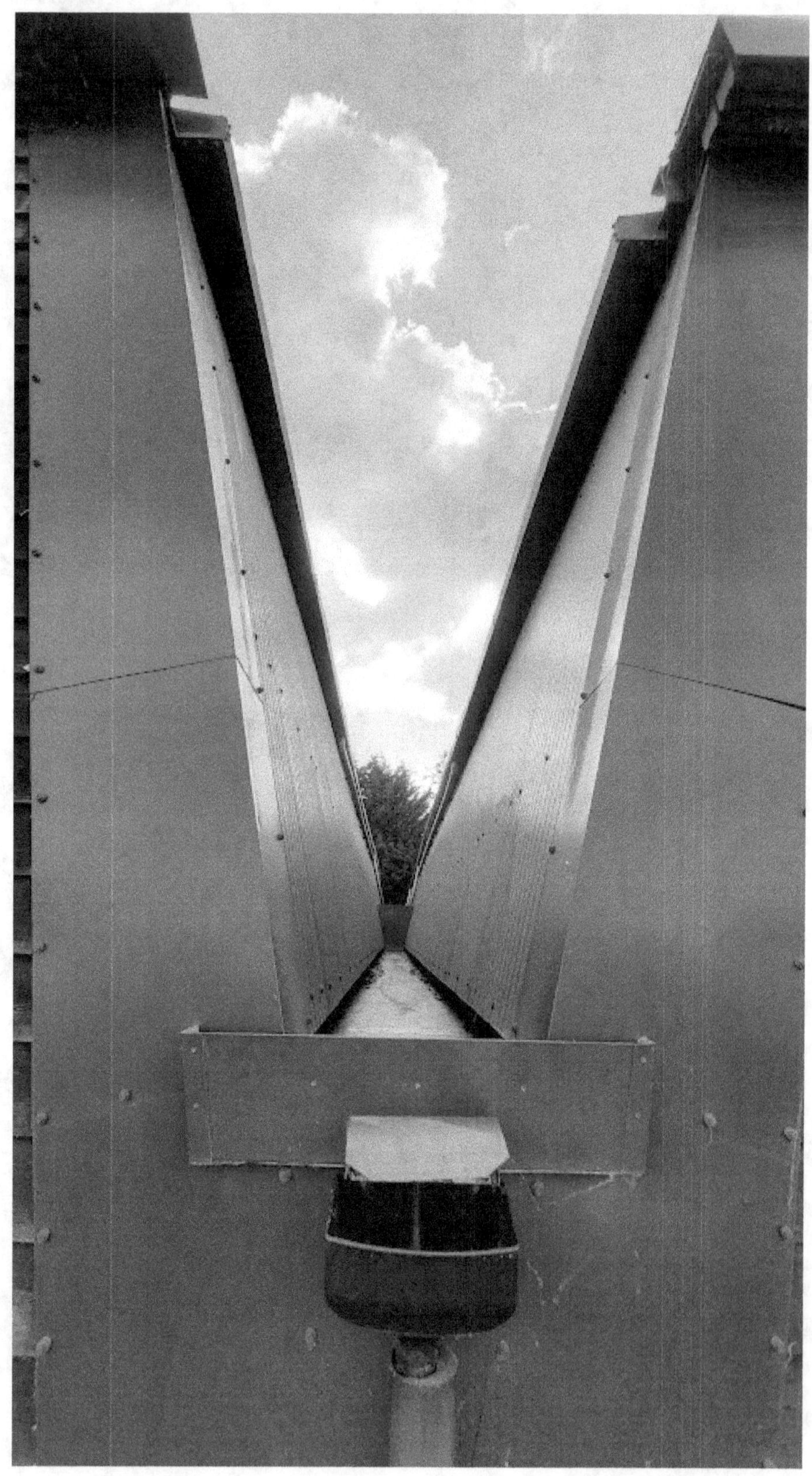

Image 45: V-sign to the clouds

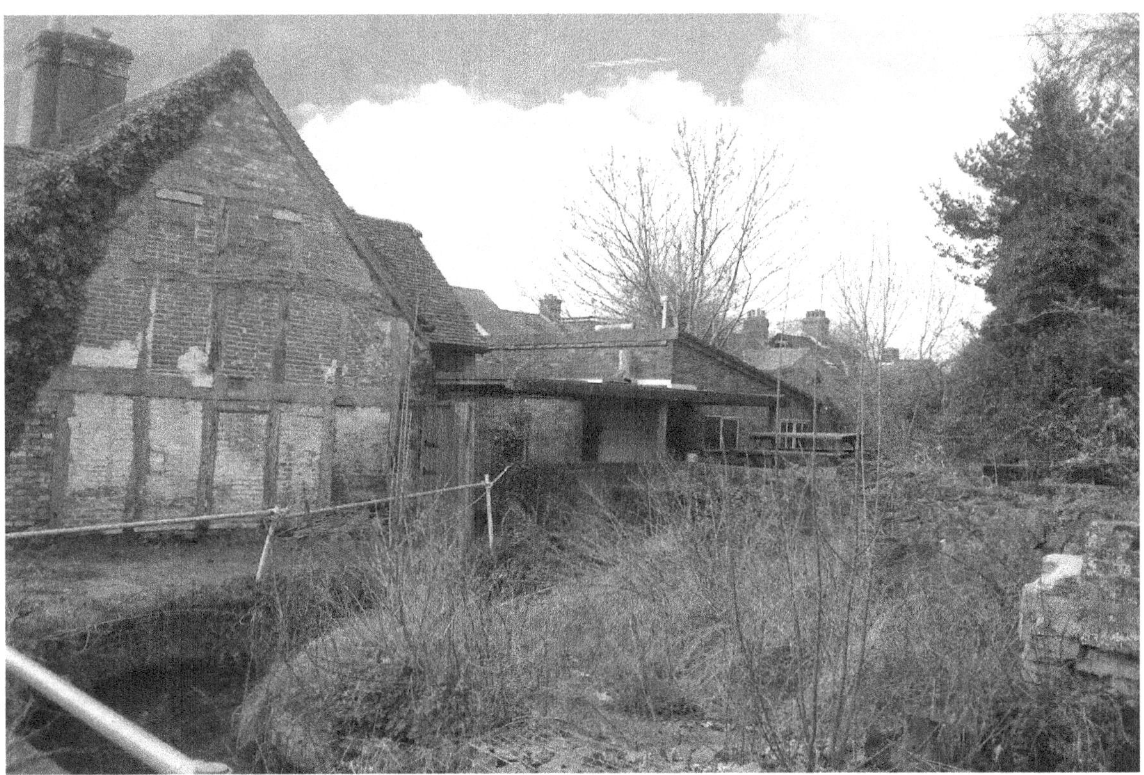

Image 46: Abandoned places, worn out faces

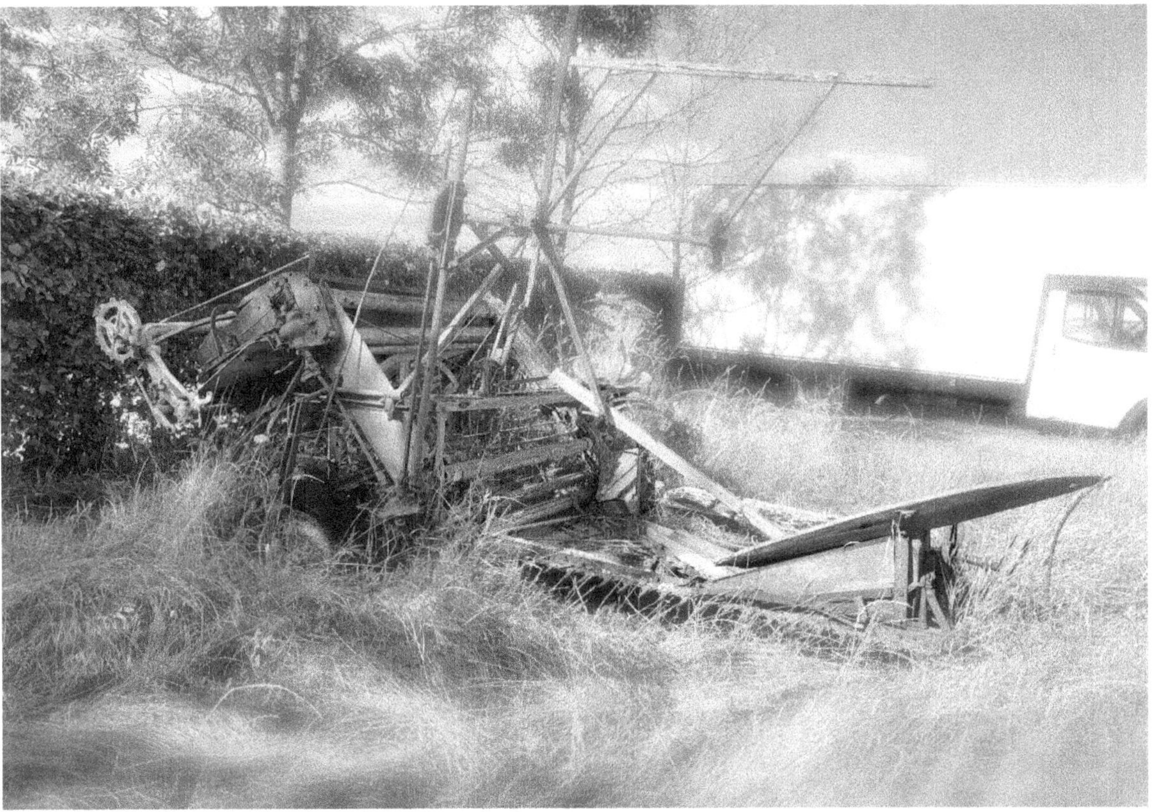

Image 47: Working the land once-upon-a time

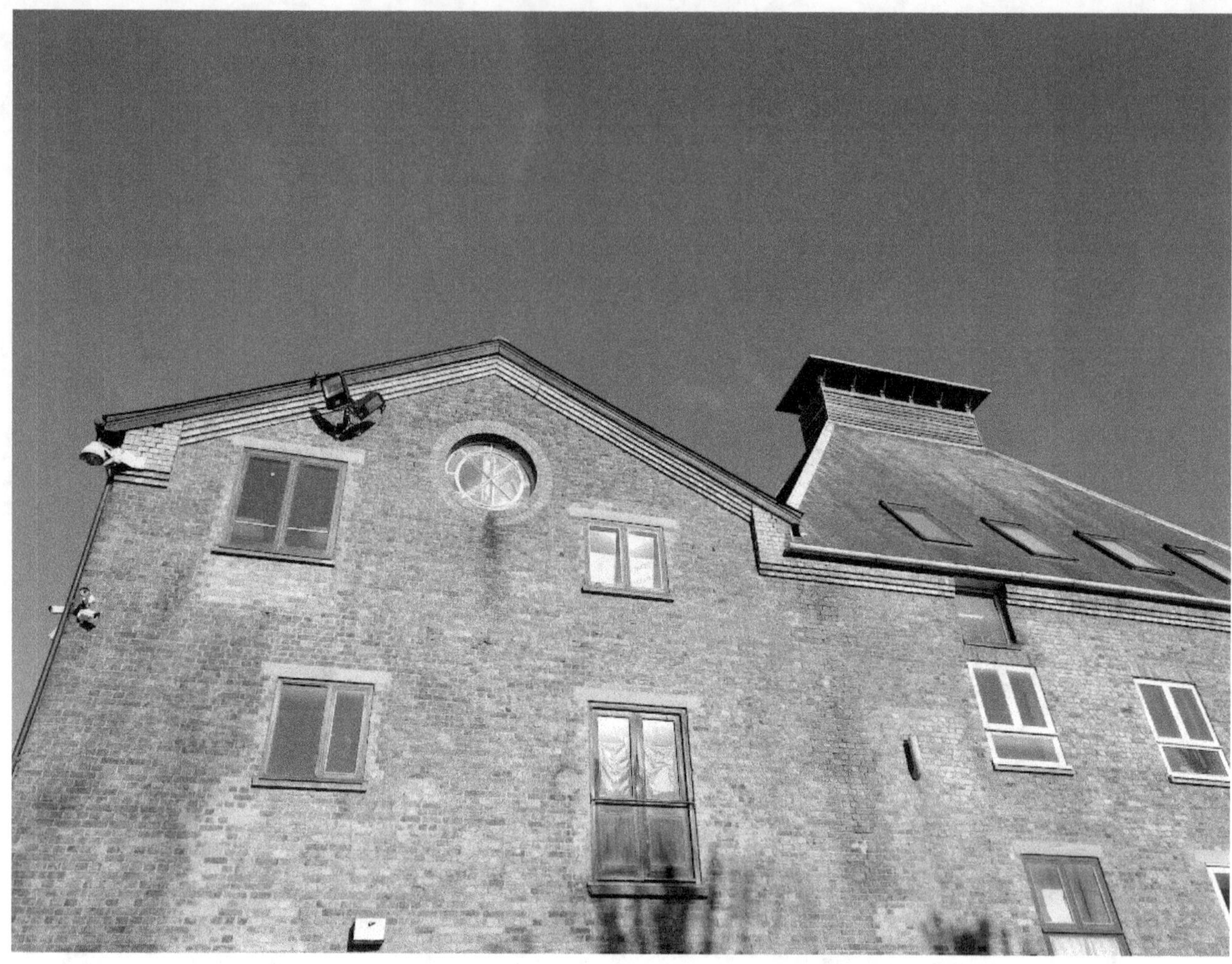

Image 48: Drying, steeping, toasting and smoking.

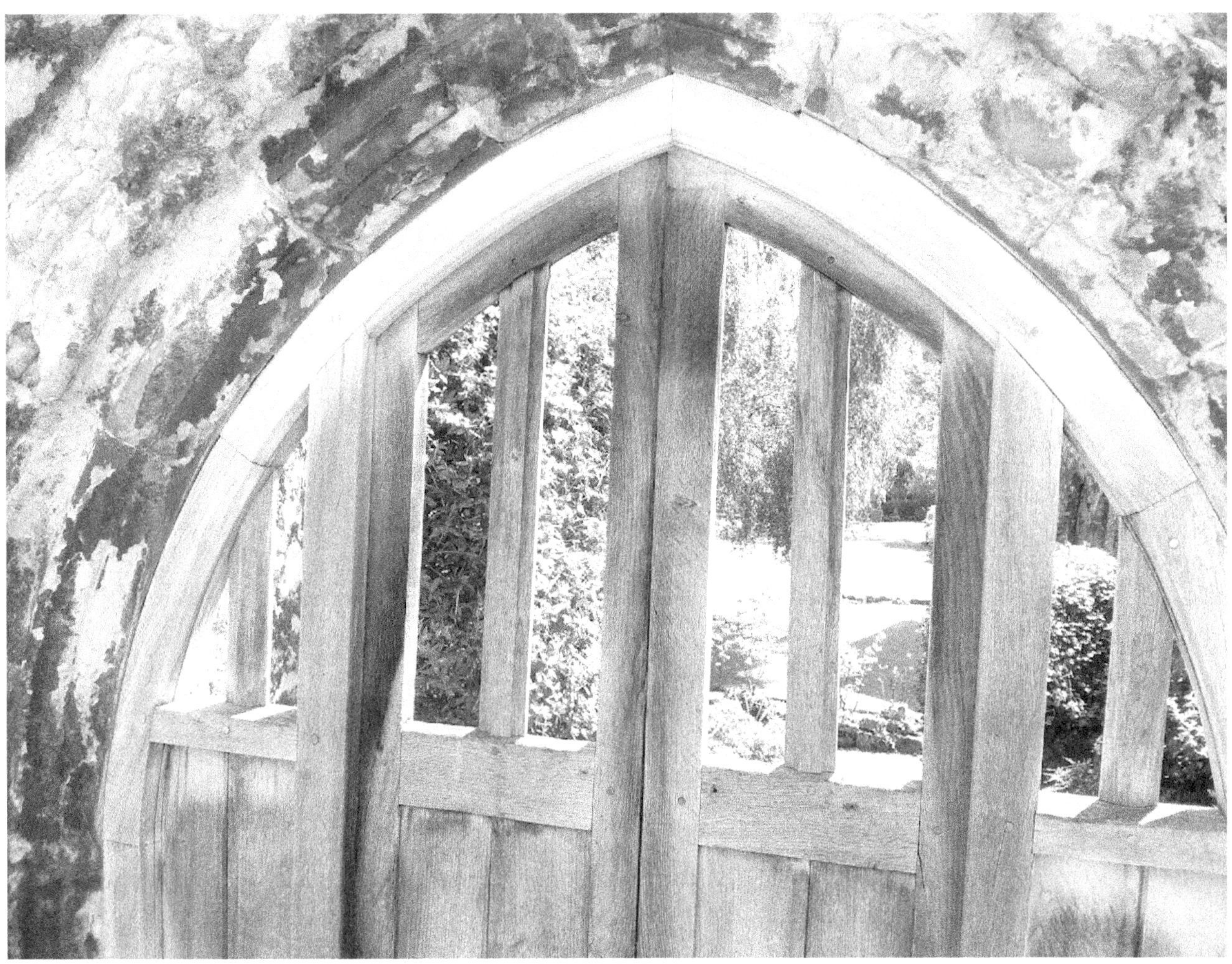

Image 49: Old door and a peak into a private garden

7 GAELS

Killashee is a village in County Longford, Ireland. It is situated on the N63 midway between Lanesborough and Longford. Killashee traces its foundation to the 5th century and is associated with Auxilius, a nephew and companion of Saint Patrick, with the Annals of the Four Masters dating its founding to AD 454.

Locating the grounds of a former monetary, Alexander Graydon settled in Killashee in 1711, when he leased the lands from Sir Richard Belling. He was sovereign of Naas in 1730 and probably built the original Georgian House at Killashee. In the grounds of the estate, which now contains a 5-star hotel, are many old and dilapidated buildings.

Images 50 to *56* are of an out-building, located outside the grounds of the hotel but within the original estate. Each room contained something different, from furniture to concrete fonts; from mattresses to oil cans. It isn't so much a question of what were these buildings originally used for, but were they used for the interim? Youth partying? A homeless shelter?

I like the light effect in *Image 54*, catching the sun at the right moment towards the corner of the camera. And the sense of abandonment is strong in *Image 55*. The oilcan left in the middle seems like the last act of something happening that should not of been happening.

Image 56 is further along. At the top of the human-made hill is a glimpse of the splendor or the hotel. Supporting it is a concrete structure that has a bridge-like function; beneath it are some oddly cut catacombs.

Parts of the hotel are still being prepared and *Image 57* is from inside, an area being developed. The building was once a school and it has a dormitory feel, sparkling porcelain everywhere.

Nearby is a town house, with a garage space underneath and this forms *Image 58*. From a distance it reminded me of Hansel and Gretel. I'm not sure why but the house becomes visible as one emerges from a wooded area. It has an edge of spookiness. The underneath area forms the next image in sequence.

The last image in this section is of an old wall on the edge of some lush grounds. John Jameson III, the grandson of the founder of the Jameson Distillery at Bow Street, moved to St. Marnocks in 1847 and occupied a manor house that is now a hotel and had the wall built, separating the property from the outside world.

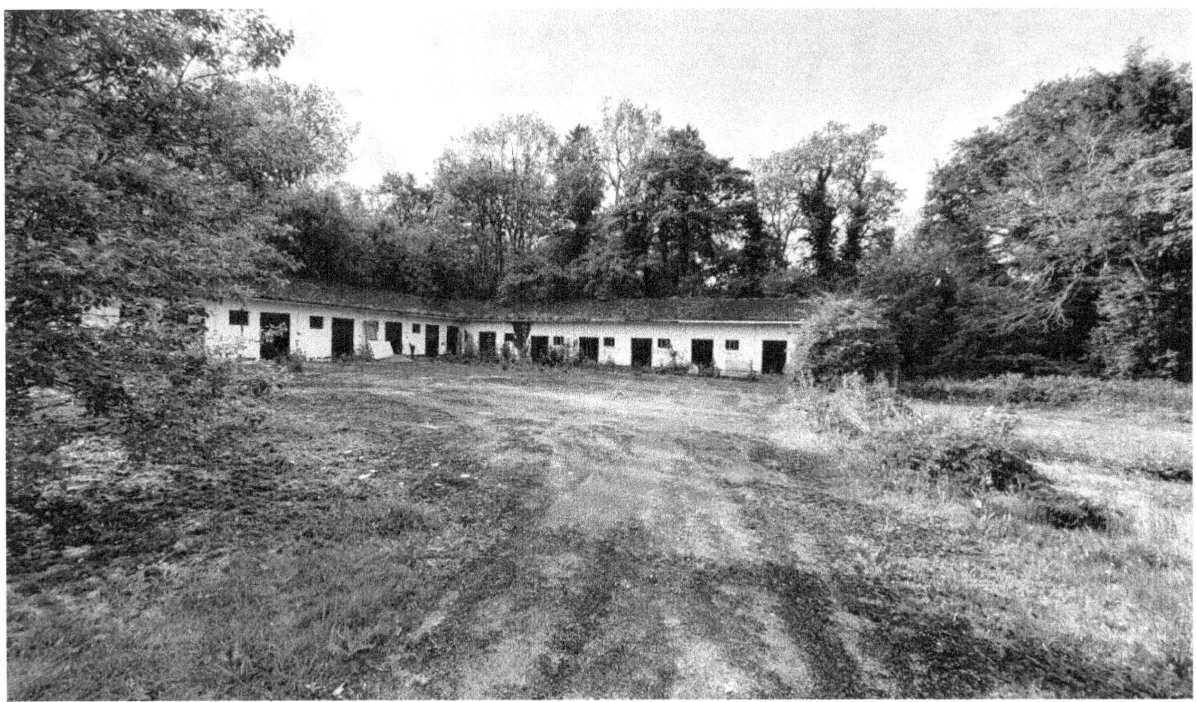

Image 50: Abandoned out buildings on the periphery of the estate.

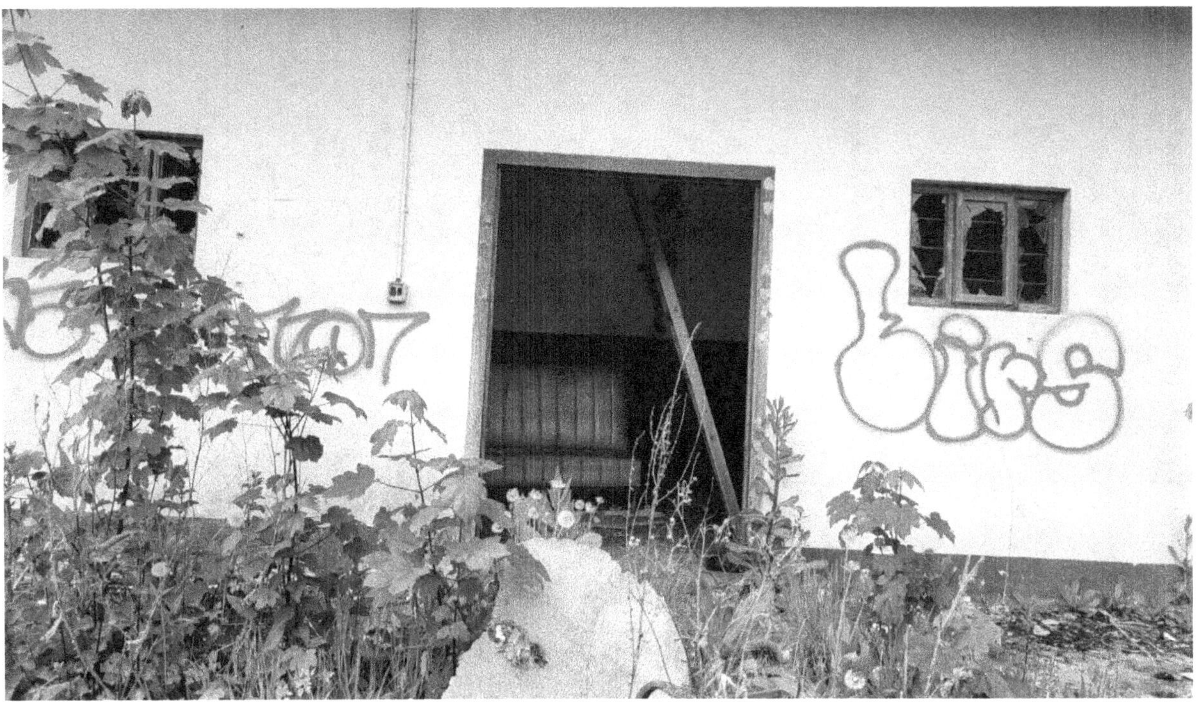

Image 51: Moving closer in, this room offers a seated experience

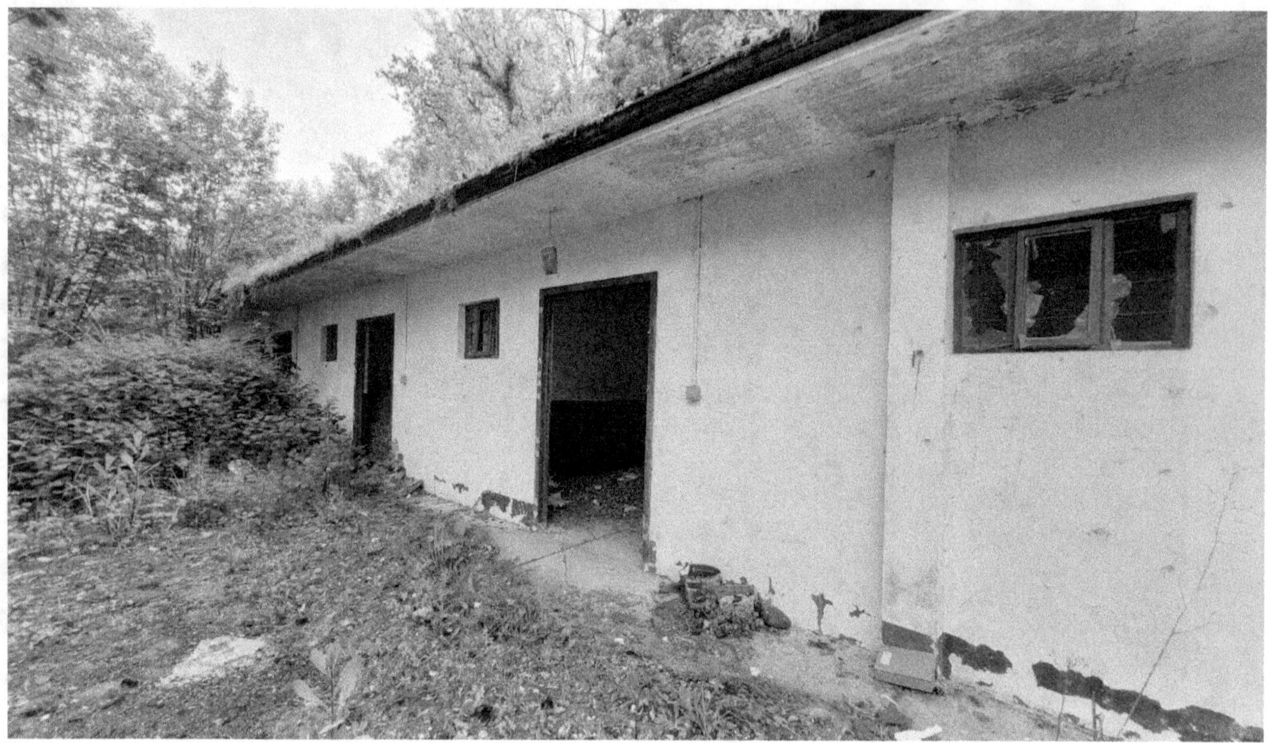

Image 52: A home from home

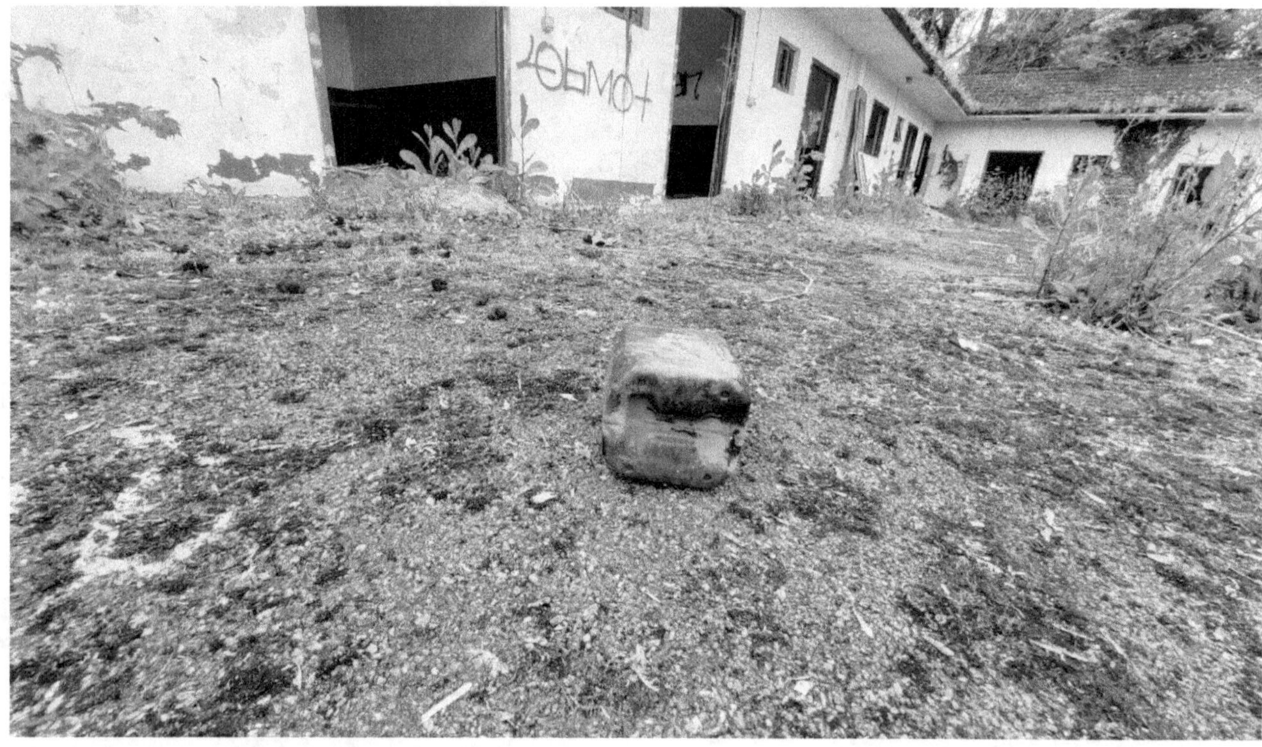

Image 53: Oilcan, center stage

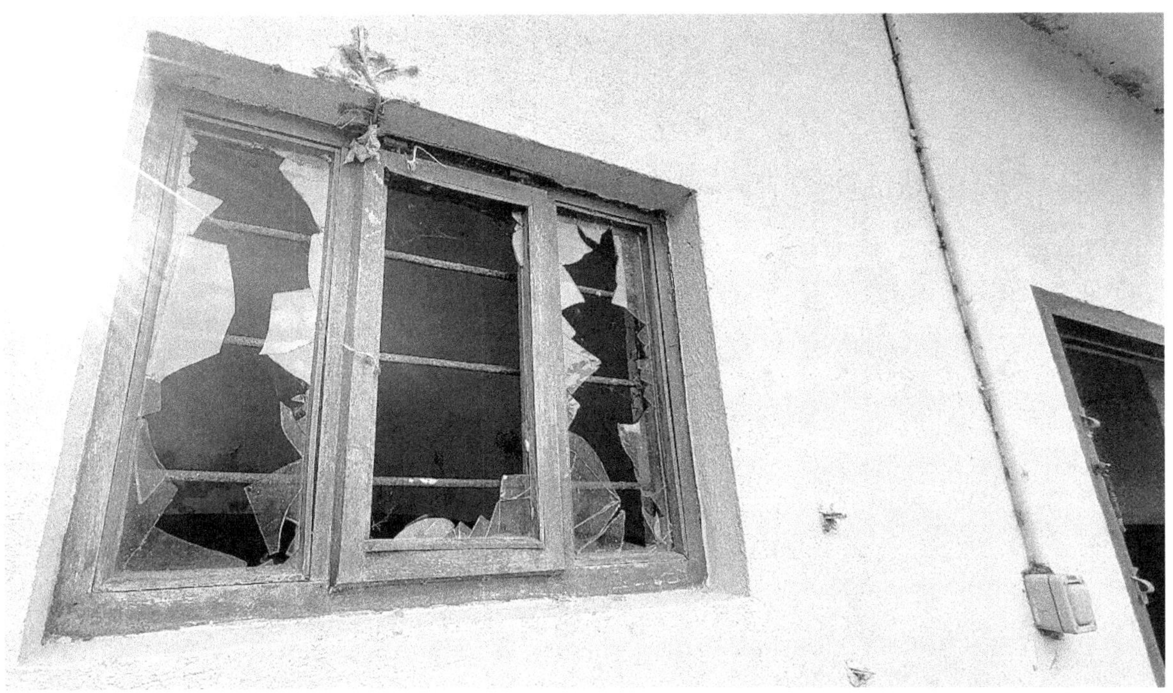

Image 54: What light through yonder window breaks?

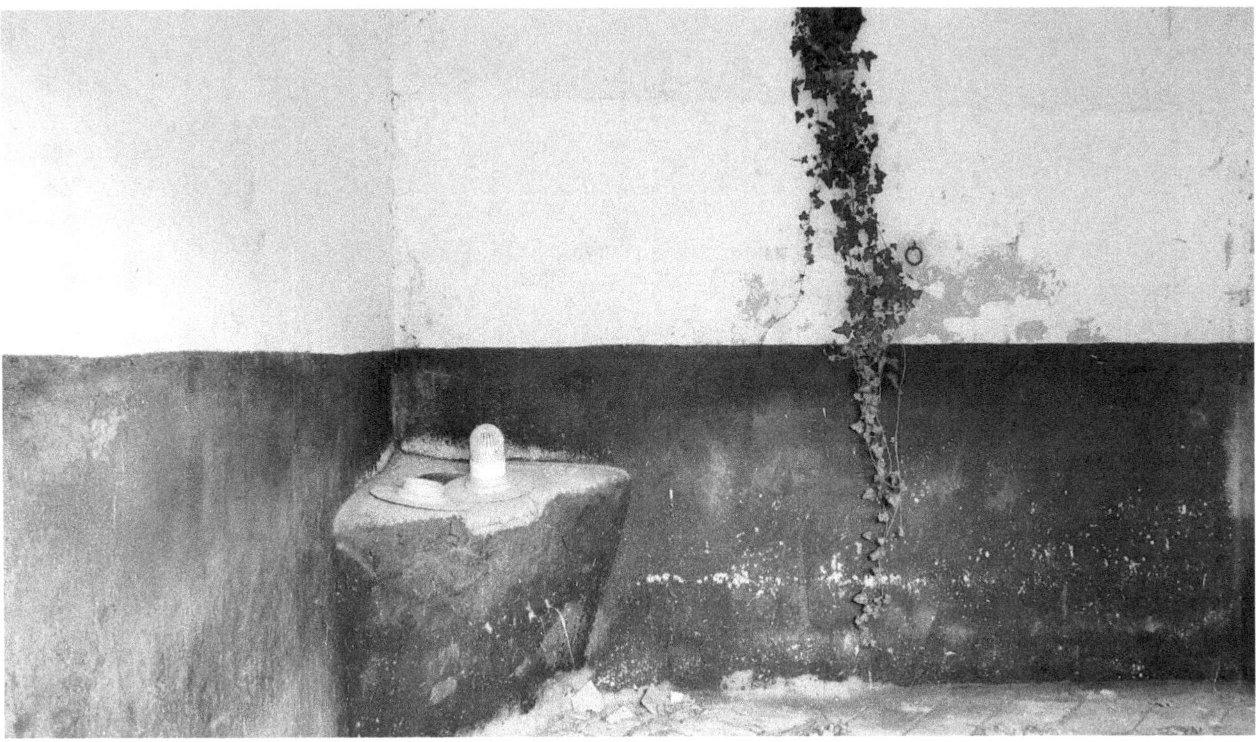

Image 55: Altar to the discarded

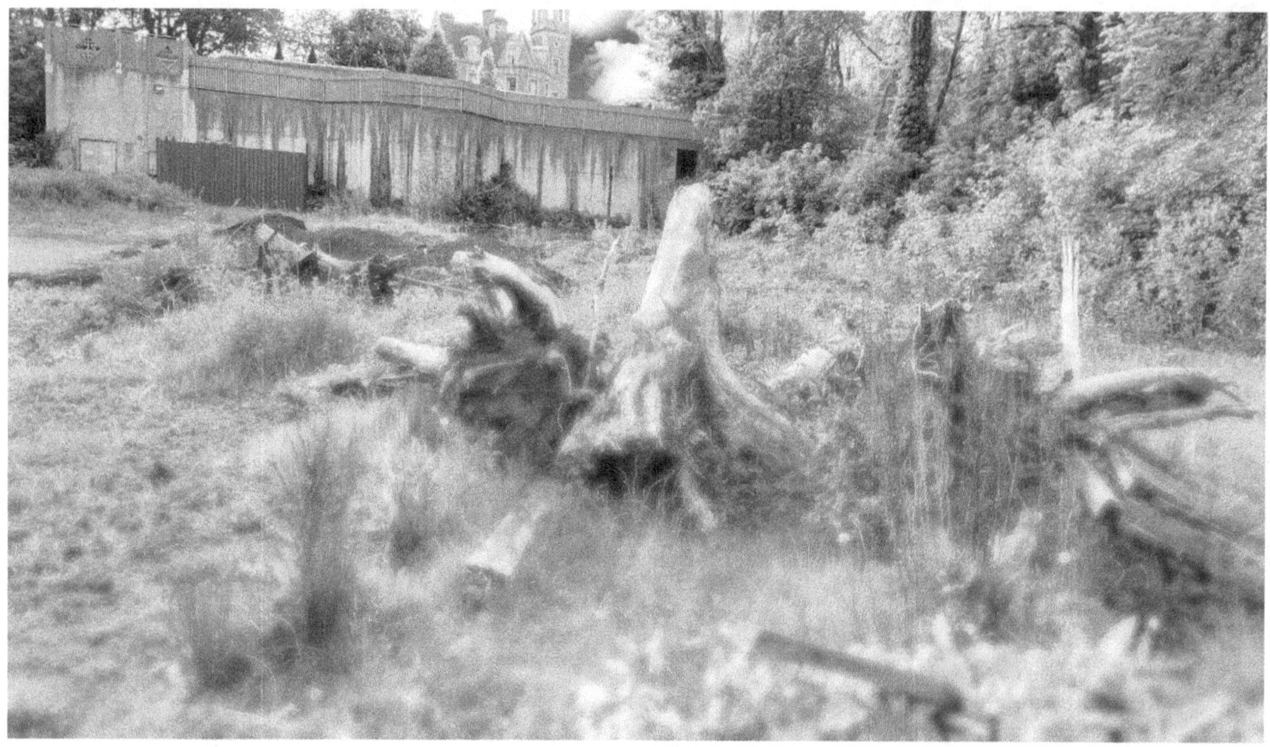

Image 56: Of concrete bridges and natural progression

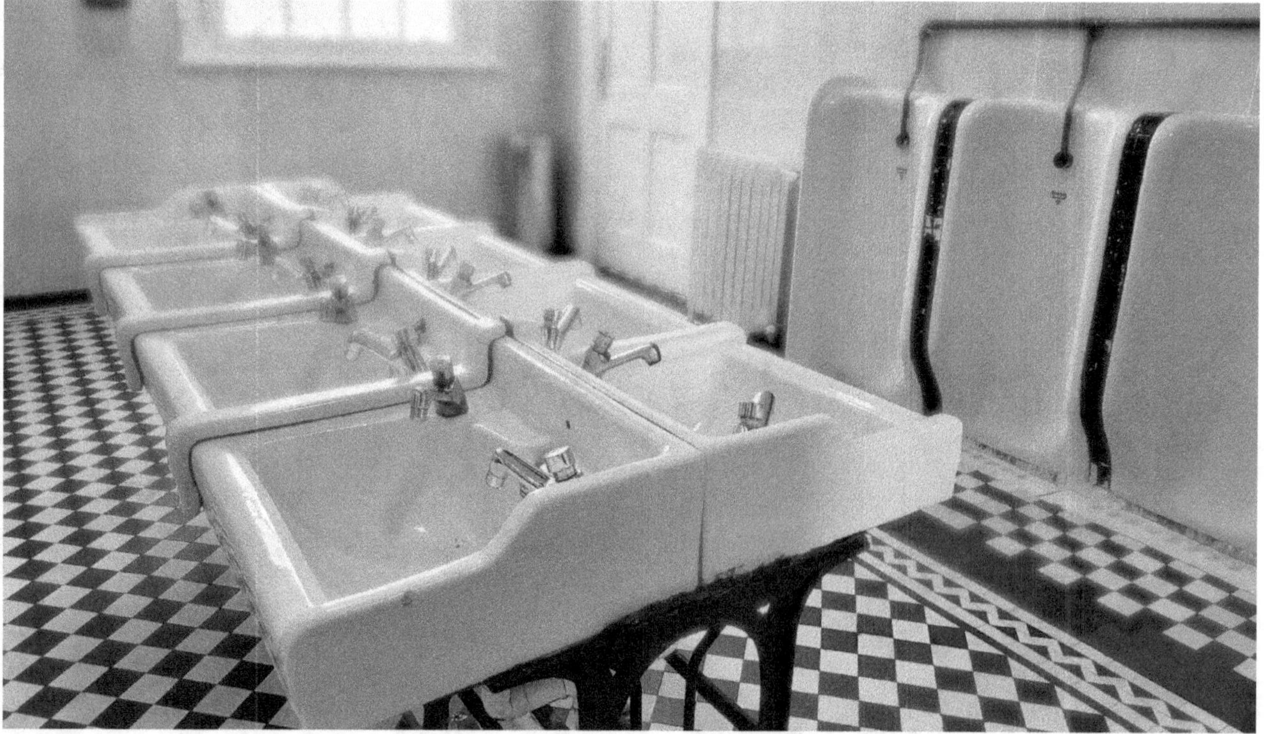

Image 57: Water babies

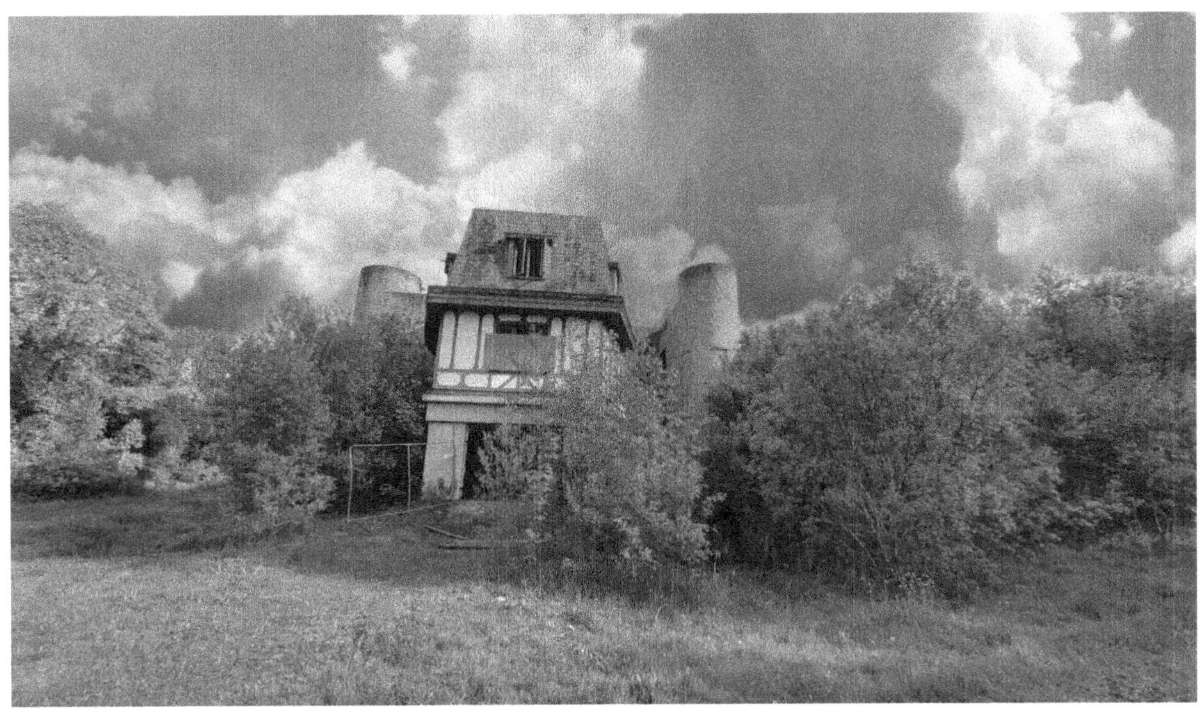

Image 58: Calling Hansel and Gretel

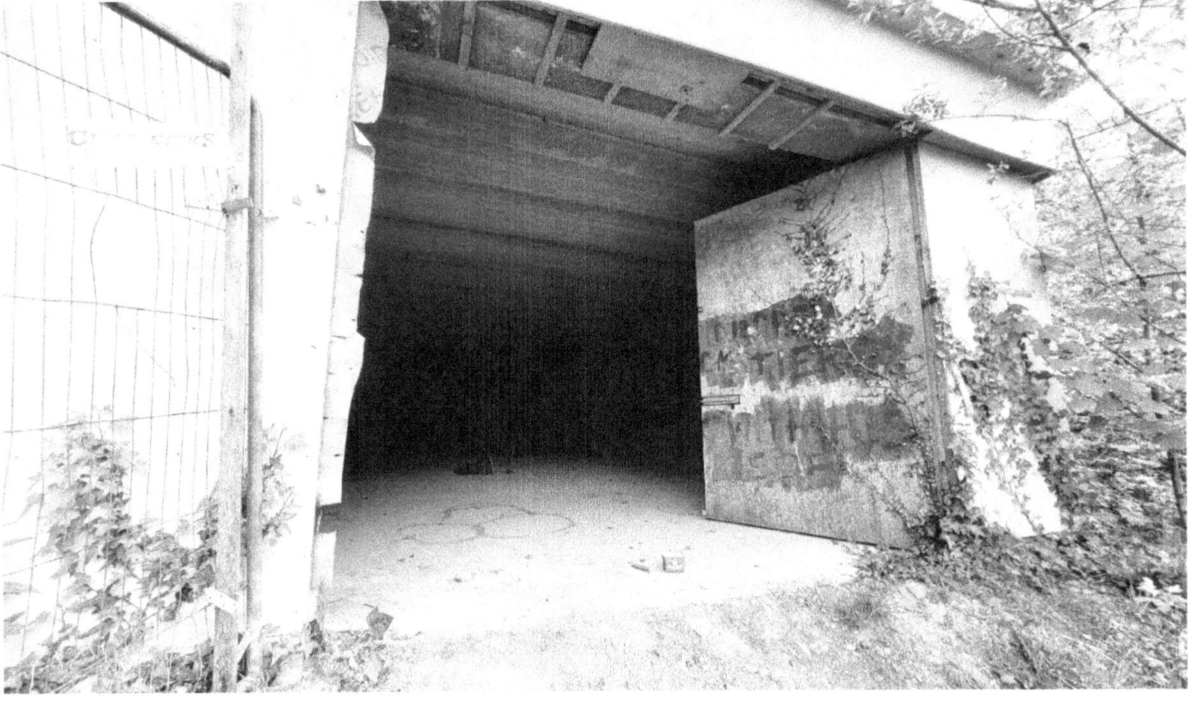

Image 59: Down below

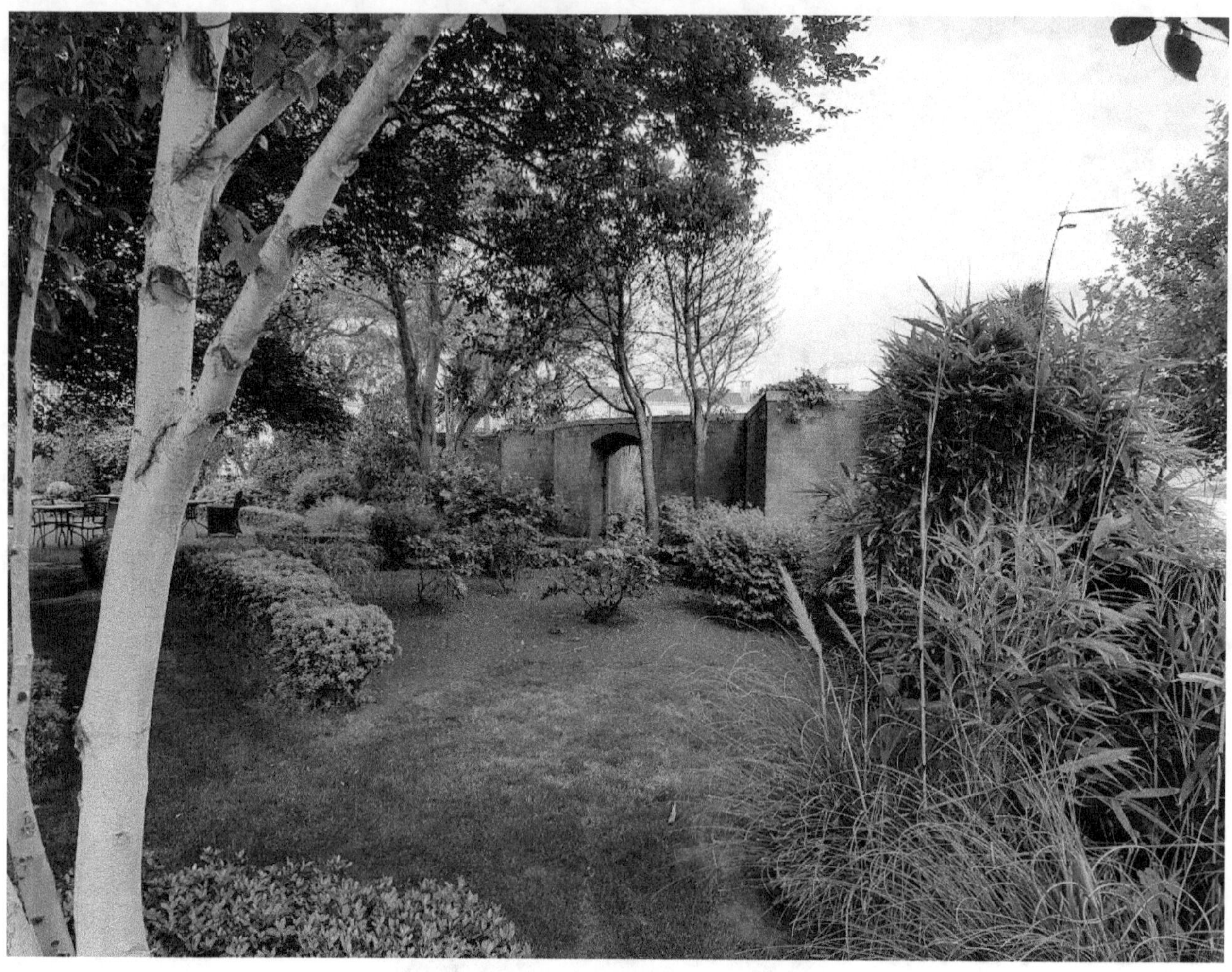

Image 60: The old wall waits

8 **GAOL**

Bodmin Gaol is a historic former prison situated in Bodmin, on the edge of Bodmin Moor in Cornwall. Built in 1779 and closed in 1927, a large range of buildings fell into ruin. Parts of the structure have since become a hotel. These images provided an opportunity to capture the crumbling structure before it underwent its conversion and process of gentrification.

Bodmin Gaol was designed by Sir John Call and built in 1779 by prisoners of war, and was operational for 150 years, in which it saw over 50 public hangings. It was the first British prison to hold prisoners in individual cells. *Image 61* captures the main prison, taken on a bright August day. I like the way that plants and vegetation have grown at the top, adding to the unkempt appearance.

Taken inside, near the top of the main prison building is a secluded alcove as *Image 62* displays. The sunlight shines brightly outside creating a nice contrast with blackness inside. The ladder laying on the attic floor makes me think of an escape route.

There were legal requirements during the 1850s to separate different classes of prisoners, such as holding vagrants in a different area to thieves; debtors from murders; and men from women. Conditions will have been horrific, yet there are parallels with the prison system today and society's enduring cultural attachment to a particular and arguably archaic material manifestation of punishment.

Architecture sends a silent message to everyone walking into any place. It tells you what to expect and where the limits of behavior are. The section of the former goal shown in *Image 63* seems to have a church like nature, connecting crime and punishment to a wider concept of power.

Image 64 allows me to quote Leonard Cohen. It's a shot I took between two buildings that form the main prison structure. The closer to the ground one goes the dark and more shadowy the vista becomes yet looking upwards the summer's light glows bright.

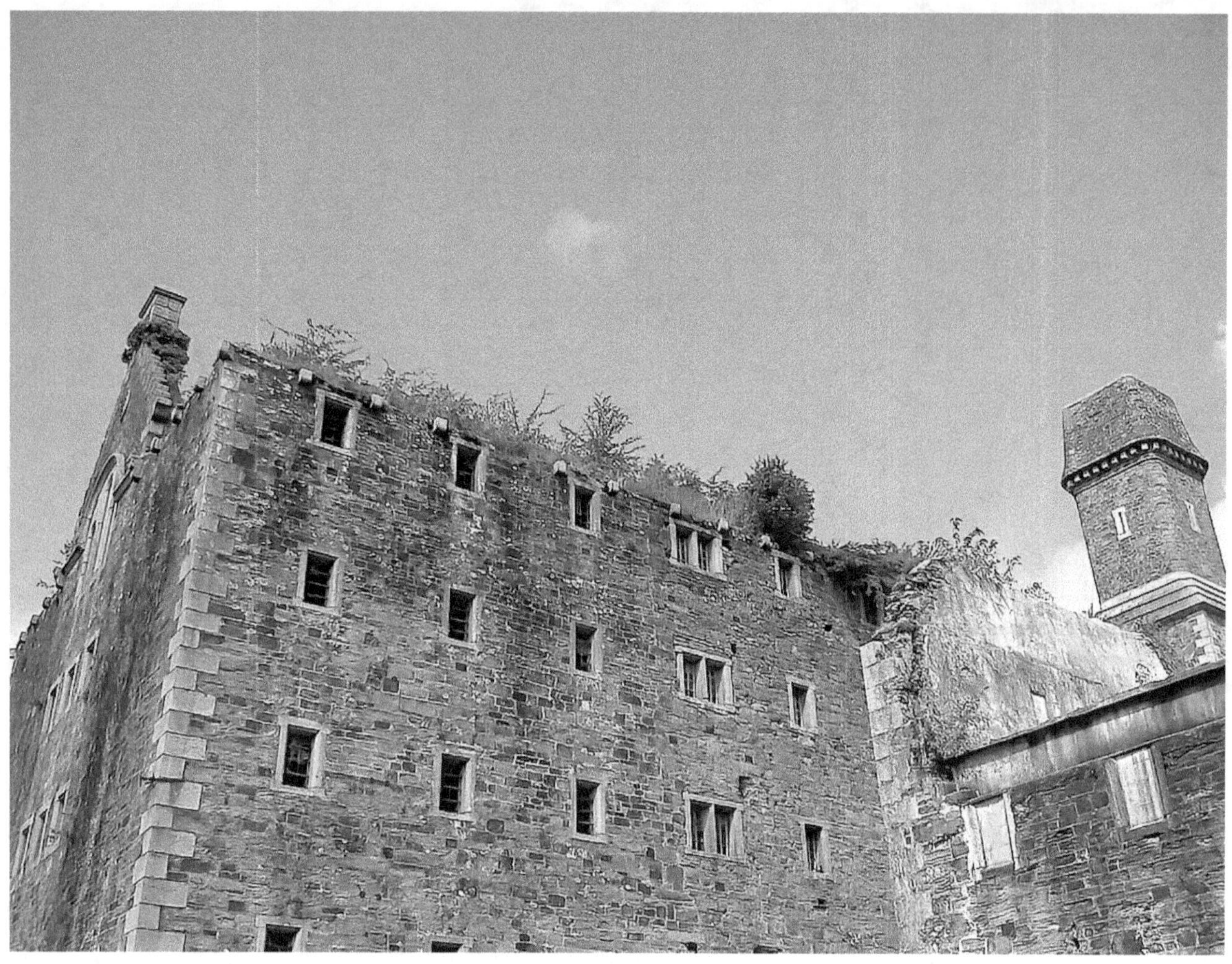

Image 61: Crumbling façade of the old prison

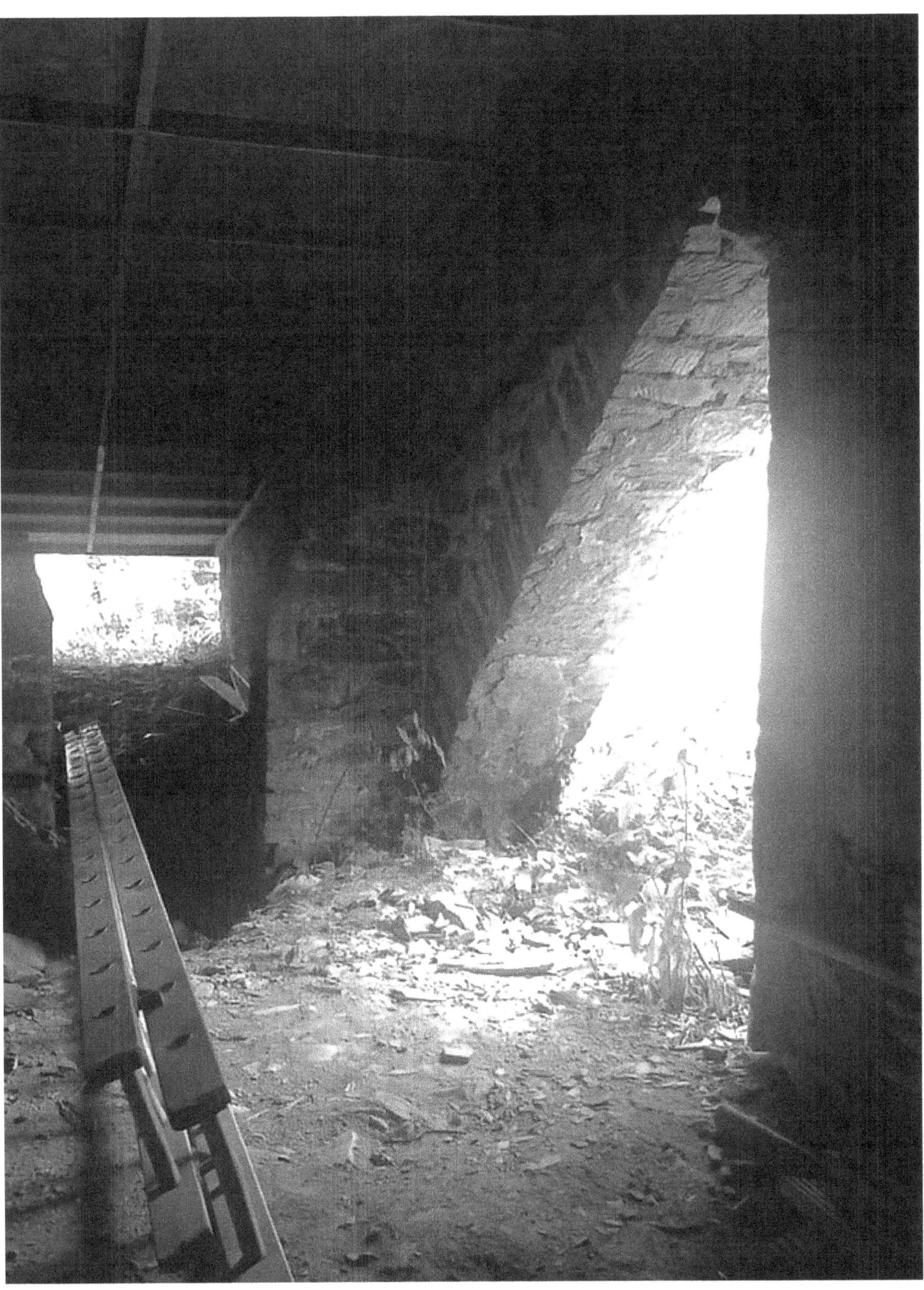

Image 62: Escape route?

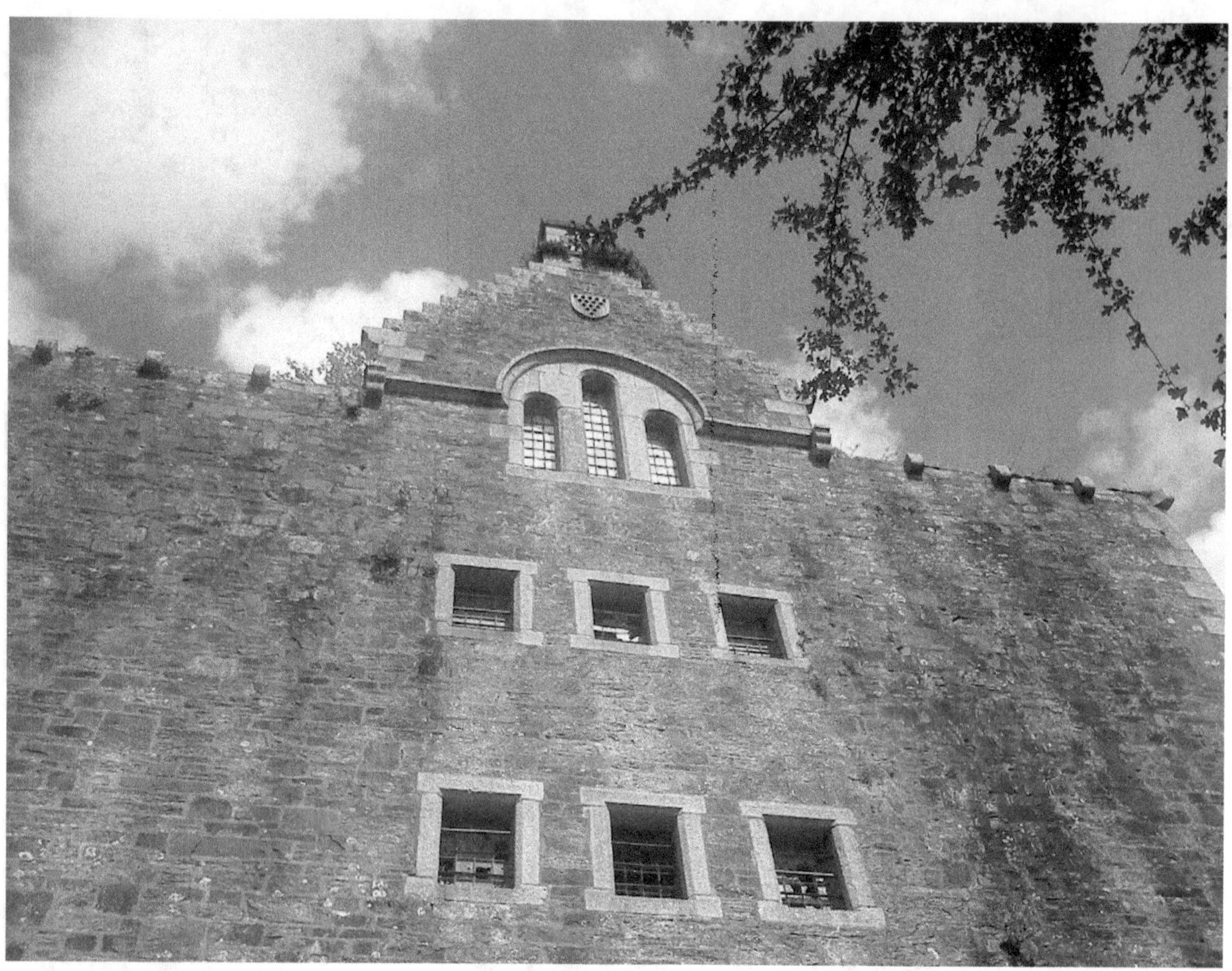

Image 63: Why do old prisons resemble churches?

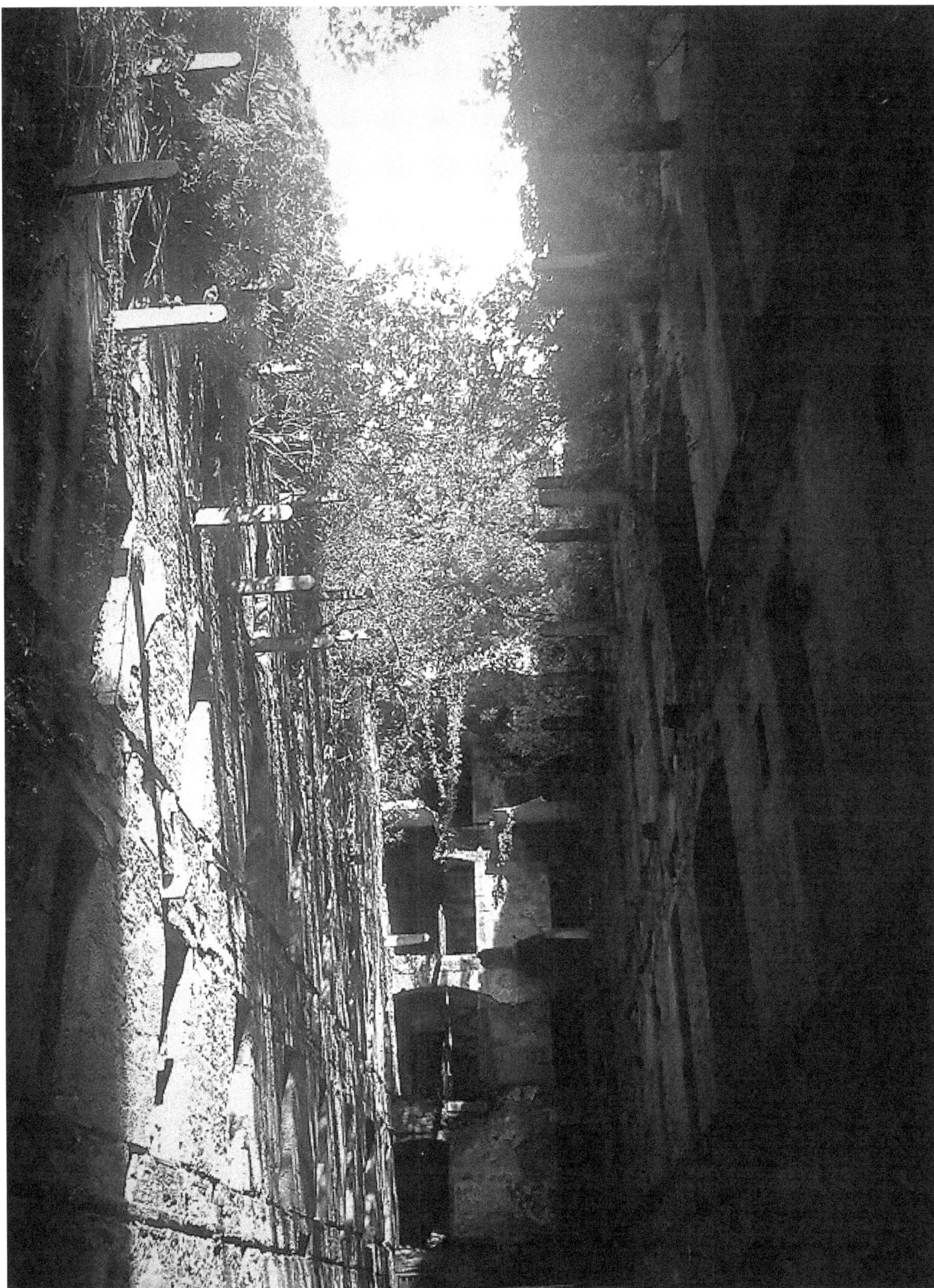

Image 64: There's a crack in everything, that's how the light gets in

9 LONDON

Think of London. The large, complex and varied city. It is impossible to seek to capture London here, but we can explore some of its hidden aspects, those areas in the shadows that you sometimes pass by without noticing or the street that seems to lead to nowhere, one where you have no reason ever to go down. Or perhaps it is simply the case of looking up, down or sideways more often.

Shoreditch today has a relaxed atmosphere and many walls are adorned with colorful graffiti. In Shoreditch there is a cool urban structure called Box Park which holds many pop up shops in reconditioned shipping containers refurbished and fitted out to act like shop space. Nearby, two former London Underground trains signal the thrills of the area – unusual, out-of-place, promising and enticing. This is what *Image 65* seeks to convey. The former train carriages are now used as art studios, positioned in place and time above an old railway viaduct.

Brutalism has a place in London, in many parts, including the magnificent Barbican Centre it is synonymous with London's post-World War II city development. There are other Brutalist (or should that be neo-Brutalist?) structures. Another eye-catching architectural triumph is the Brunswick Centre. The Brunswick Centre (today rebranded as 'The Brunswick') is a grade II listed residential and shopping center in Bloomsbury, London, England. It is located between Brunswick Square and Russell Square. Within the complex is a Curzon cinema, underneath the structure and the cinema contains many winding corridors. These retain the features of concrete and some are not currently in use, hence the inclusion of this (*Image 66*) skylight within the overarching theme of this book.

Image 67 is an old sign – not one enforceable today whatever 'nuisance' is supposed to convey – located in Lambeth. The area was once known as 'Lambeth Marsh' (or 'Lambeth Marshe'). This area was marshland and the place south of the river Thames that poorer members of society lived. I doubt the sign dates back that far, but it conveys, perhaps, the attitudes of law enforcement through street like The Cut throughout the Victorian era.

The Brunel Museum contains the history of the building of the Thames Tunnel. The museum contains the grade II listed Tunnel Shaft. The Thames Tunnel is a tunnel beneath the River Thames in London, connecting Rotherhithe and Wapping, the first tunnel in the world to have been constructed successfully underneath a navigable river. The tunnel was built between 1825 and 1843 by Marc Brunel and his son Isambard using a novel tunnelling shield, and *Image 68* is of the gloomily lit tunneling shaft.

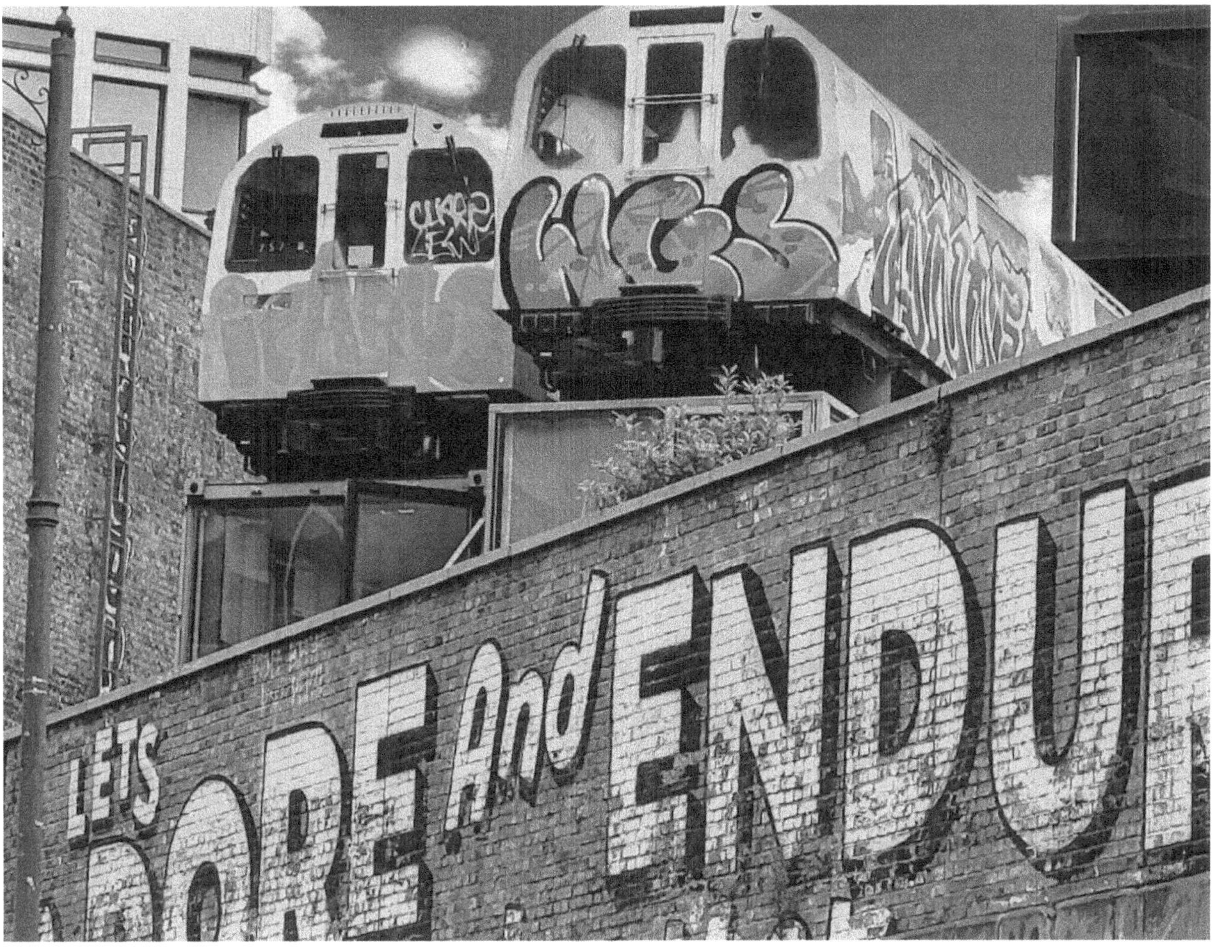

Image 65: Slow train coming

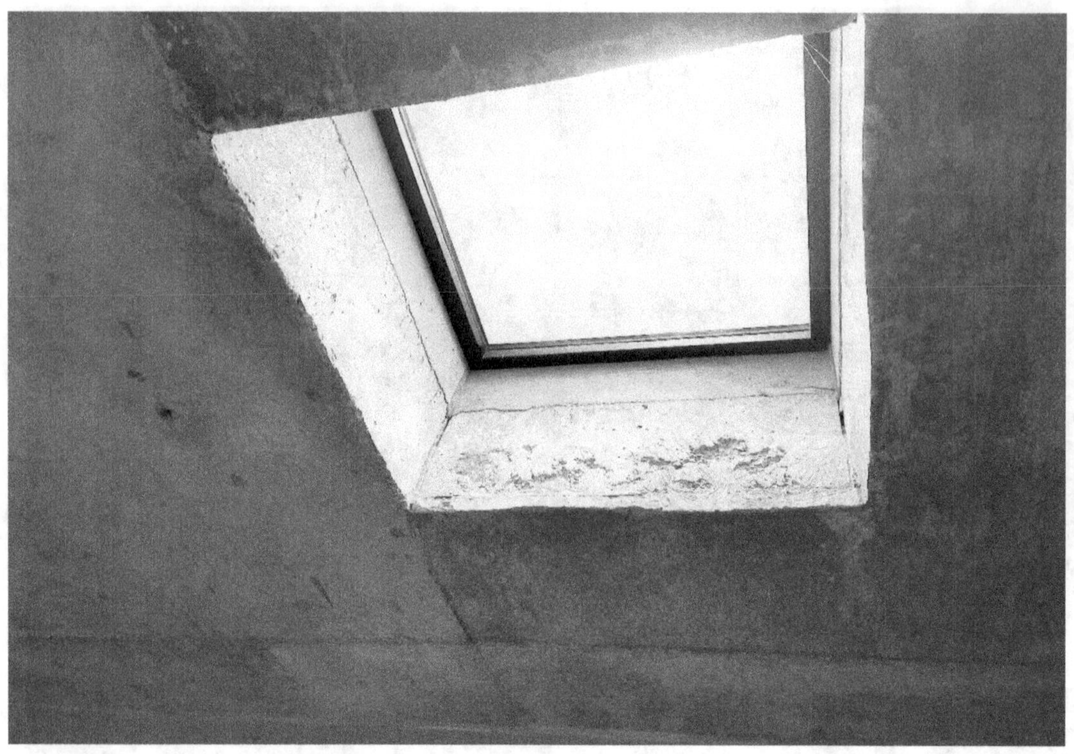

Image 66: Brutal casting

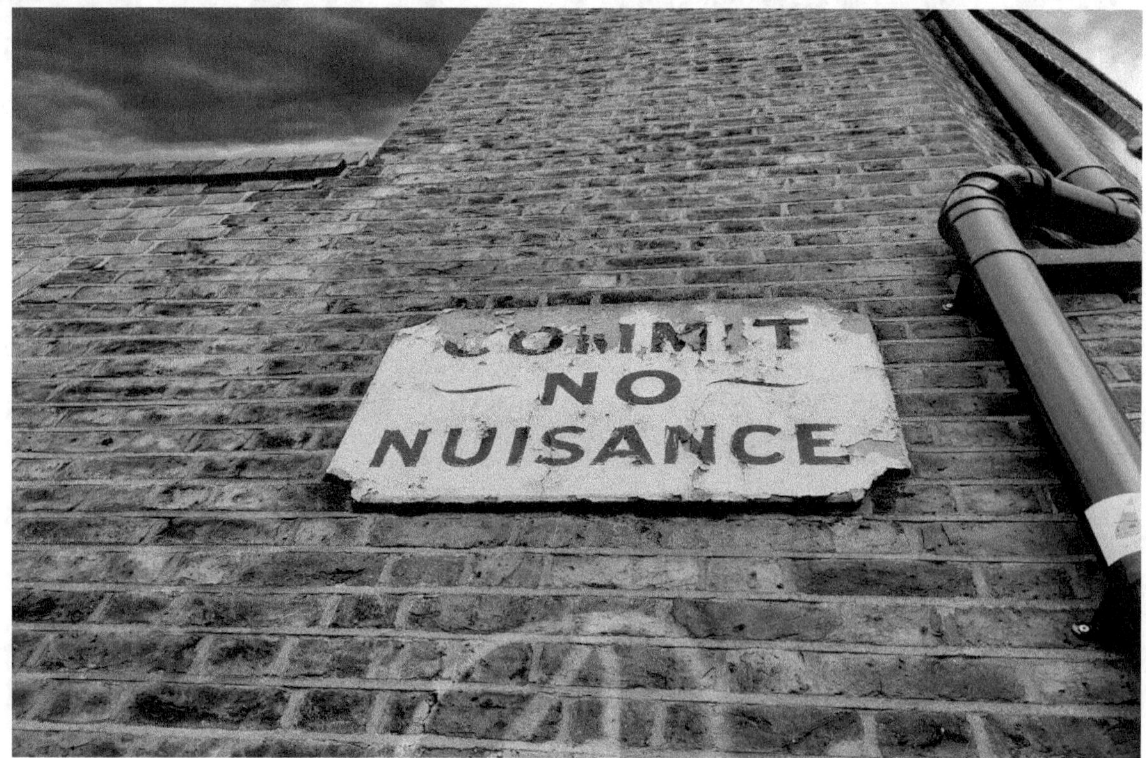

Image 67: Lambeth Marshes

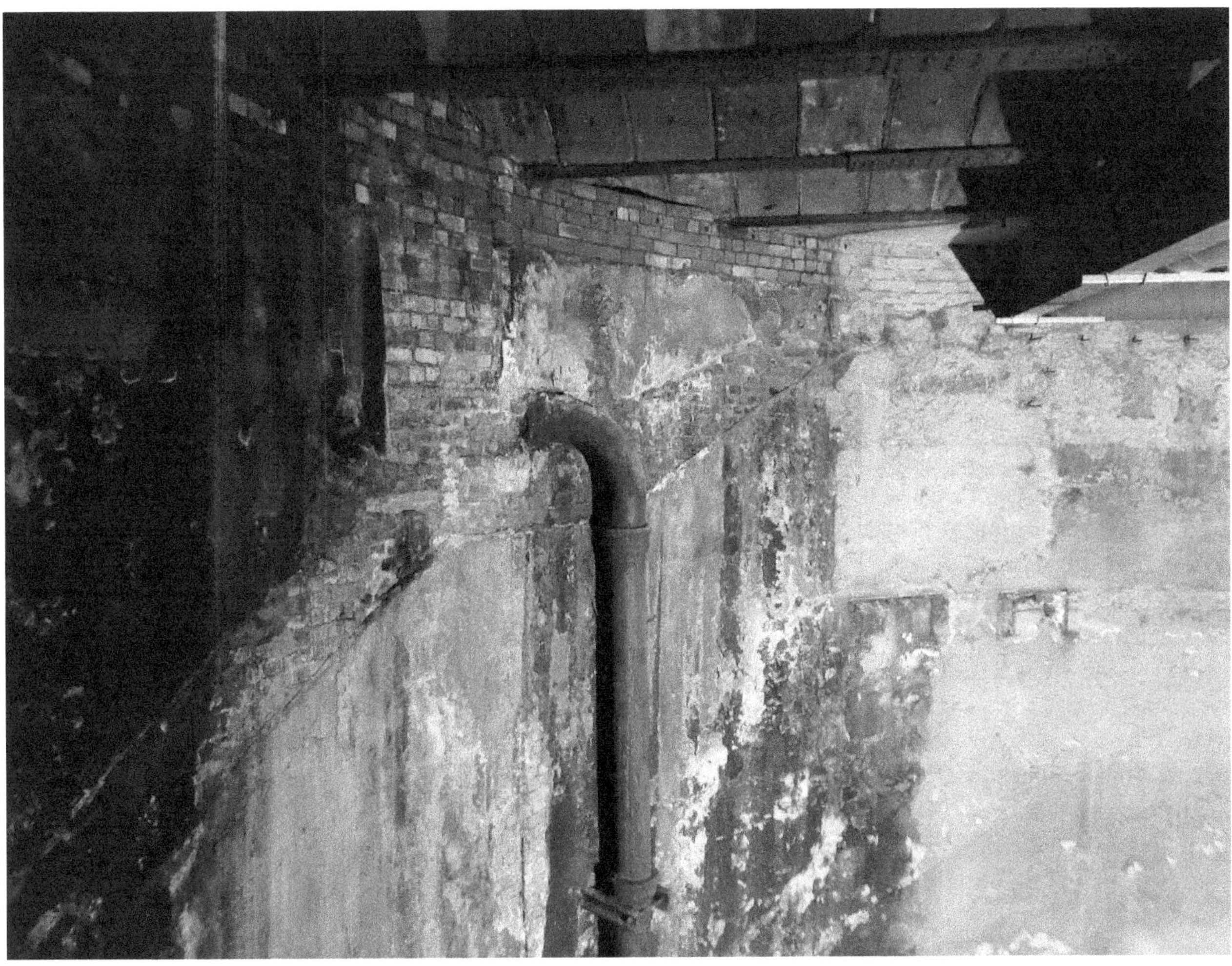

Image 68: Salute to Victorian engineering

The London Transport Museum Depot at Acton holds the majority of the Museum's collections which are not on display in the main Museum in Covent Garden. Outside is the oldest carriage in the collection, dilapidated, beaten-up and made of wood and iron. The first underground passenger services started in 1863 when the Metropolitan Railway opened using steam locomotives hauling gas-lit wooden carriages, braked from a guards' compartment. It is likely that the structure in *Image 69* is from around that era, although I couldn't find any signage to pinpoint the exact age.

Image 70 is of an abandoned wooden structure, probably used to wrap up cables. It looks like a giant cotton wheel. It is situated between two railway tracks at Finsbury Park train station. The intermodal interchange station in North London opened in 1869. It's not the most interesting of stations, especially on Sunday afternoons.

Icehouses and ice wells are structures used to store ice throughout the year, commonly used prior to the invention of the refrigerator. One very large icehouse structure still exists in the Canal Museum in London. Carlo Gatti (1817-1878) built the ice well in 1857, the year in which his first cargo of 400 tons of imported Norwegian natural ice was brought to London. During the course of building this well, one of the workers, John Parker, fell to his death. *Image 71* is taken by peering into the vast brick structure.

King's Cross in London was once a thriving centre of activity, connected to the coal trade. The two massive Victorian coal drops sheds were used to receive coal from South Yorkshire and trans-ship it to narrowboats on the Regents Canal and to horse-drawn carts. At their height, the sheds were processing 8 million tons of coal per a year. With deindustrialization it fell into disrepute. It is now an area buzzing with restaurants and bars (branded 'Coal Drops Yard'. Many of the industrial buildings have been converted. *Image 72* was taken before the conversion, capturing the buildings in their disused state, although still remaining resolute.

North of the Tower of London stands sections of the London Wall. The wall was built around 200 CE to provide defense and security to the citizens of London. The wall also helped to create a sense of identity for London. The wall was once two and a half miles long, those sections that remain acts as a monument that defined the size and shape of the city. *Image 73* shows a section of the wall, during a summer month.

Image 74 depicts an old work area, covered with rust tools. This was taken inside a warehouse called the Bargehouse that forms part of the Oxo Tower Wharf complex.

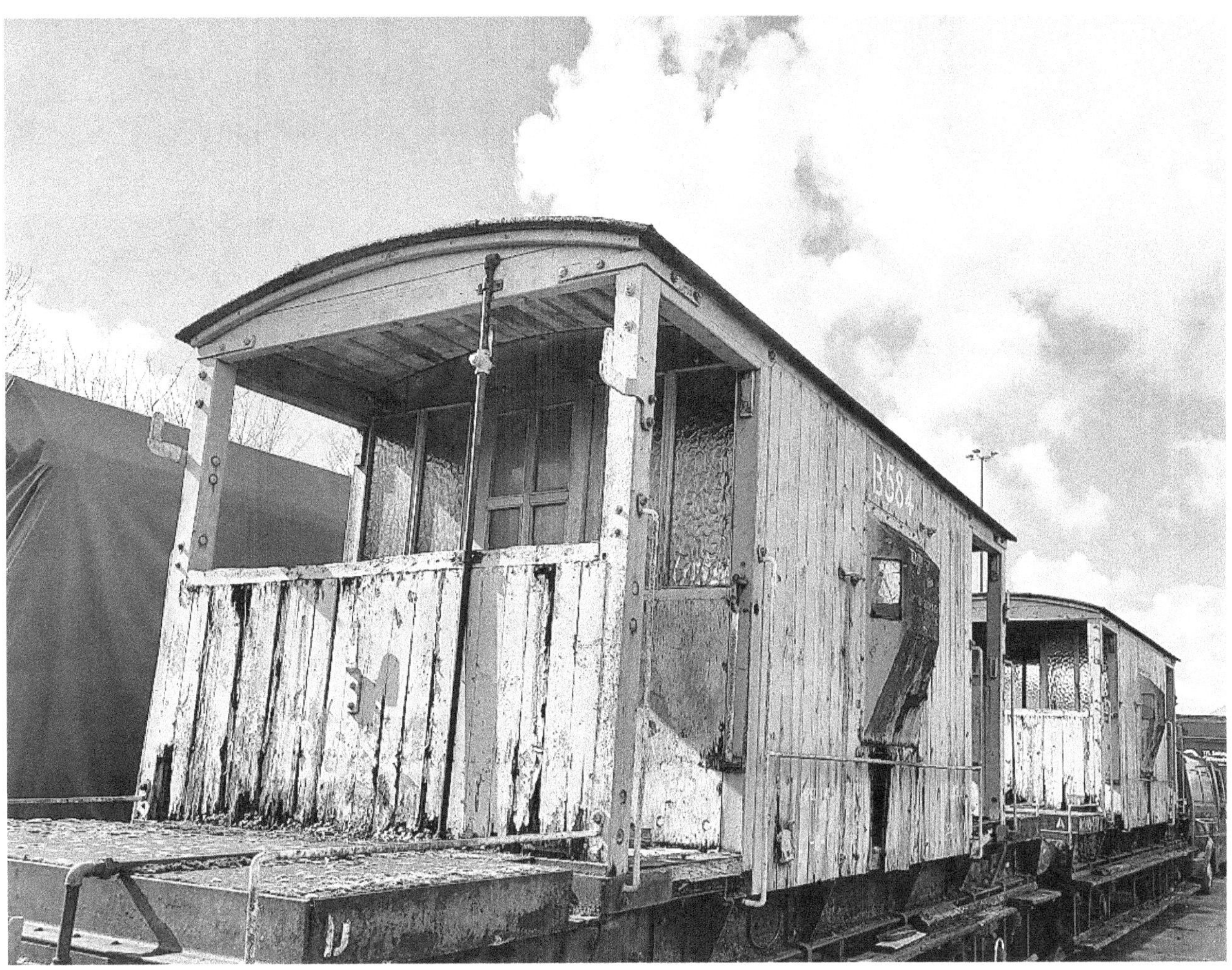

Image 69: Train, train

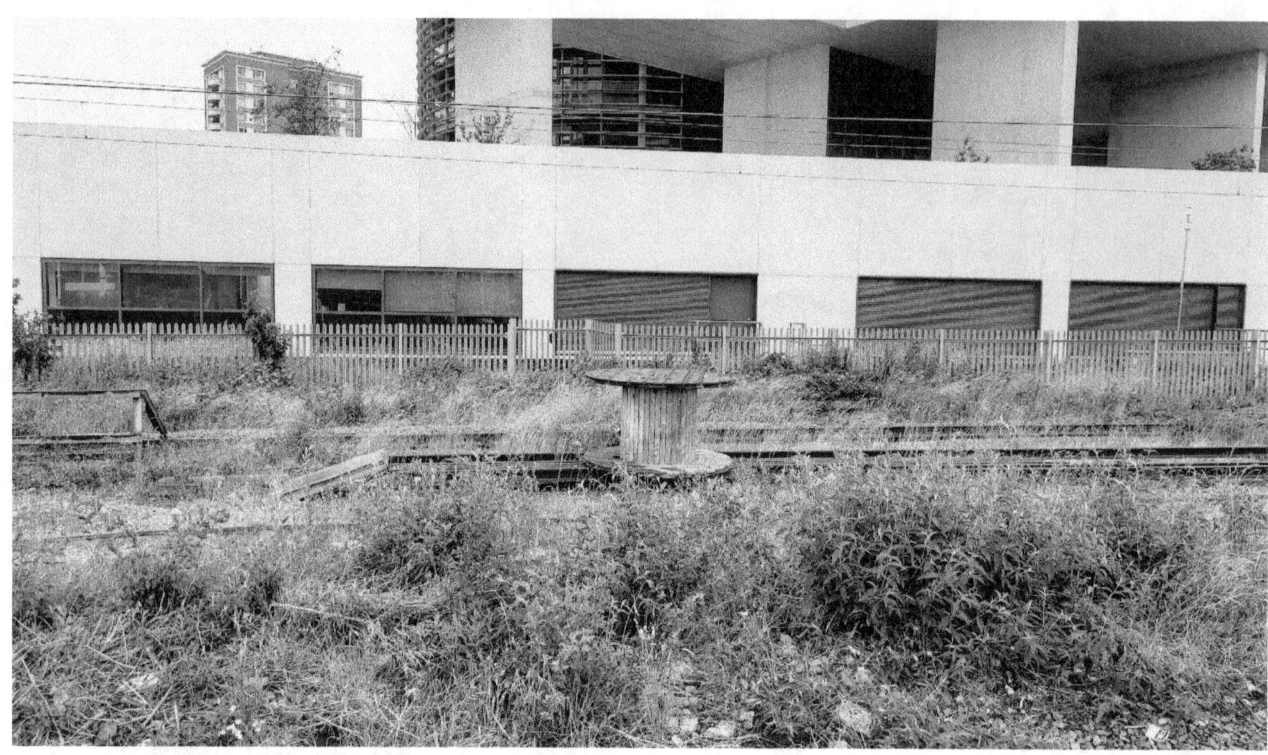

Image 70: One big cotton wheel?

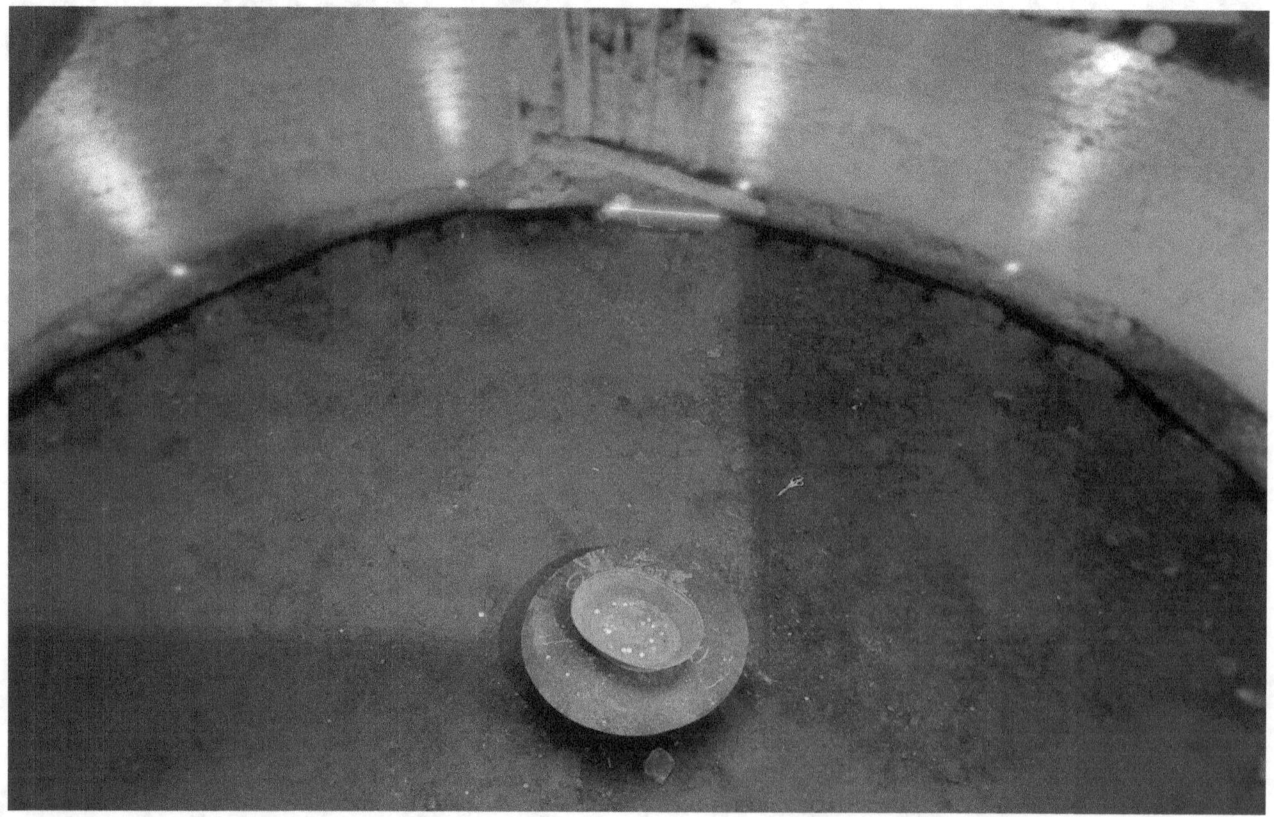

Image 71: No ice in the icehouse

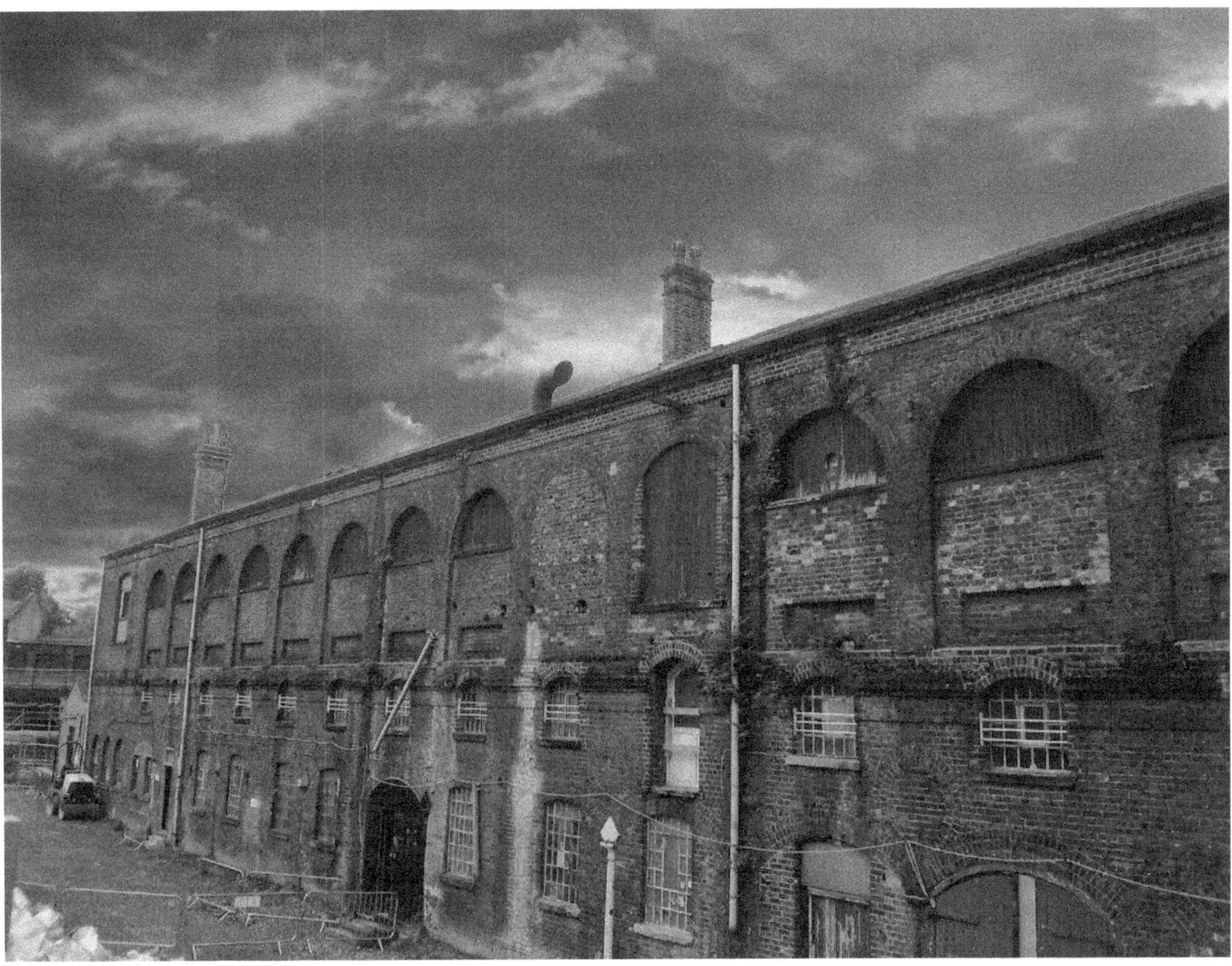

Image 72: Coals for Newcastle?

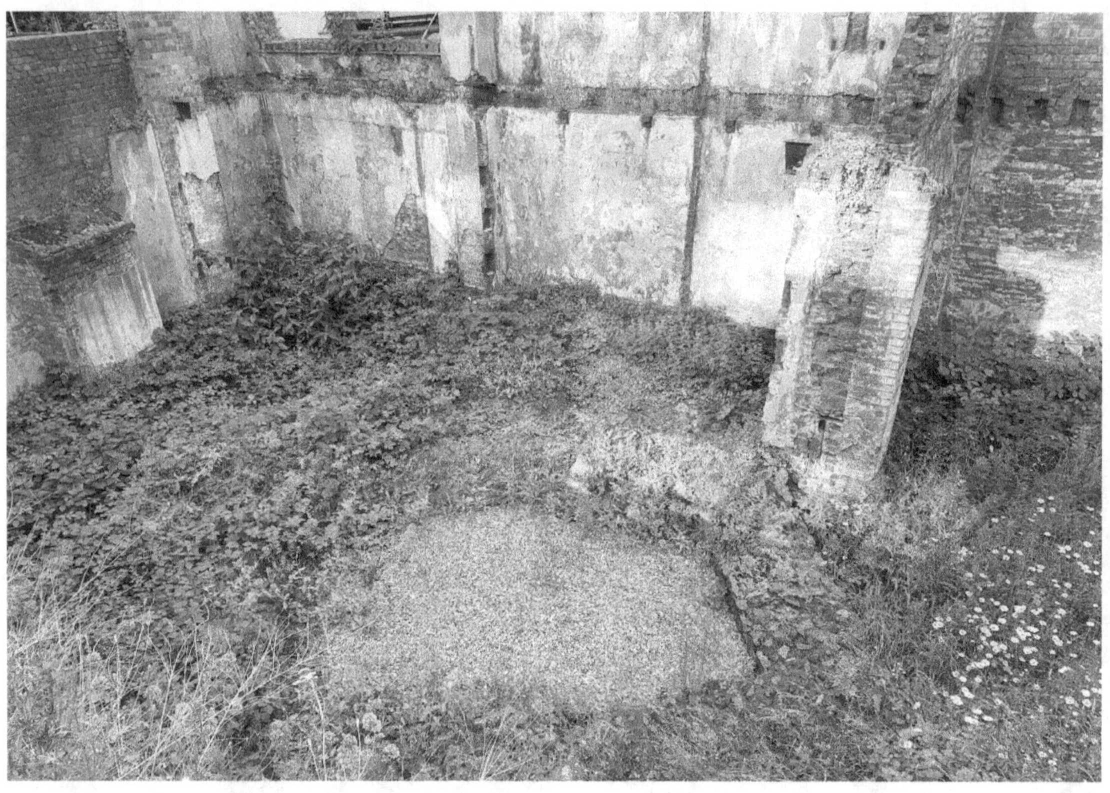

Image 73: What did the Romans ever do for us?

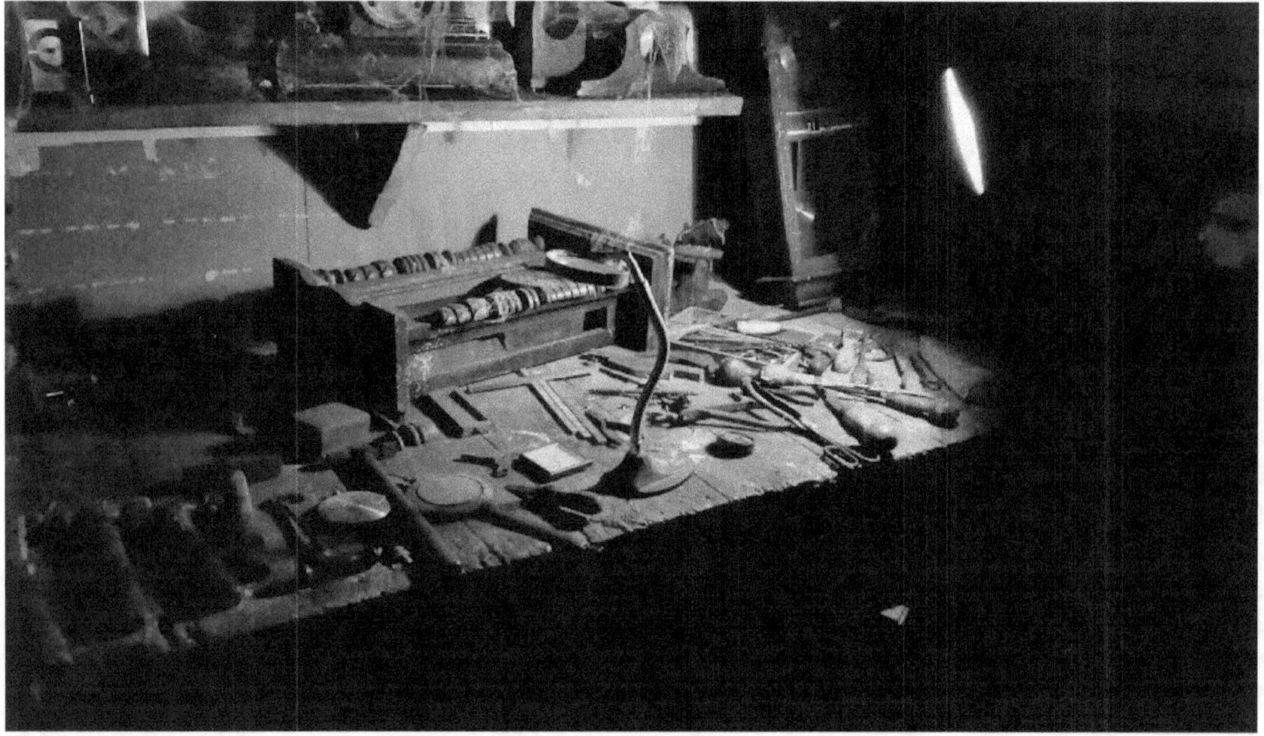

Image 74: Oxo

A buzzing part of London is Petticoat Lane market and there are plenty of antique shops. The history of Petticoat Lane Market can be traced back to the 17th century and the name derives from the street being home to several weavers and tailors. There are also many old buildings and other signs of yesteryear. *Image 75* attempts to capture an old street sign above an empty building. There is a faded look to the image, taken on an October afternoon.

The building in *Image 76* is a storehouse of some sort. It is located next to Westfield, a shopping complex in Shepherd's Bush. In this image I like the way the shopping mall is blurred into the background and the older building given prominence, a sort of reverse of what the those responsible for marketing the shopping complex would be hoping for.

The Royal Arsenal, Woolwich was located on the south bank of the River Thames in Woolwich in south-east London, England. It that was used for the manufacture of armaments and ammunition, proofing, and explosives research for the British armed forces. As a well as being along the Thames for transportation, the Thames, through much of British history, was recognized as means for invaders to enter. For this reason canons and forts were situated at strategic points along the river. This cannon – *Image 77* - is within the Woolwich area.

Image 78 is a roof garden, although the 'garden' part is unintentional. Most of the building is no longer in active use, although it was once the headquarters for the entirety of London Transport. 55 Broadway is a Grade I listed building close to St James's Park in London. Upon completion in 1931, it was the tallest office block in the city. The building has an *art deco* style and it is faced with Portland stone.

Underneath Waterloo Station are various vaults. Some are now used to host bars and clubs; many of the walkways have been put to use by graffiti artists. There is a maze of disused railway arches and tunnels. *Image 79* is The Leake Street graffiti tunnel, founded by Banksy.

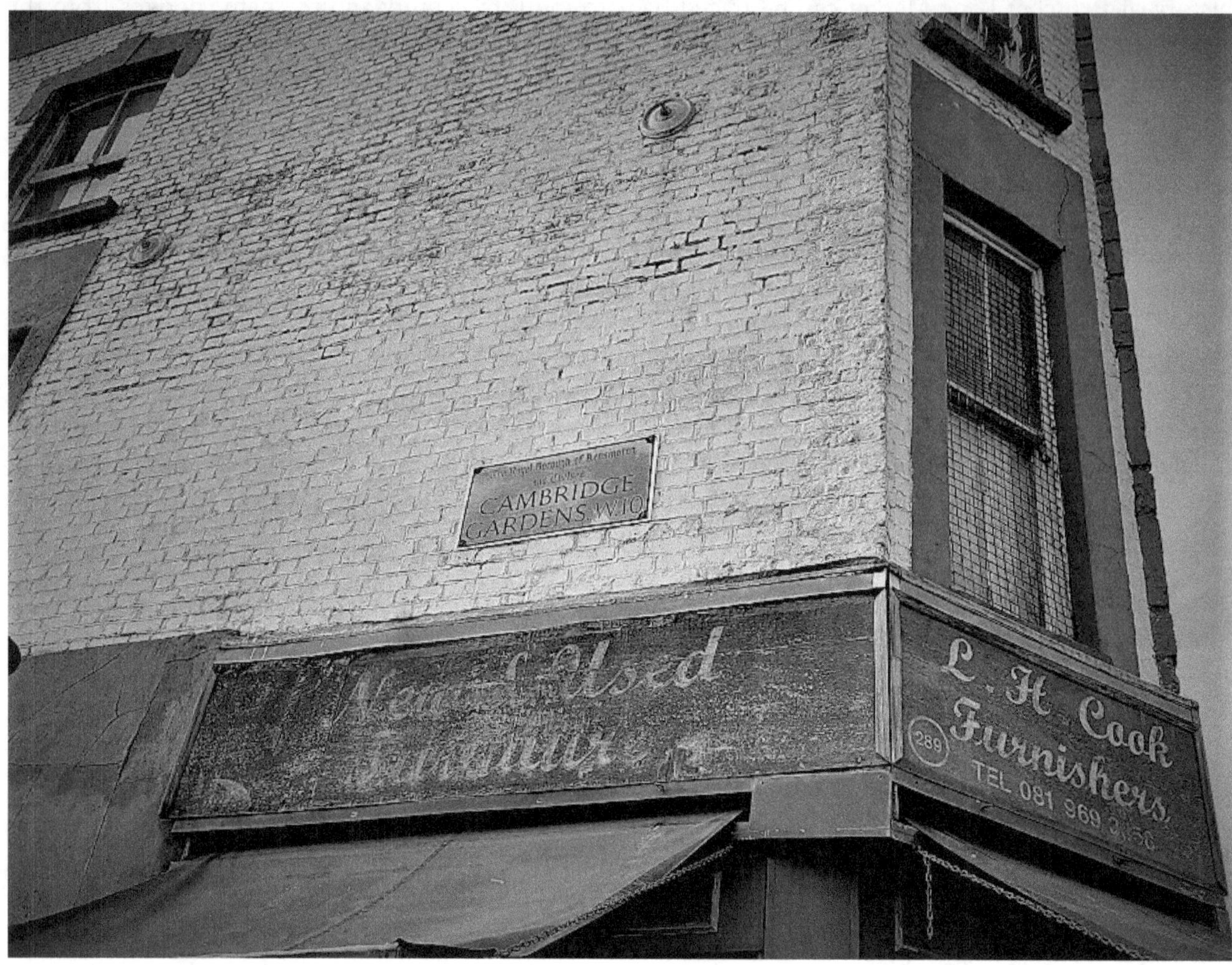

Image 75: Market towers

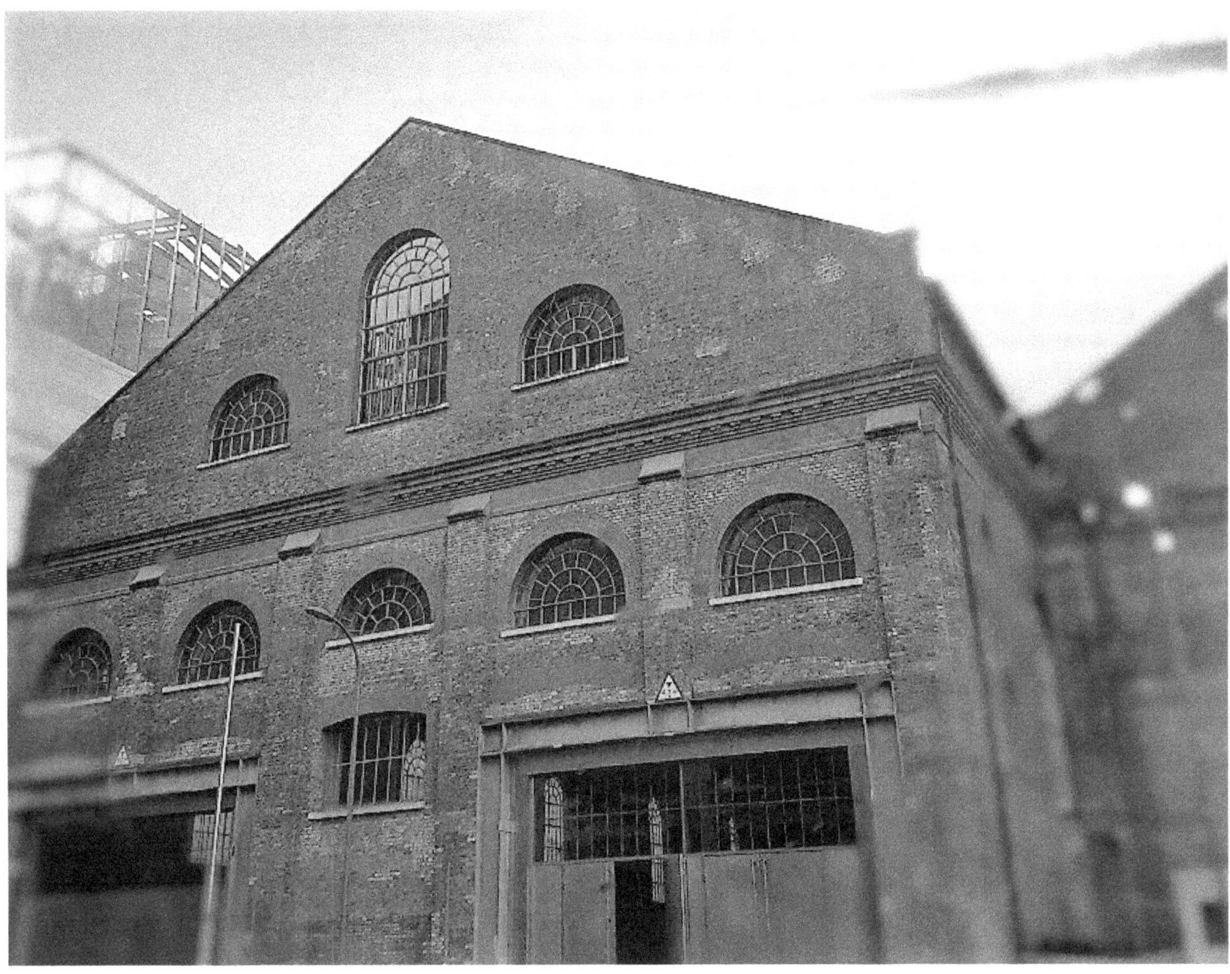

Image 76: Sherpa

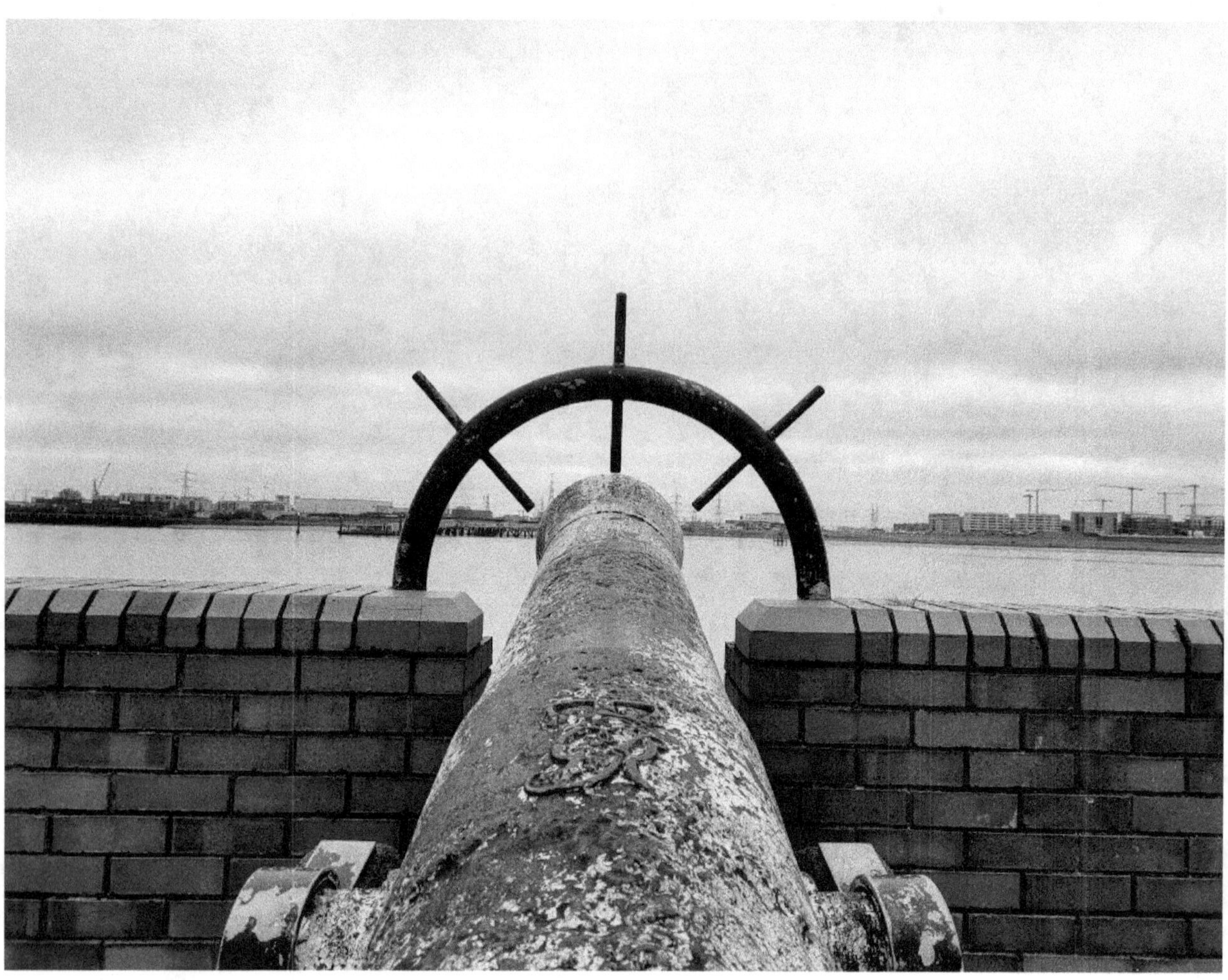

Image 77: Your Arsenal

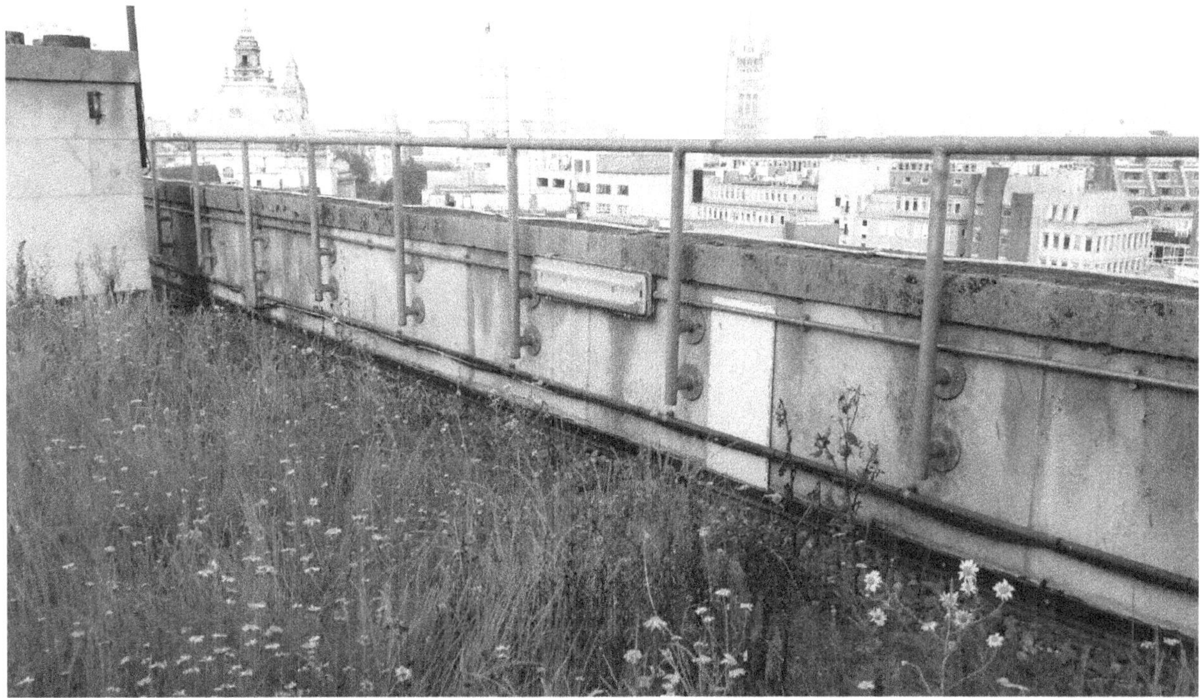

Image 78: Roof garden

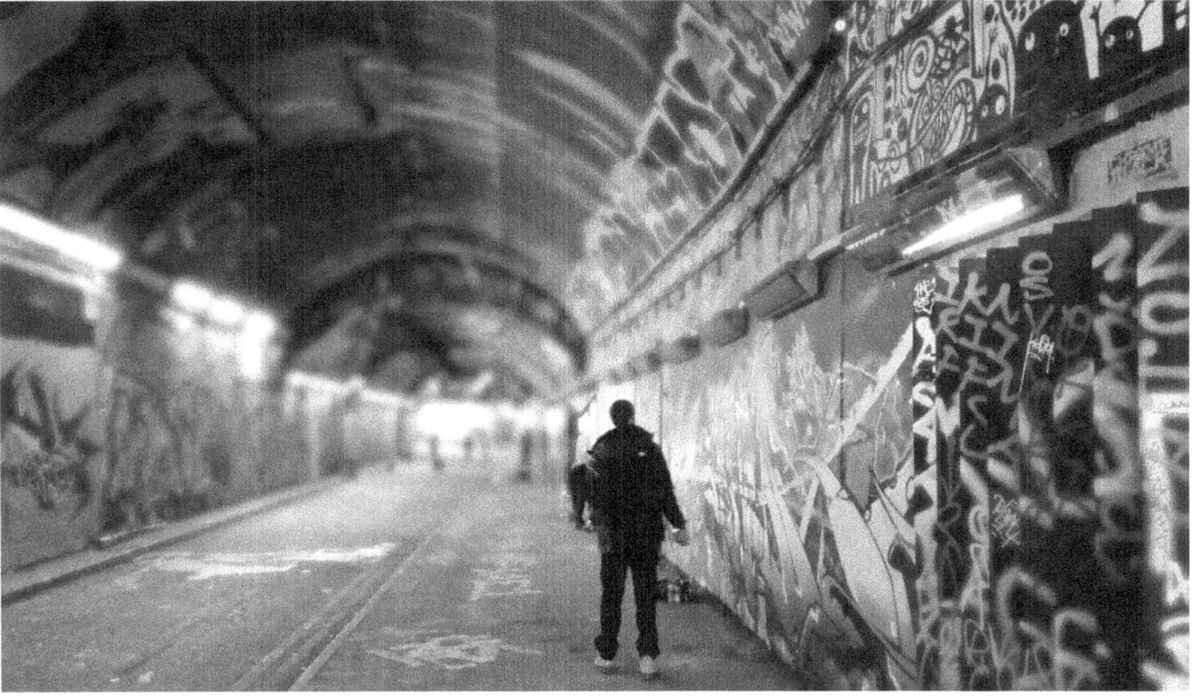

Image 79: One for the vault?

10 **UNDERGROUND**

London Underground's tube network is vast, sprawling, and has been subject to changes and modifications. Over time, stations have closed; other shave been expanded or sections rebuilt, leaving other parts closed off. The London Transport Museum periodically opens up sections of the abandoned spaces for small groups visitors. Most of the images in this chapter come from such events.

The first image (*Image 80*) is of a disused underground station, from street level. This a station that was first called 'Strand' (until 1915) and then renamed as Aldwych tube station. This was a terminus for a section of the Piccadilly Line, which began to see a reduced service from 1962 and which was finally closed down in 1994. The station was built by the architect Leslie Green, who worked in the Modern Style, which is a style of architecture, art, and design that first emerged in the United Kingdom in the mid-1880s. It is the first *Art Nouveau* style worldwide.

Images 81 to 84 continue to journey through the passageways of the station and the platform, showing an unusual 'end of the line'. The variances of lighting enhance the shadows, providing a sense of quiet in a structure that is normally associated with the bustle of people.

A different type of underground tunnel, used for transportation, forms the next series of images. These are from the former postal railway.

The Post Office Railway was a 2 feet (610 millimeters) narrow gauge, driverless underground railway in London that was built by the Post Office with assistance from the Underground Electric Railways Company of London, to transport mail between sorting offices. The route consisted of 6.5 miles (10.5 kilometers) of track and eight stations. The railway operated between 1927 and 2003.

The images are taken in the area underneath the Mount Pleasant sorting office. This remains one of the largest sorting offices in the world. *Images 85 to 87* show different shots of the postal rail tunnels, including older train set never to run again. The shadows and lighting provide the feel of the past.

Image 88 is the way out of the Kelvedon Hatch Secret Nuclear Bunker. Unfortunately photography is not permitted inside most of the structure. The bunker was built as an RAF Rotor Station, then it became a civil defense center and as a Regional Government HQ. The bunker was designed to allow up to 600 people survive the aftermath of a nuclear war. I like the spiral of the exit, pointing to escape?

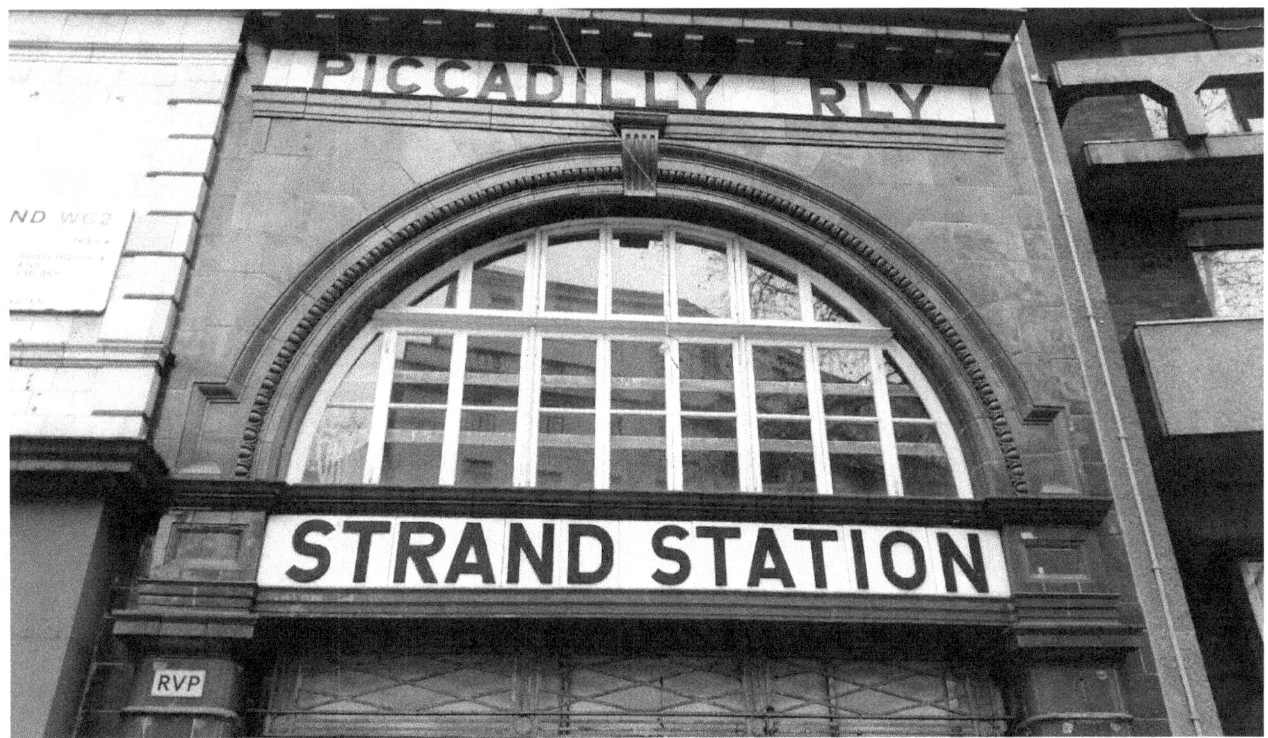

Image 80: A former underground station

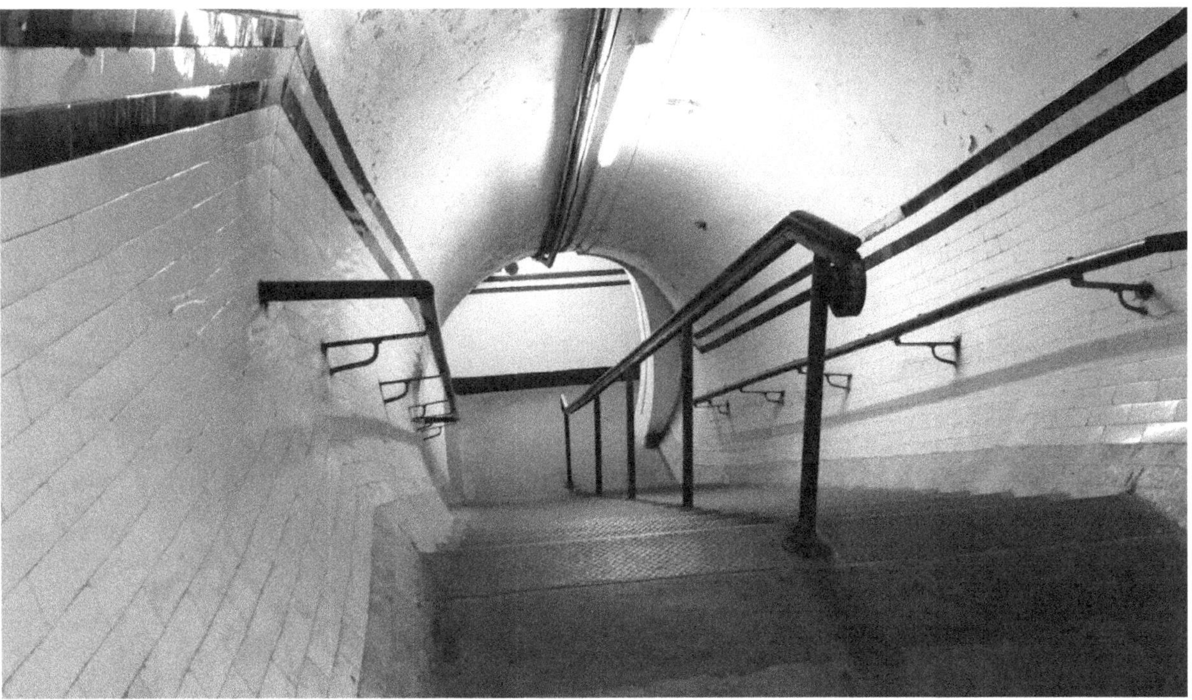

Image 81: Down we go

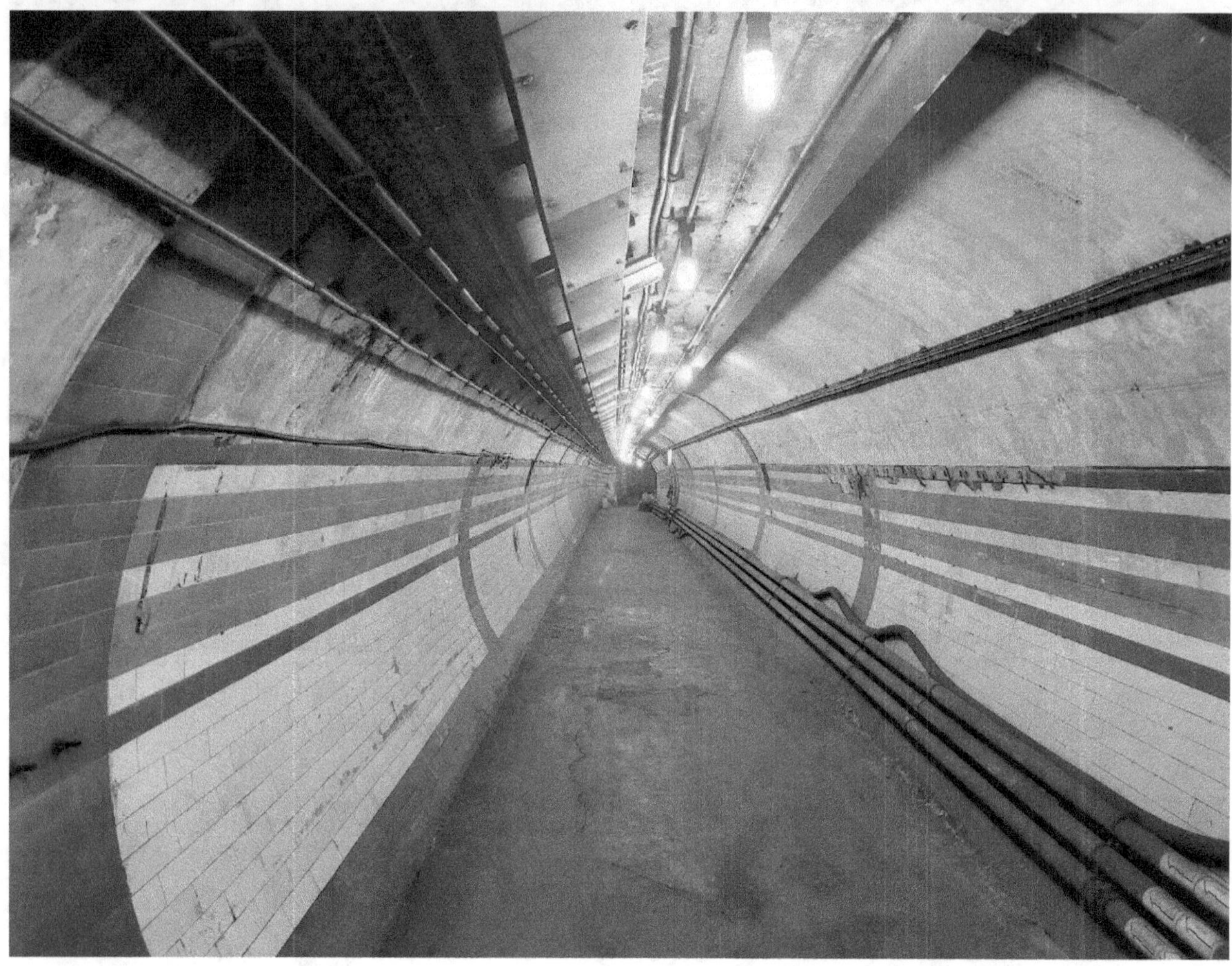

Image 82: Which way now?

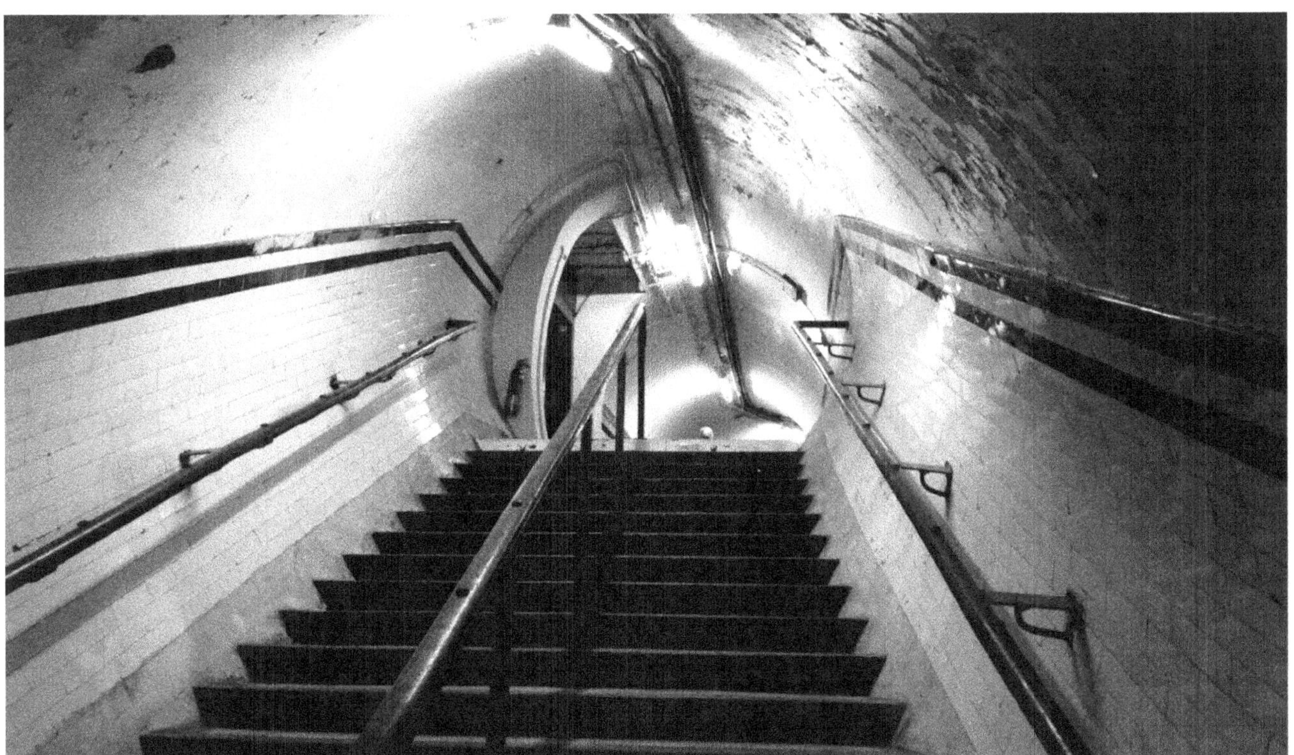

Image 83: Stairway to?

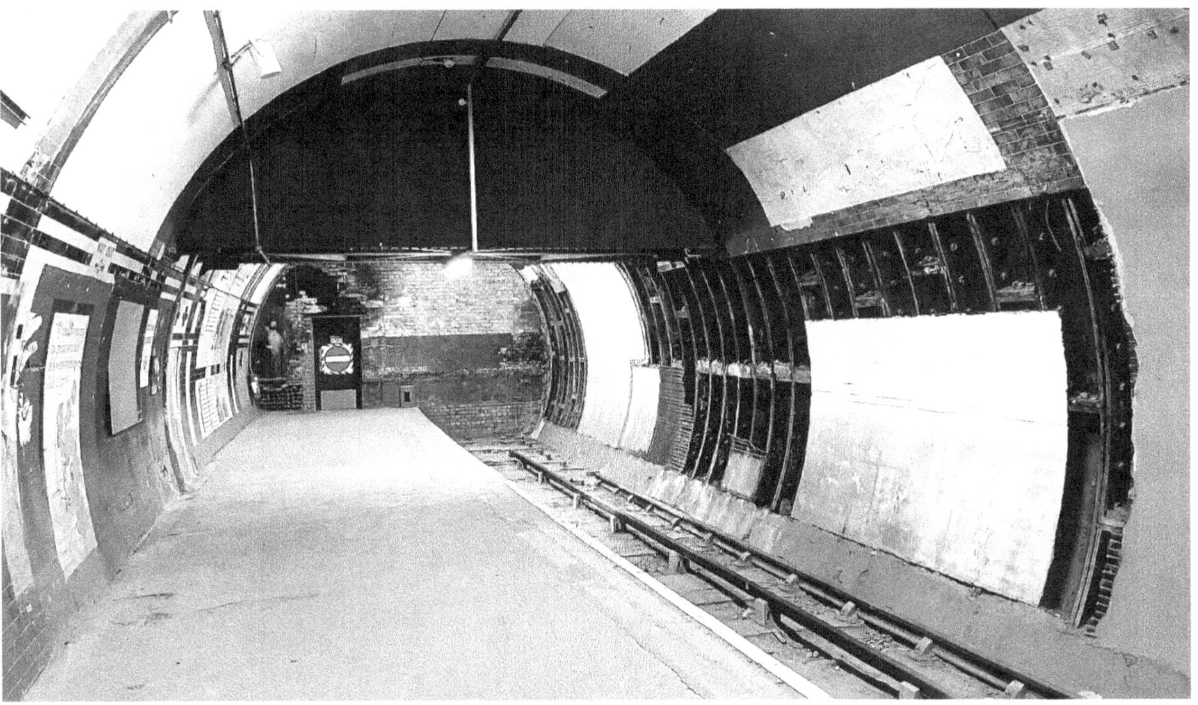

Image 84: Terminus

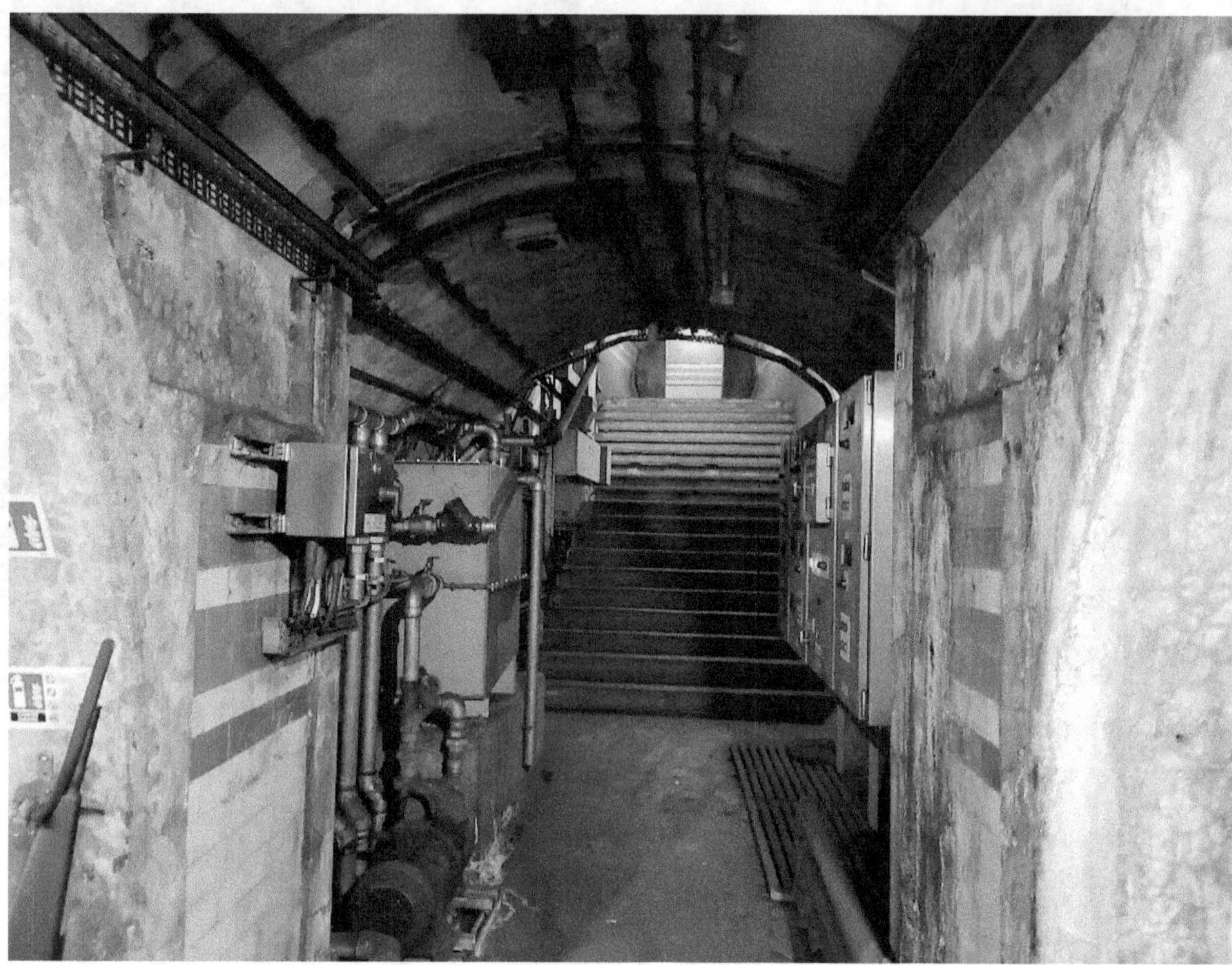

Image 85: Powering the mail trains

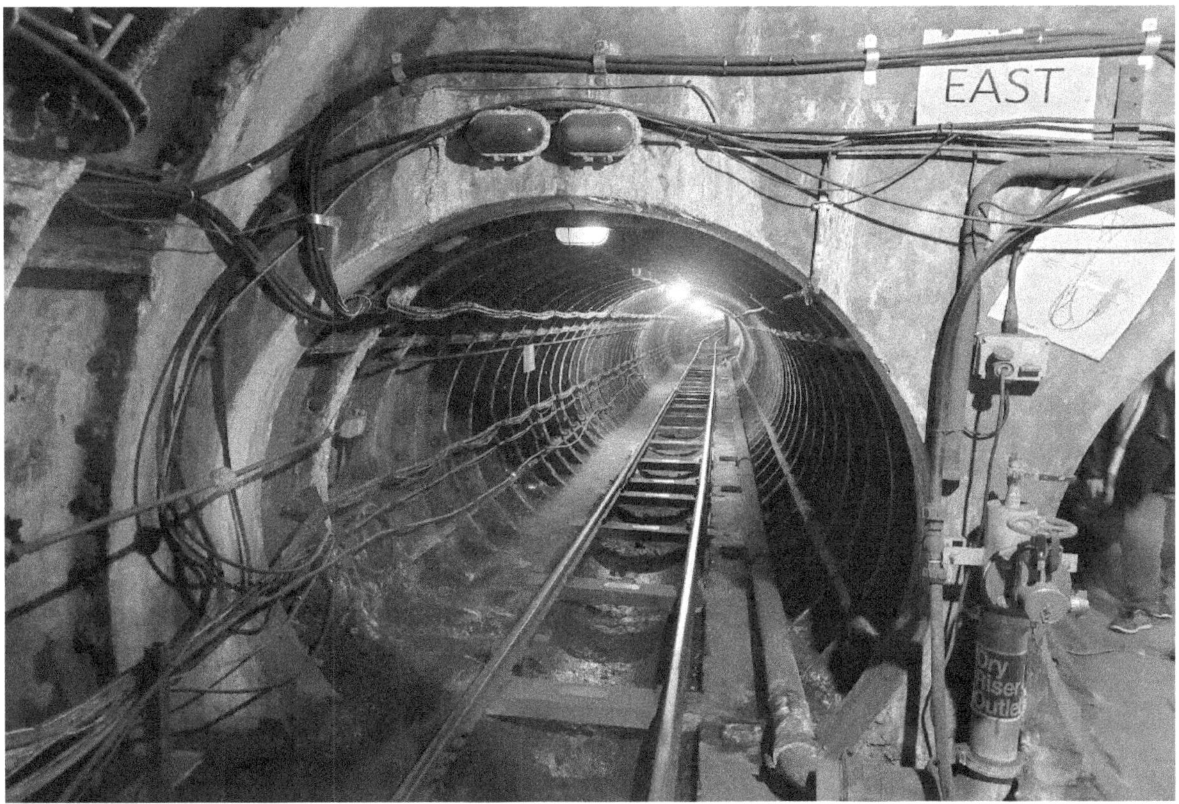

Image 86: Tunnel to who knows where?

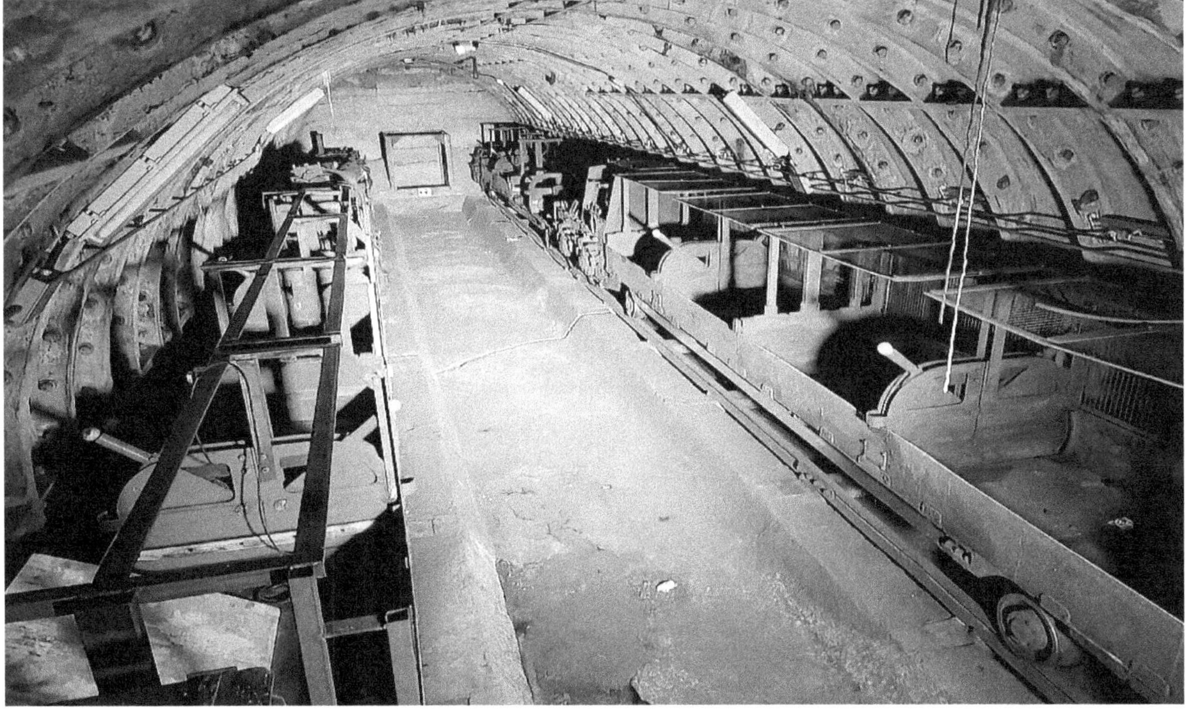

Image 87: Trains await

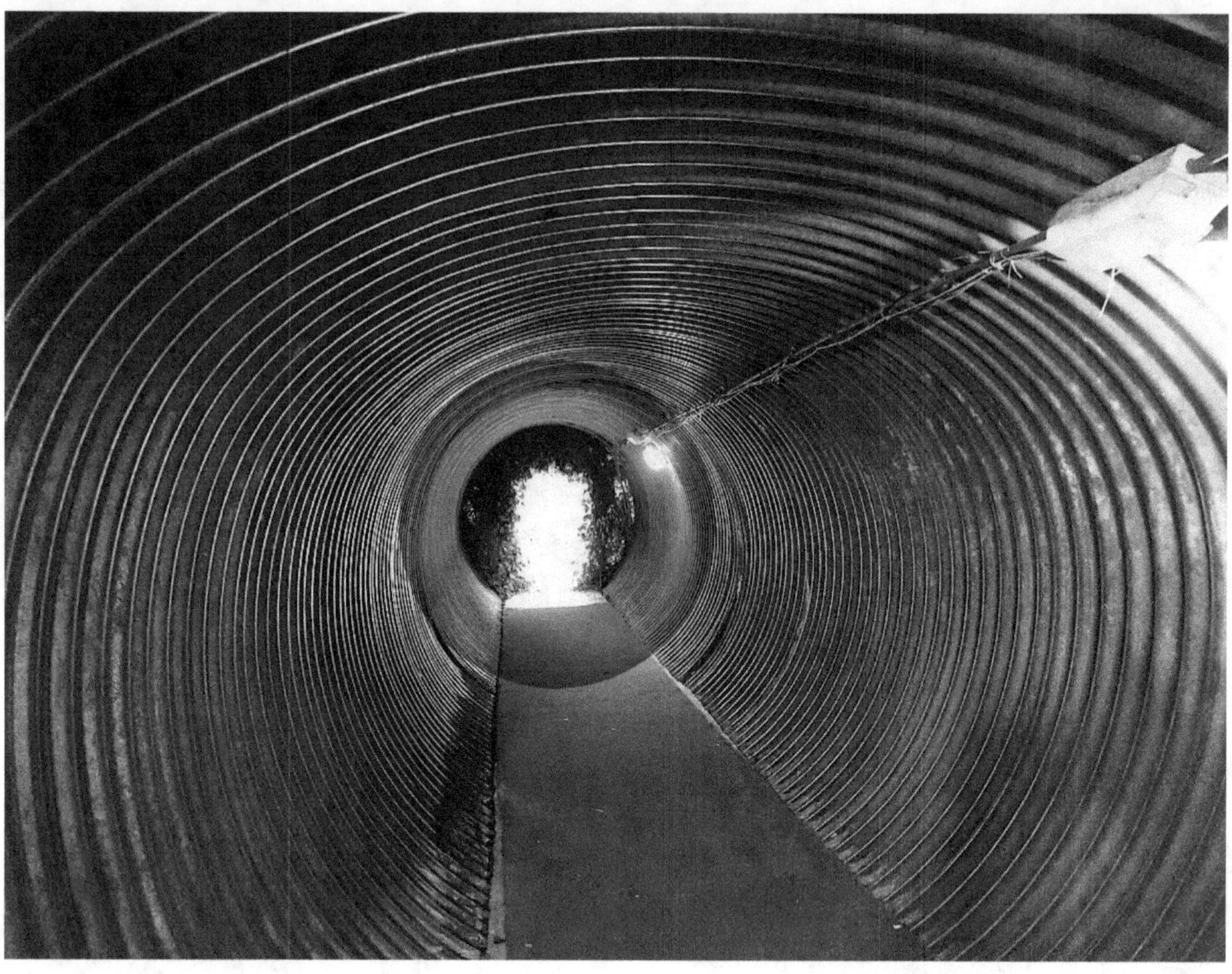

Image 88: On rabbit holes

11 **ROMANESQUE**

Verulamium was a town in Roman Britain. It was sited southwest of the modern city of St Albans in Hertfordshire, England.

Verulamium contained a forum, basilica and a theatre. Most of the images in this section are from the remains of the amphitheater. The theatre is built on a site that is only slightly sloping, and it was constructed in about 140 CE. By the 5th century the theatre had fallen into disuse. It was excavated in the 19th century. The arena would have been used for anything from religious processions and dancing, to wrestling, armed combat and wild beast shows.

Image 89 shows a closeup of part of the theatre structure, displaying what is mainly flintstone, interspaced with grass. There are some interesting contrasts among the different contours of the terrain. The flint theme continues with *Image 90*, which is a close up of the top of a wall against the clouds.

A hazy pattern of light predominates the main structure as seen in *Image 91*. The summer light actually looks a little spooky. *Image 92* shows some vegetation, with grass extending upwards from the stone.

To give a sense of perspective with some of the surviving structures, *Image 93* shows a long section of wall.

Stones of different shapes form *Images 94 and 95*, contrasting a solid foundation stone with a jagged edge of flint. An array of different decorative effects can be achieved by using different types of knapping and combinations with the stone.

The wall depicted in *Image 96* is from the nearby park and of a different Roman-built structure, providing the basis to separate a out a settlement. I like the combination of foliage, wall, tree and grassland.

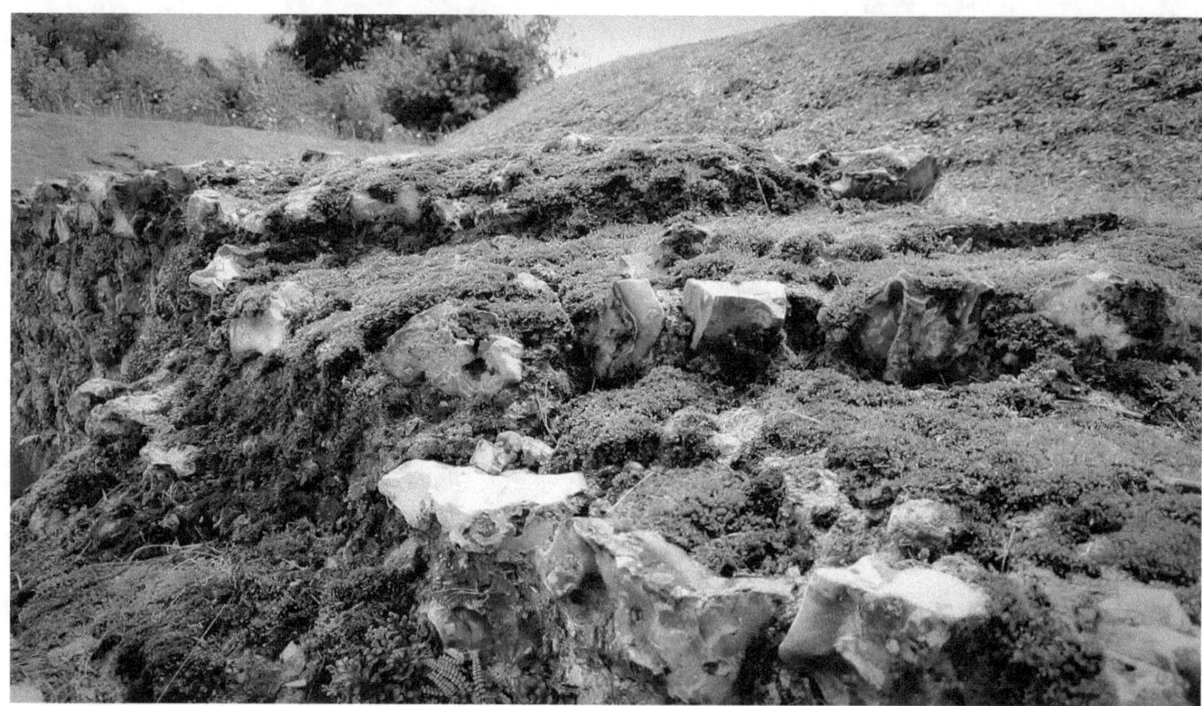

Image 89: Close up of part of the formation of the Roman theatre

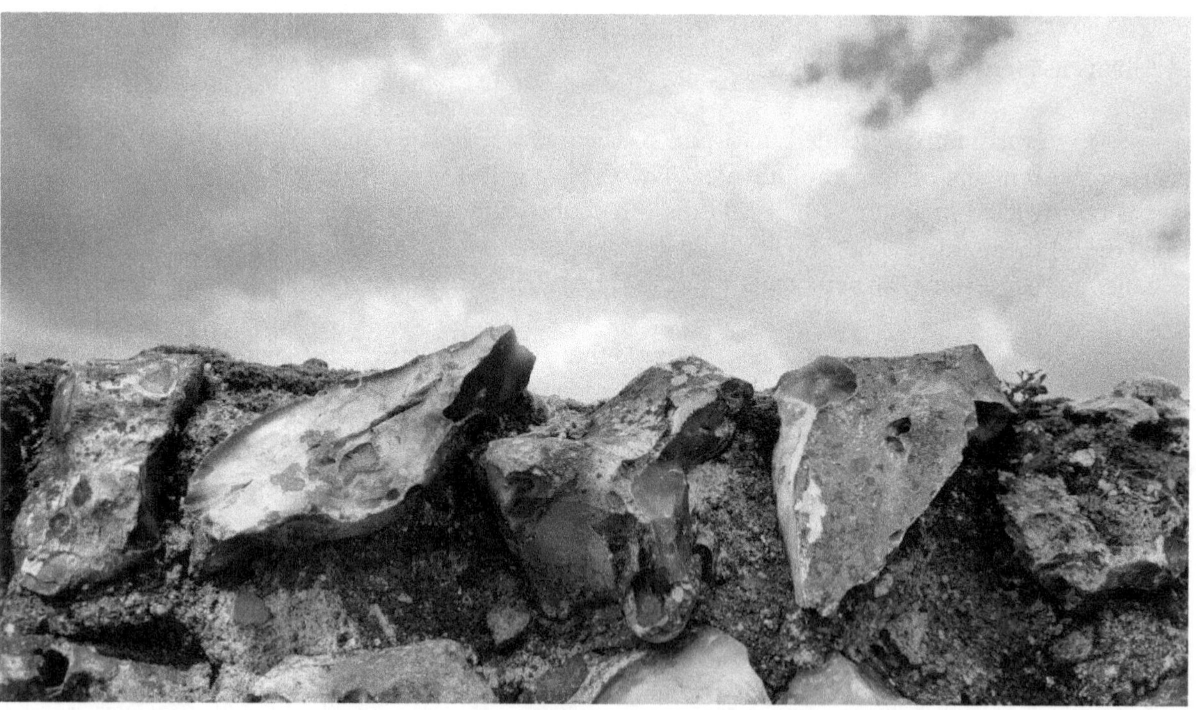

Image 90: Stone wall, close up on a wet July day

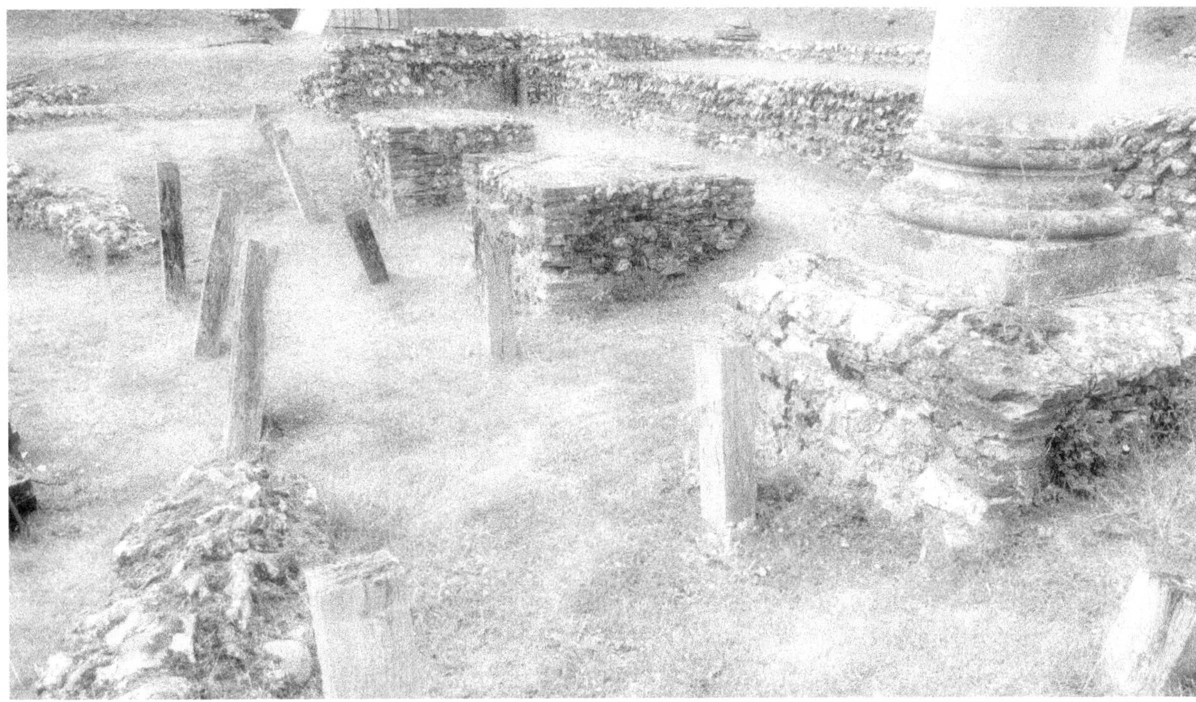

Image 91: Foundations

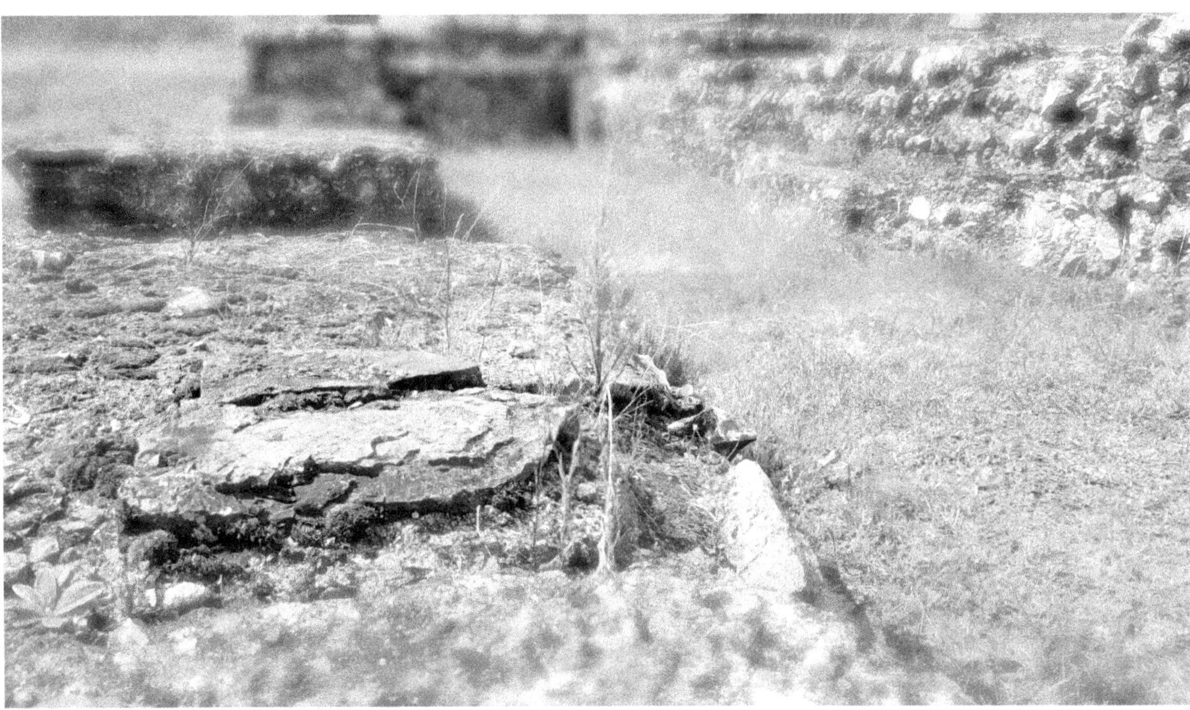

Image 92: Life

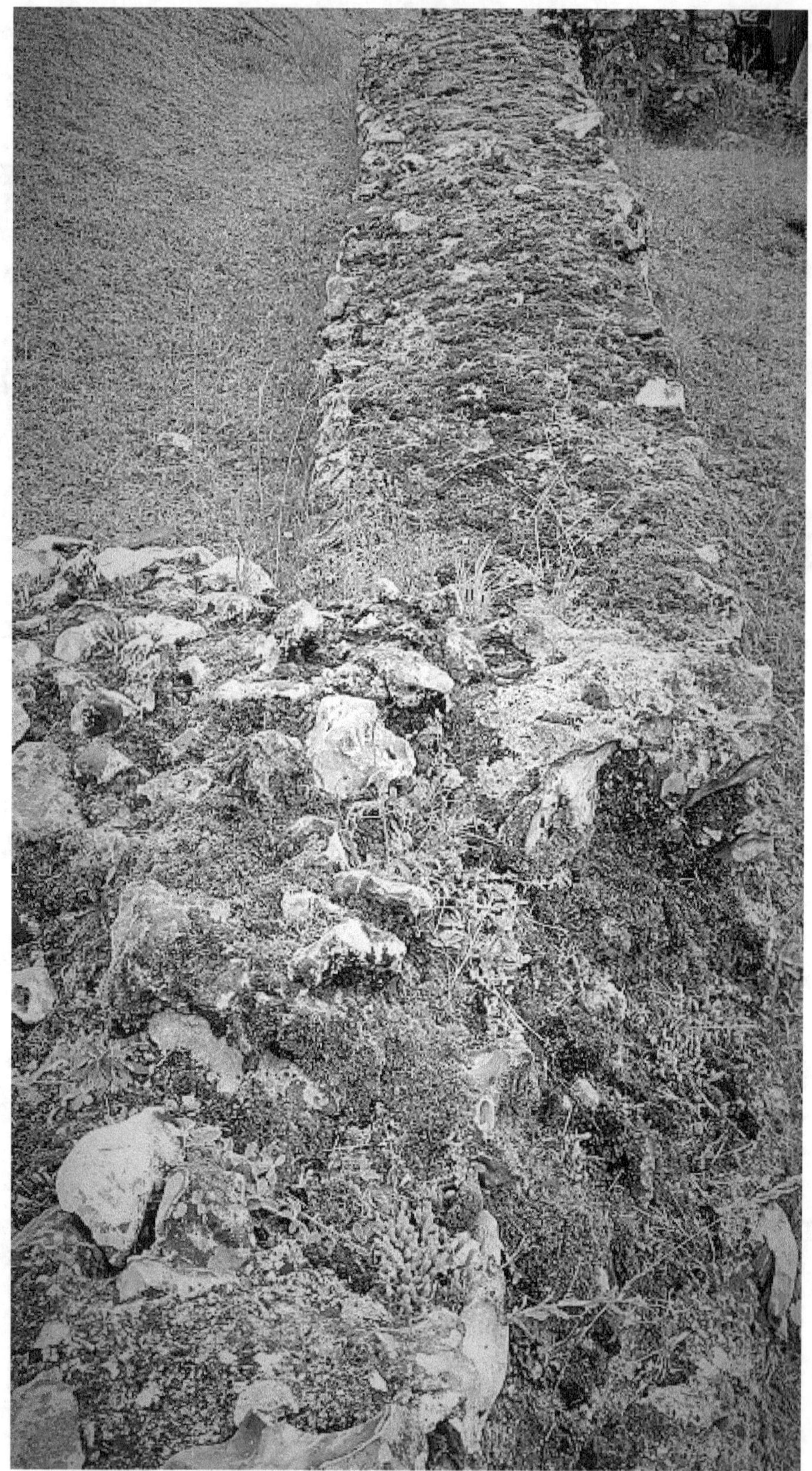

Image 93: Long walled section

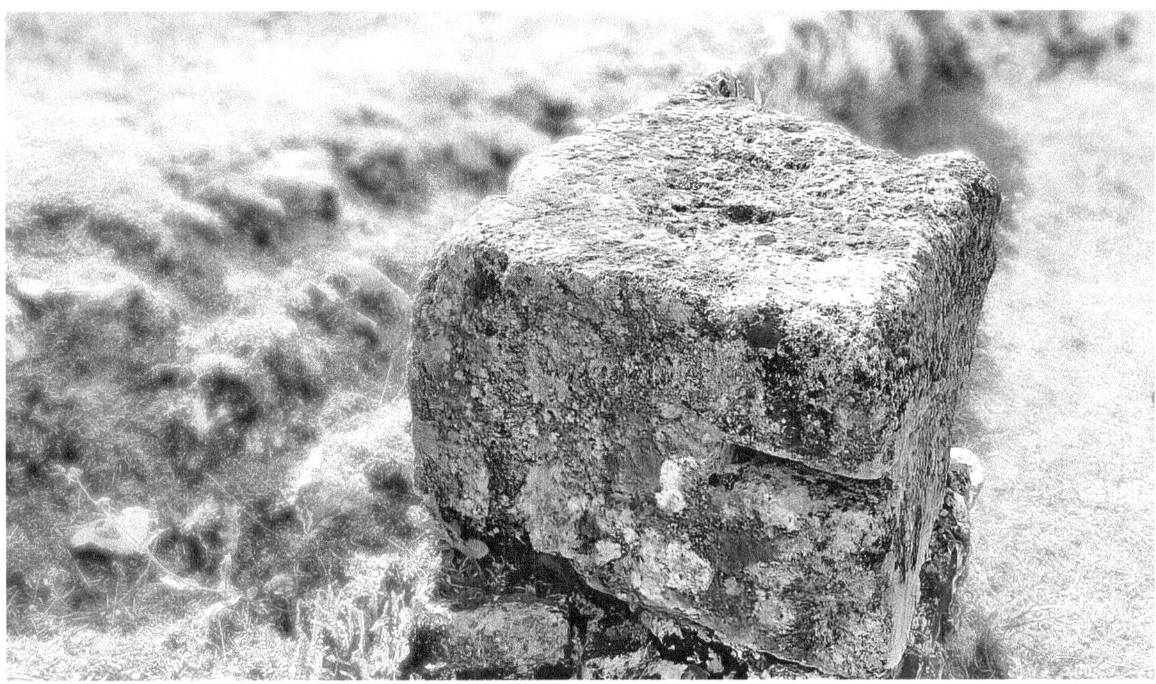

Image 94: Base and superstructure

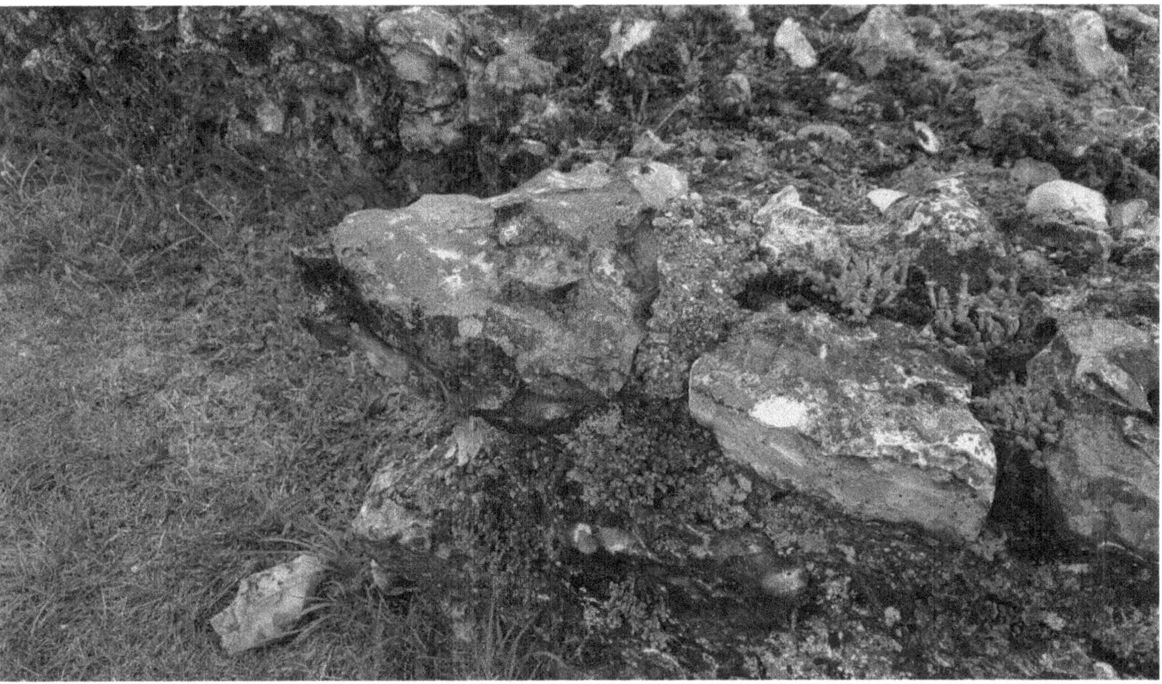

Image 95: Jagged edge

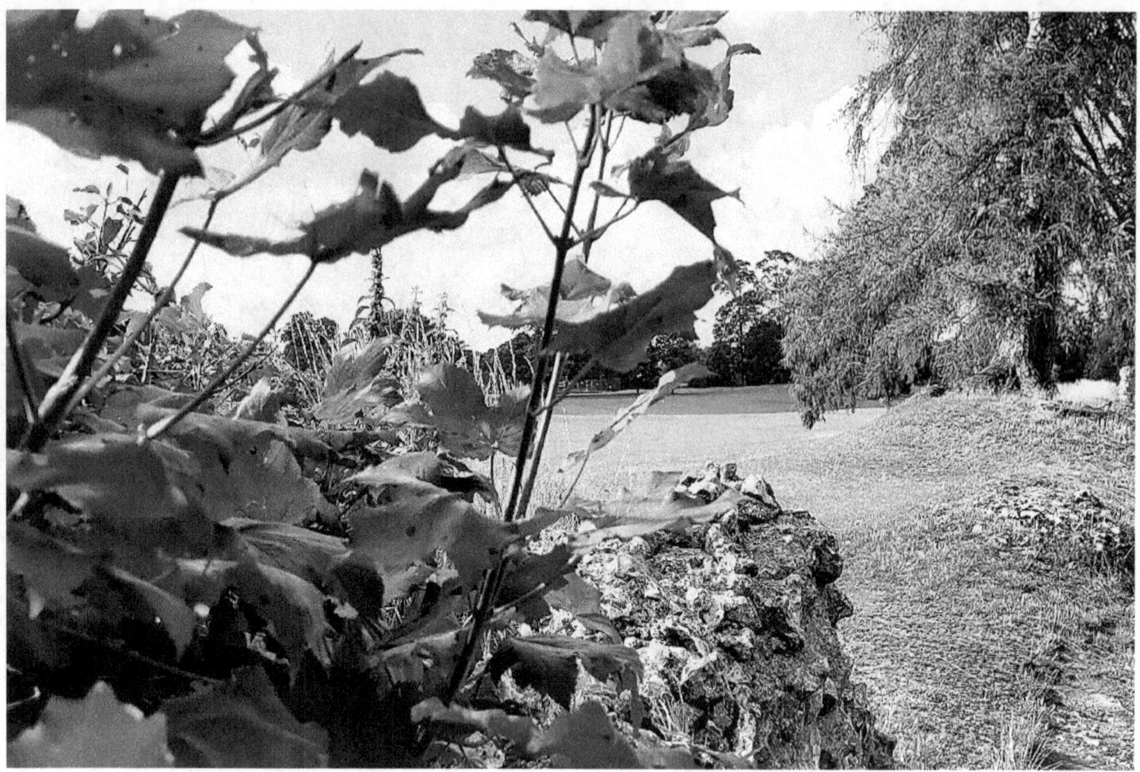

Image 96: Remains of the day

12 **UNUSUAL**

This closing chapter is an assortment of images, disparate and unrelated, but interesting, nonetheless.

A neolithic stone structure forms *Image 97*. This is located in Jersey, one of the Channel Islands. I like the contrast in light and dark, with the summer sun trying to break through and light up the twists and turns of the structure inside.

Sticking with Jersey, there are a few stone churches and chapels. *Image 98* shows one of the smallest, situated atop of a hill. The photograph was taken on a very hot day at the start of August. The chapel is being repaired, hence the scaffolding.

A hexagonal building in an area of parkland in Hertfordshire is shown in *Image 99*. The shape is unusual. A peek inside suggests the building is not in use, hence its inclusion here.

A forlorn looking building attached to the side of house form *Image 100*, illuminated by a summer's evening cast of sunlight.

A parkland area in Hertfordshire, where a rewilding project is in progress, contains a wooden seat that is gradually decaying. The seat can be glimpsed among the overgrowth in *Image 101*. Close by is a stone font that was once repurposed as a flowerbed. *Image 102* shows some weeds emerging, the flowerbed left unkept.

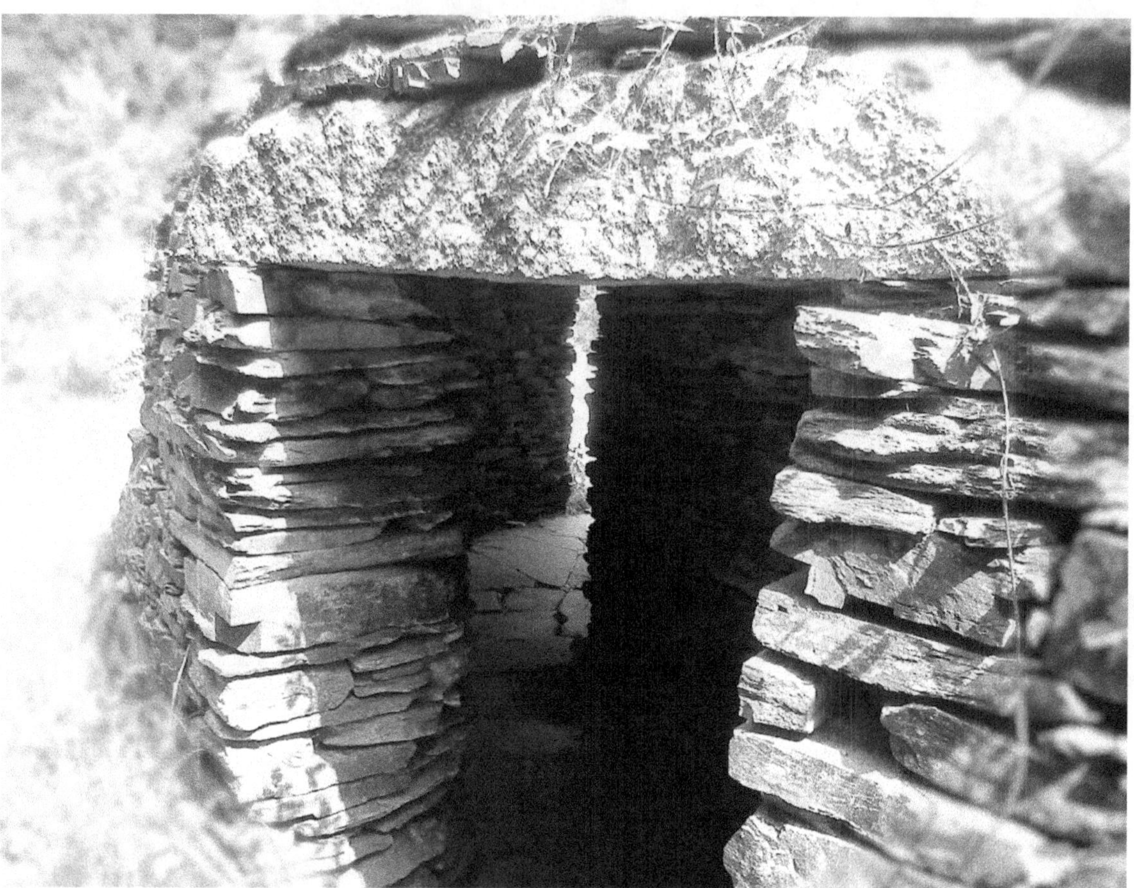

Image 97: Light and dark

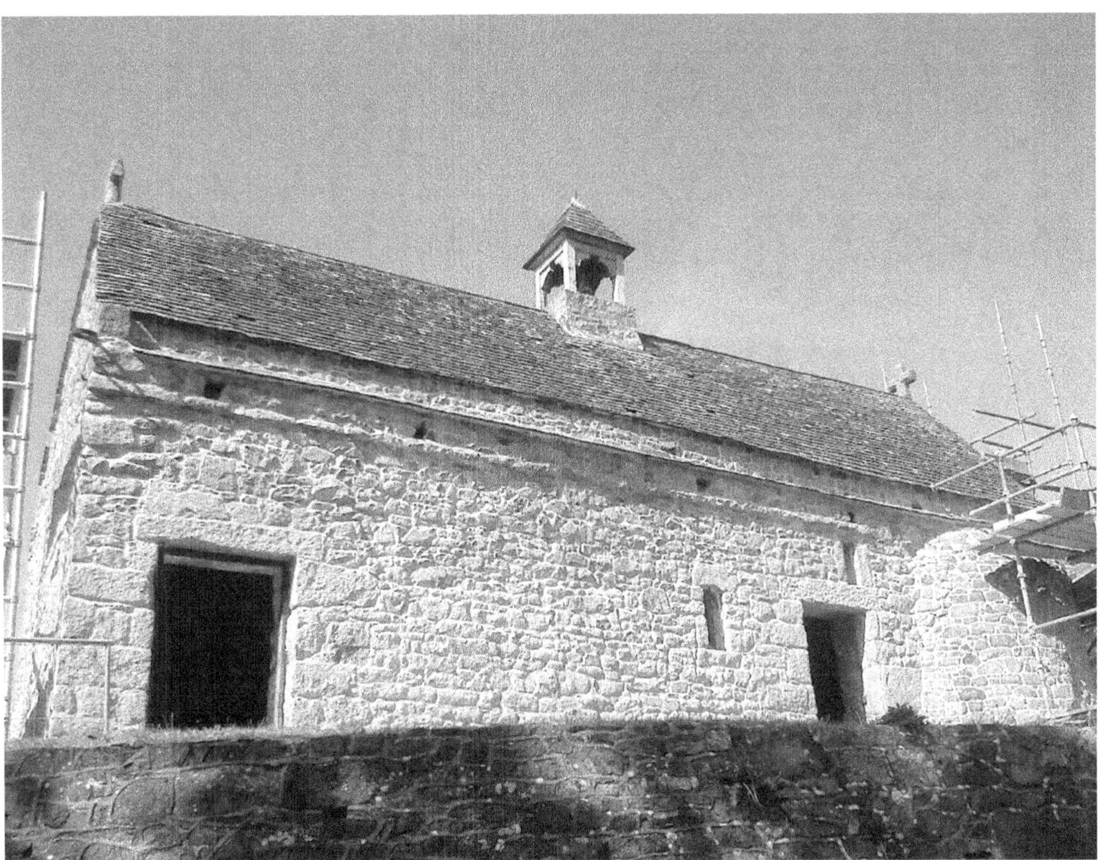

Image 98: Get to the church on time

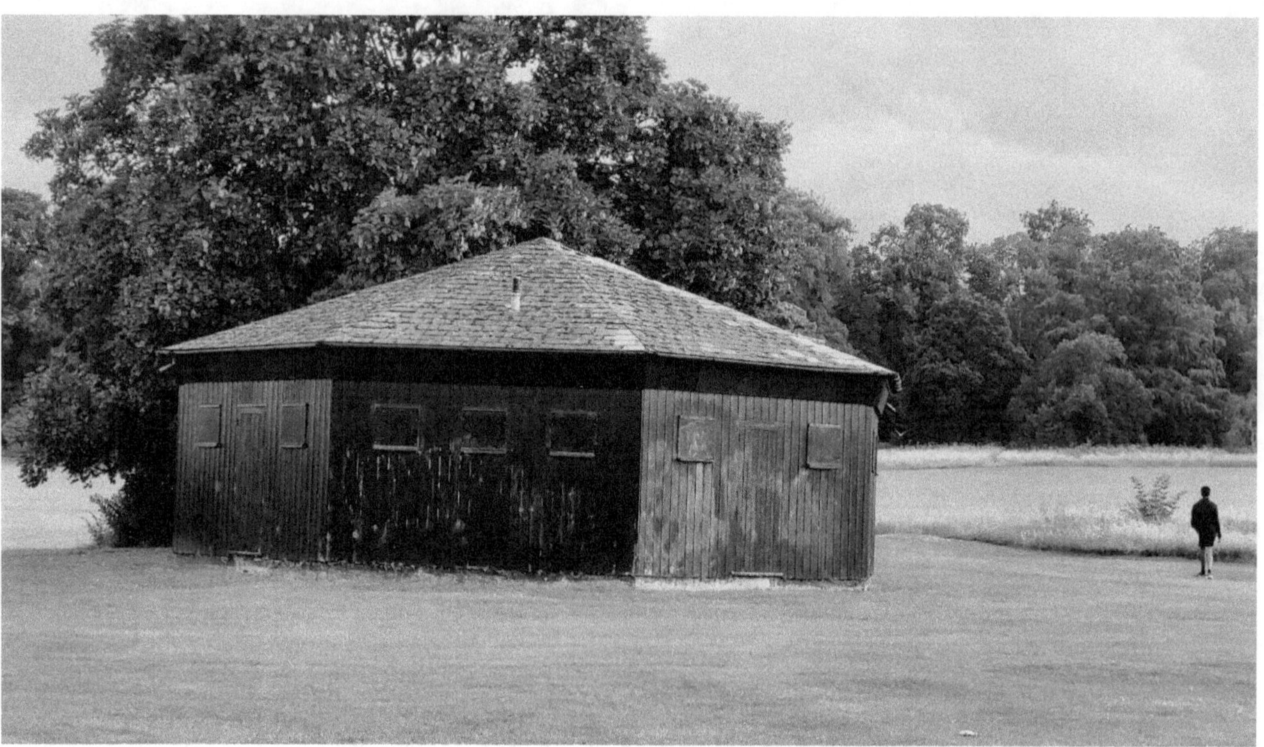

Image 99: Hexagonal

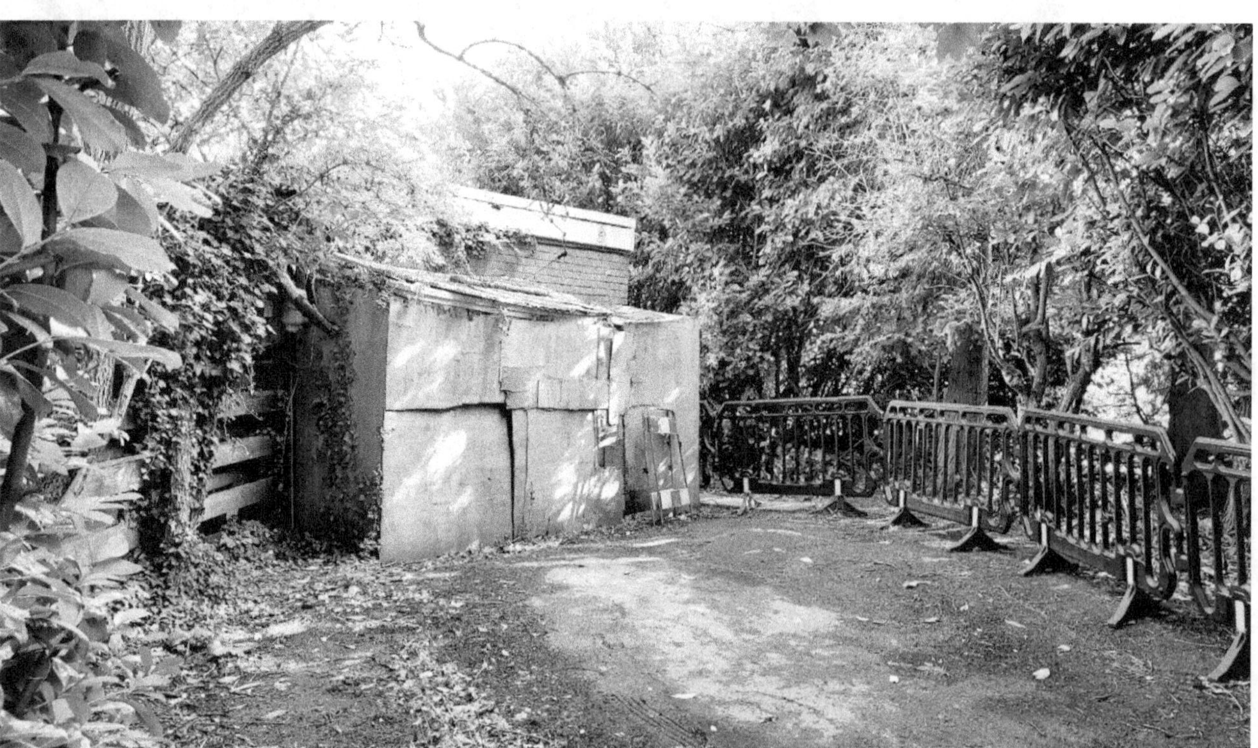

Image 100: Derelict

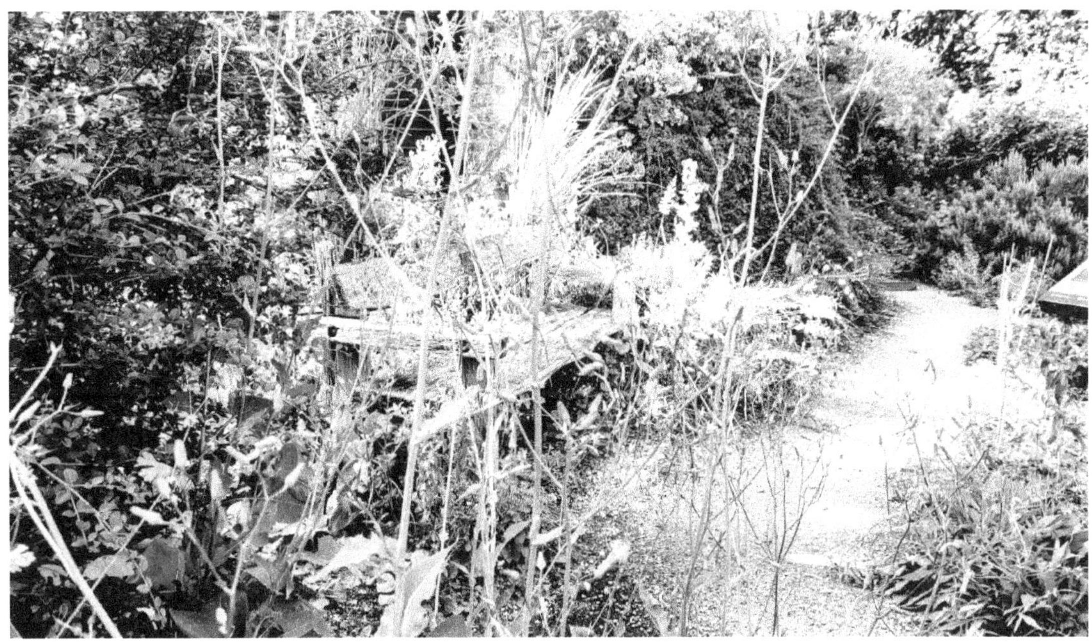

Image 101: Creaking

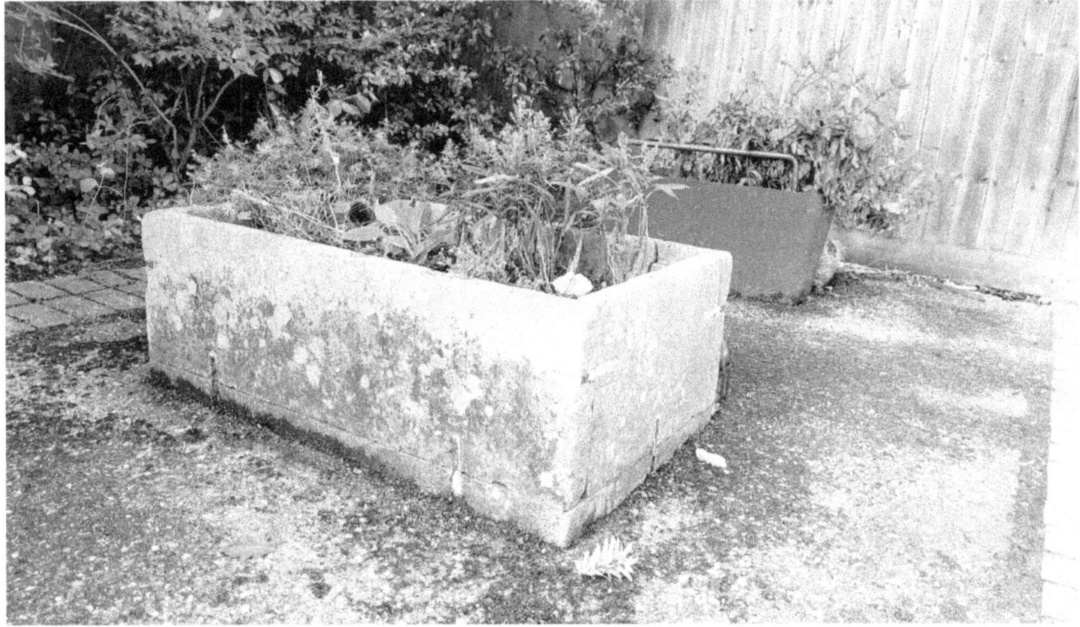

Image 102: Font of all knowledge

A pair of grotesques provide *Images 103 and 104*. These were taken inside Ely Cathedral, in the county of Cambridgeshire. A grotesque is a fantastic or mythical figure used for decorative purposes. In the Middle Ages, these types of babewyn were quite common. Both of these grotesques so signs of erosion, which adds to their character.

Image 105 is of some steps leading to an overgrown and unkempt wooded area. To go to the top of these only leads to thick overgrowth, mostly nettles and thorns. This belies the attractive look of the steps and lush light that illuminates the base.

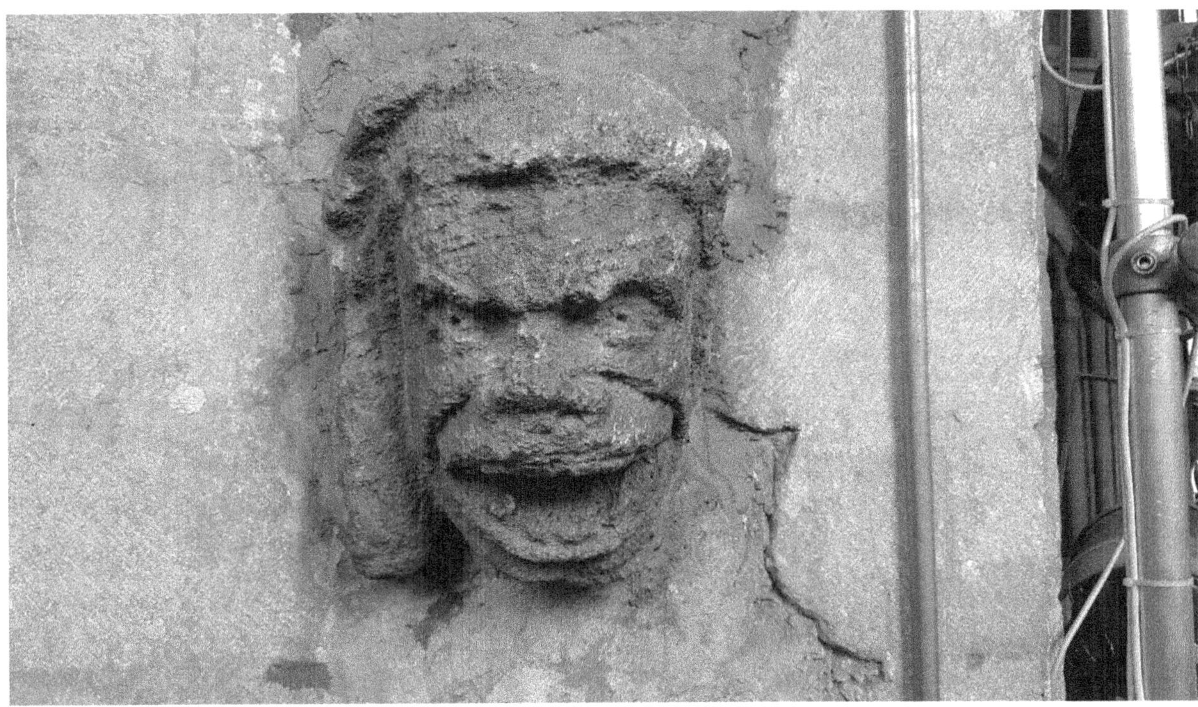

Image 103: Smile for the camera

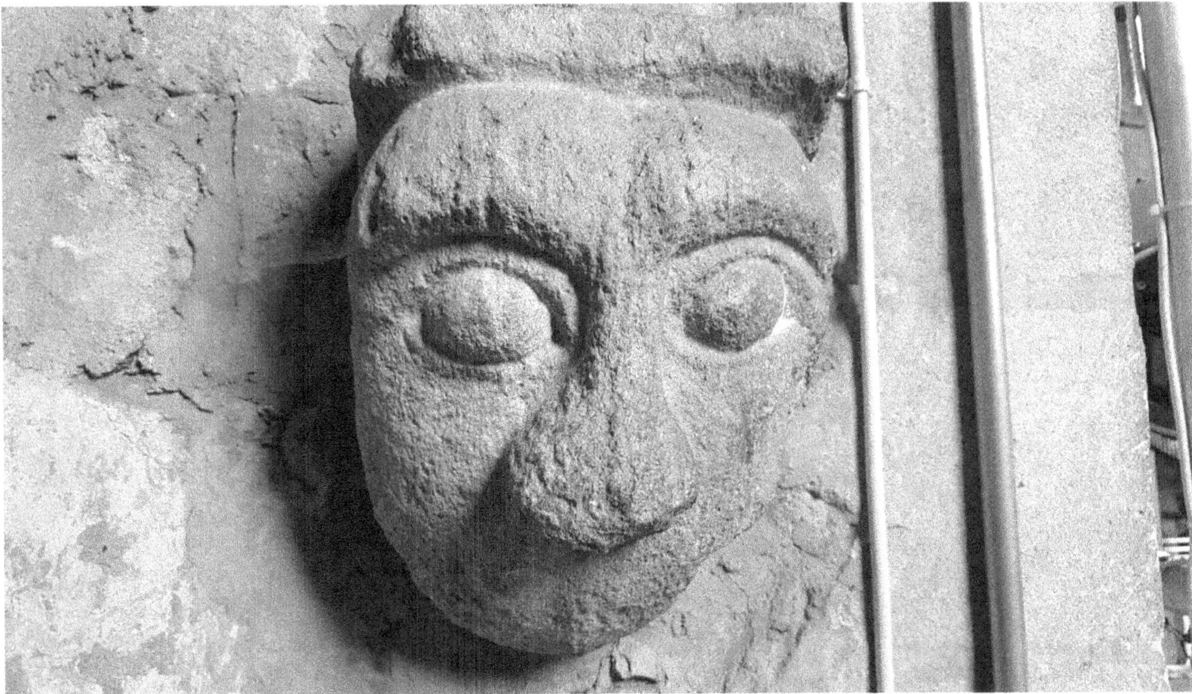

Image 104: The smile has eroded.

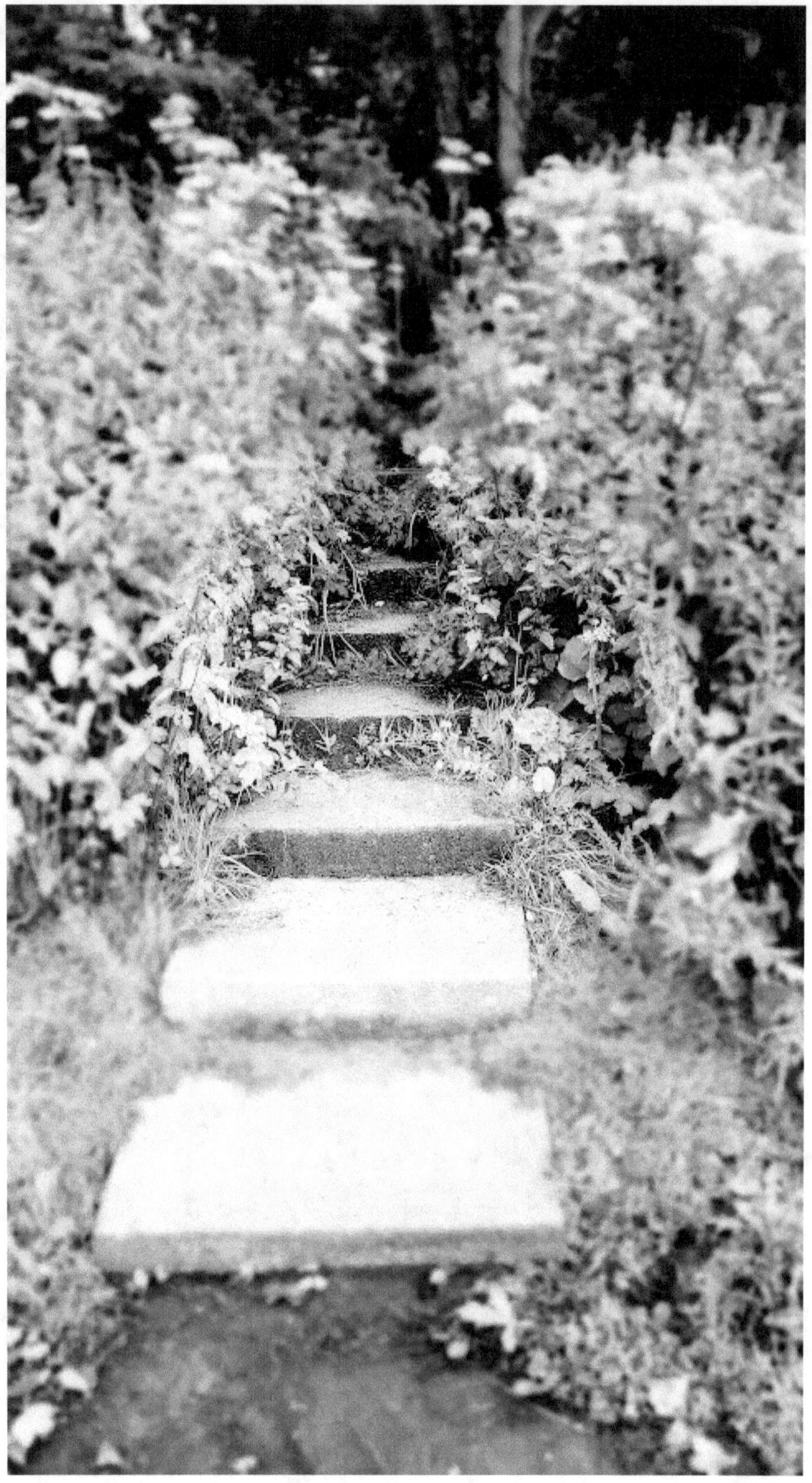

Image 105: The unkempt steps

An old section of garden, untouched for some ten years, forms *Image 106*, an old pot, gravel and a grotesque weathering away.

A seven-arched brick bridge which carries Barnet Road over the river Colne is shown in *Image 107*. Whether it should be in this book is debatable as the upper section – the road – remains in use. However, parts of the lower section are blocked off and on this basis I've decided to include it. The bridge is called Telford's Bridge and it was completed in 1774.

A coal tax post is shown in *Image 108* (this one is from Hertfordshire). Coal-tax posts are boundary marker posts found in southern England. They were erected in the 1860s and form an irregular loop between 12 and 18 miles from London to mark the points where taxes on coal were due to the Corporation of London. These posts were cast by Henry Grissell at his Regents Canal iron works and originally 280 were cast.

Some old looking bottles (that are not particularly old) are shown in *Image 109*. The wax-seal capped whiskies have long been drunk and left on a shelf. They remind me of potions ready for a passing wizard.

Winter descends on a poorly maintained urban garden, as *Image 110* reveals. The effect of the frost and the combination of light create an enchanting picture. What lies ahead?

The final photograph is of a building that no longer exists, it has since been demolished. The brick and iron structure shown in *Image 111* was located on the Napsbury estate in Hertfordshire.

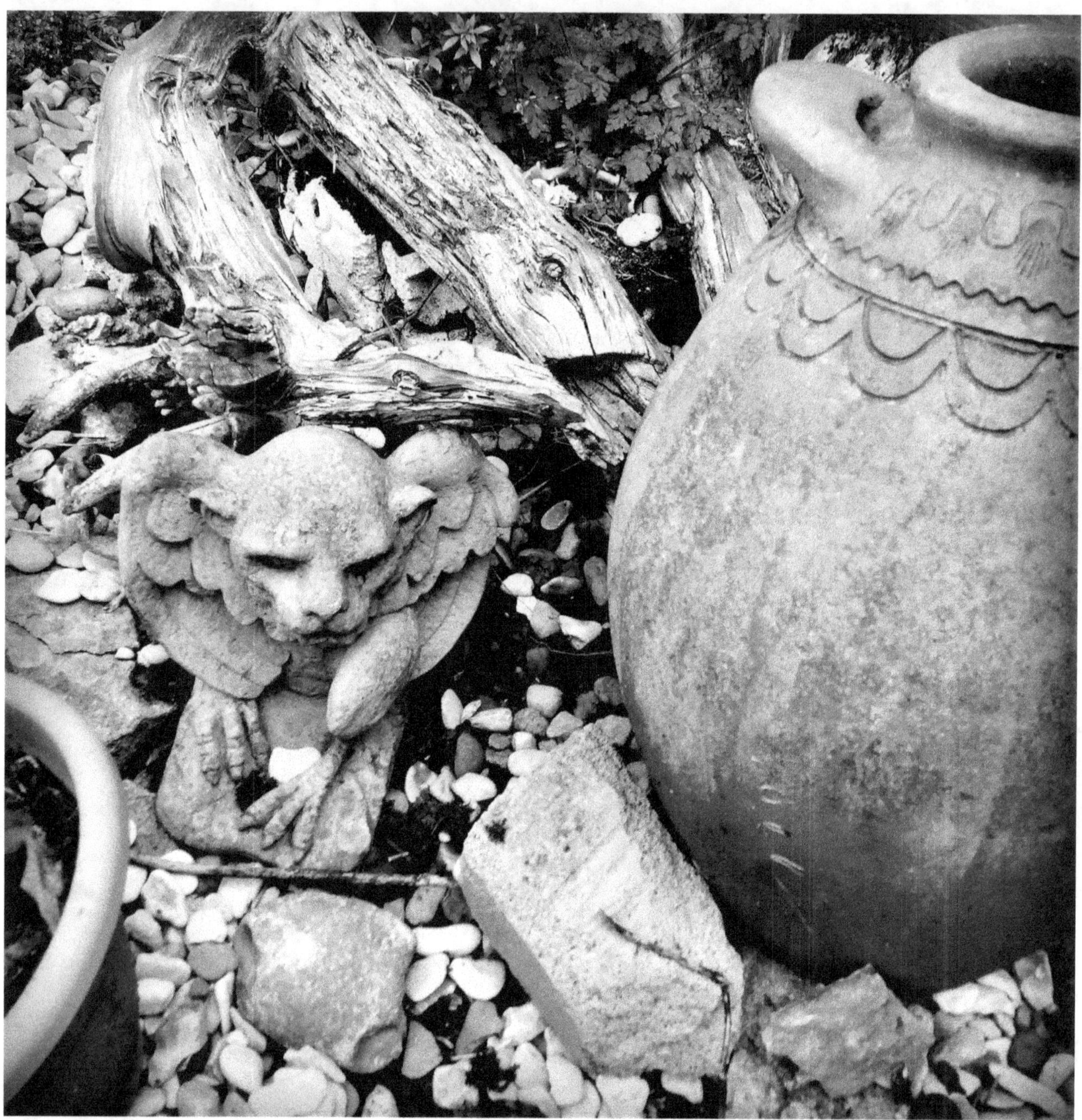

Image 106: The old garden

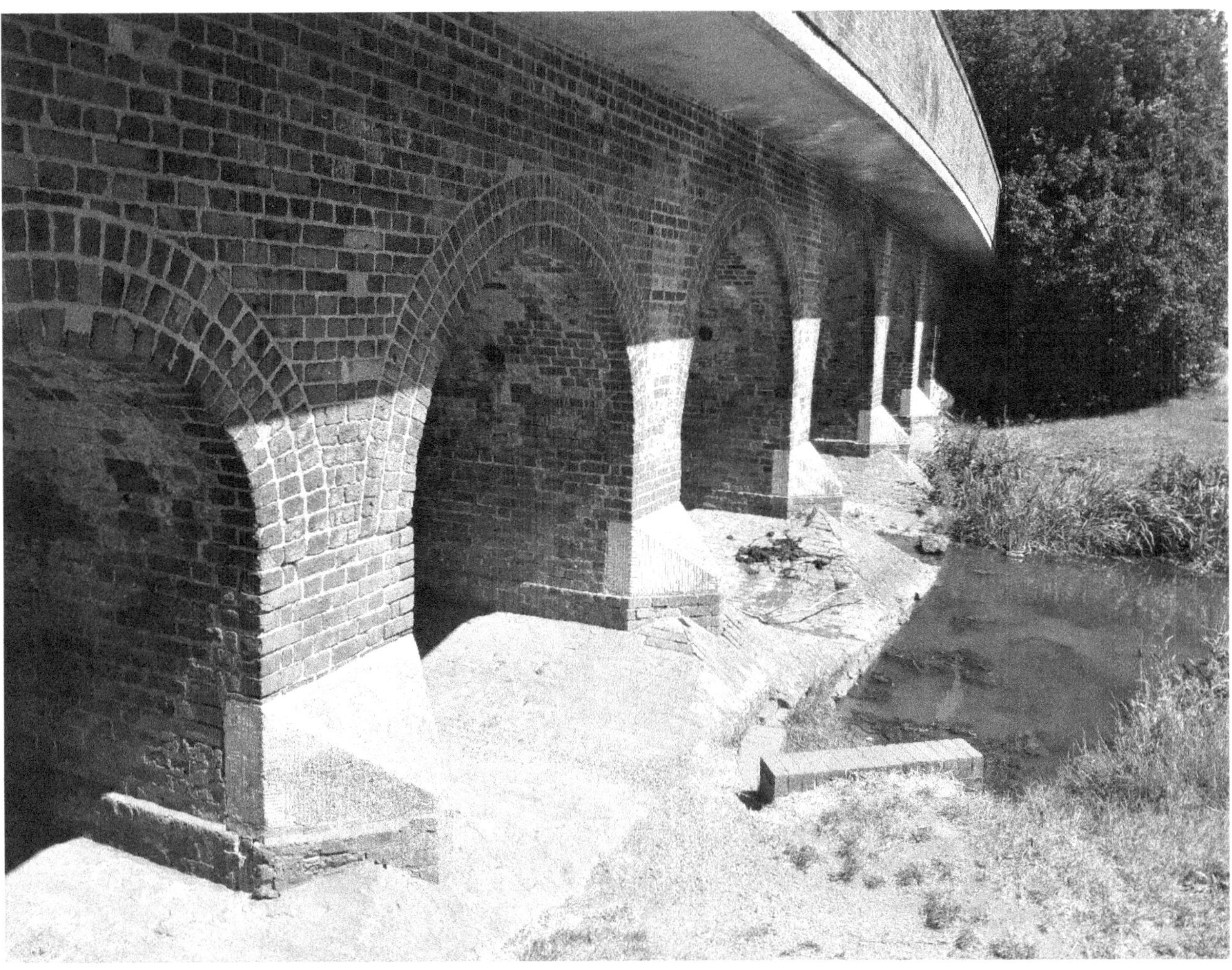

Image 107: Telford's Bridge

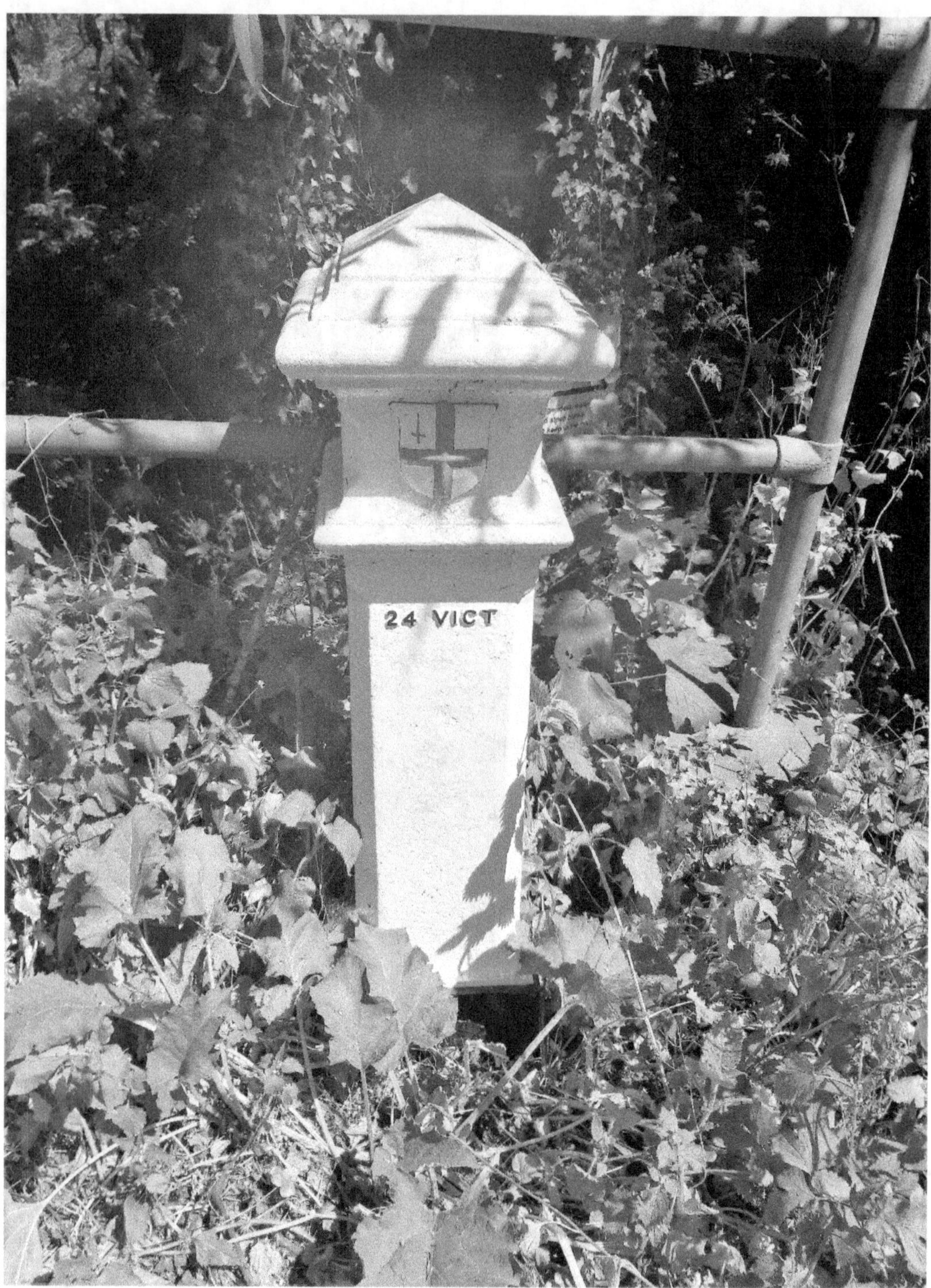

Image 108: Coal post

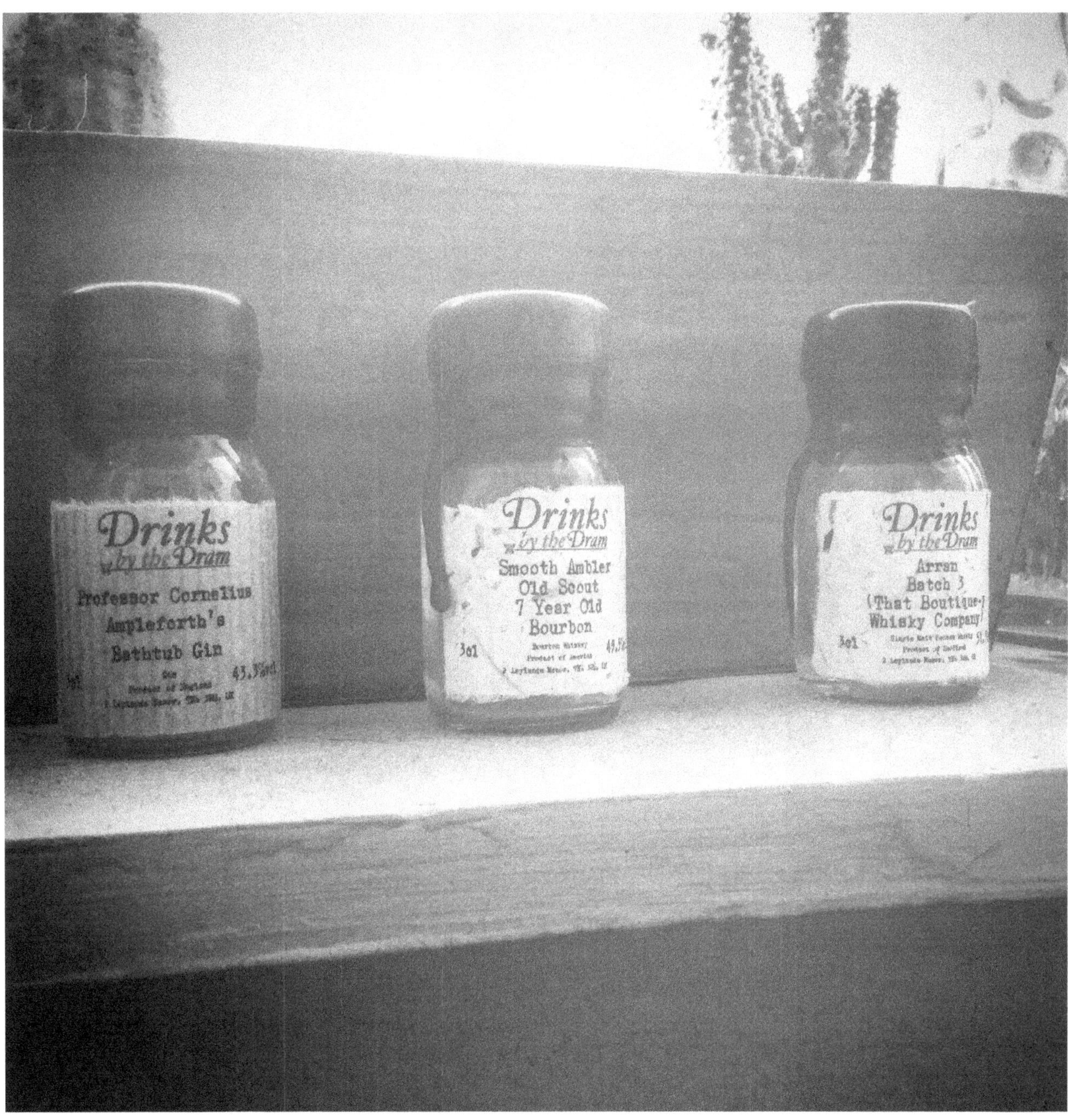

Image 109: Old looking bottles

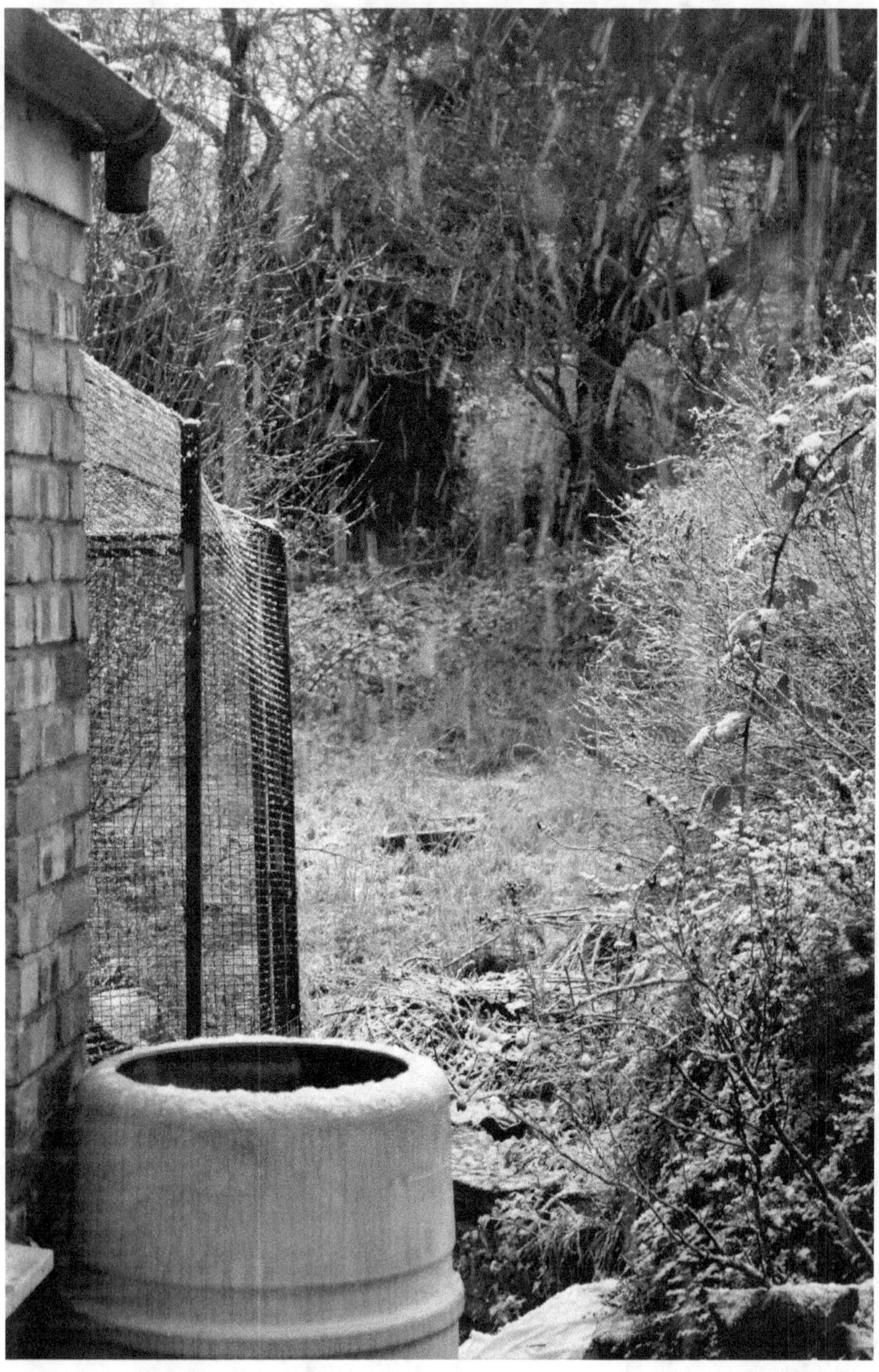

Image 110: Going wild in the winter

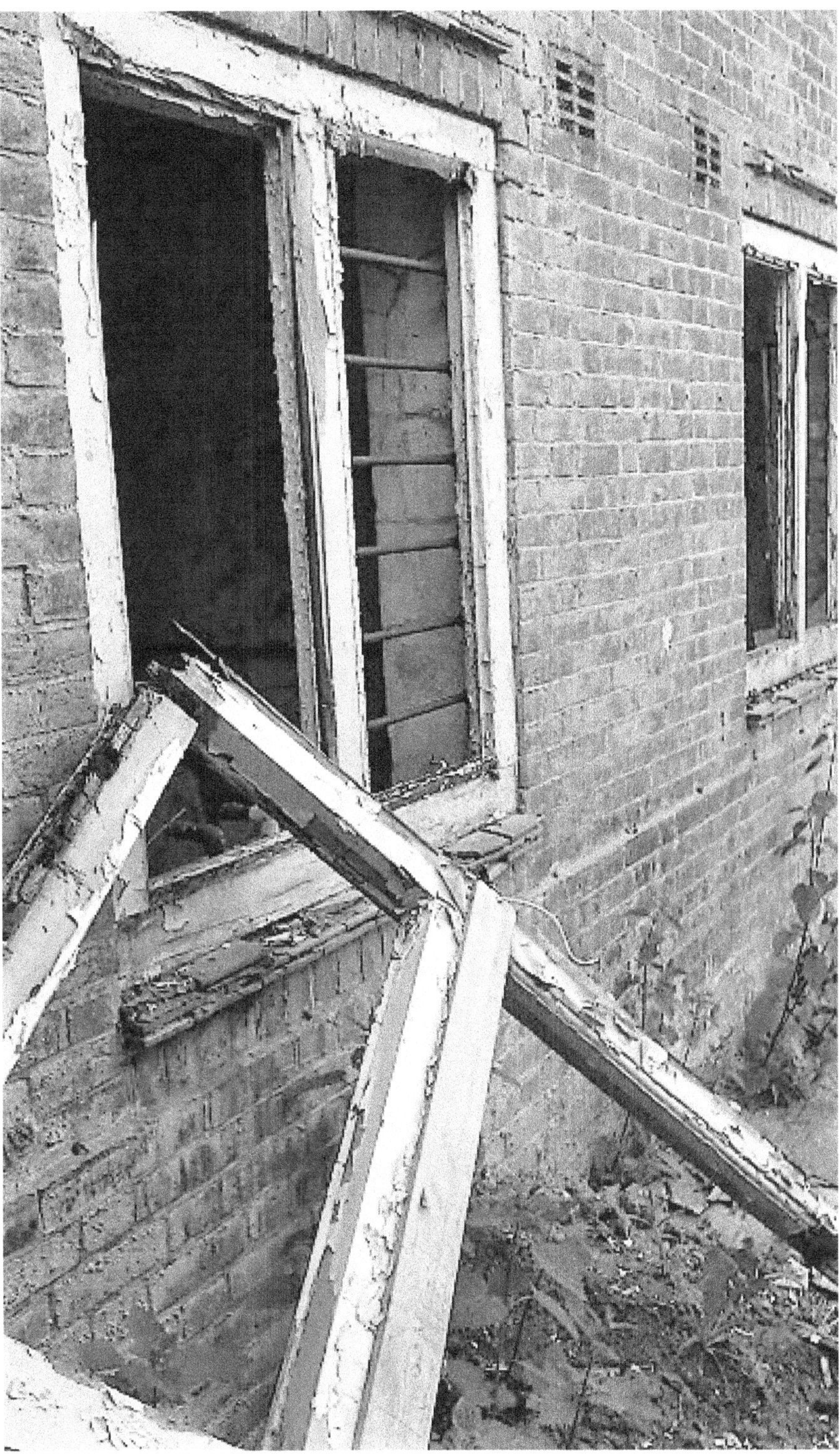

Image 111: Crumbling

ABOUT THE AUTHOR

Tim Sandle is a microbiologist by profession. He is also an author and a journalist. He lives in Hertfordshire. This is his first photography book.

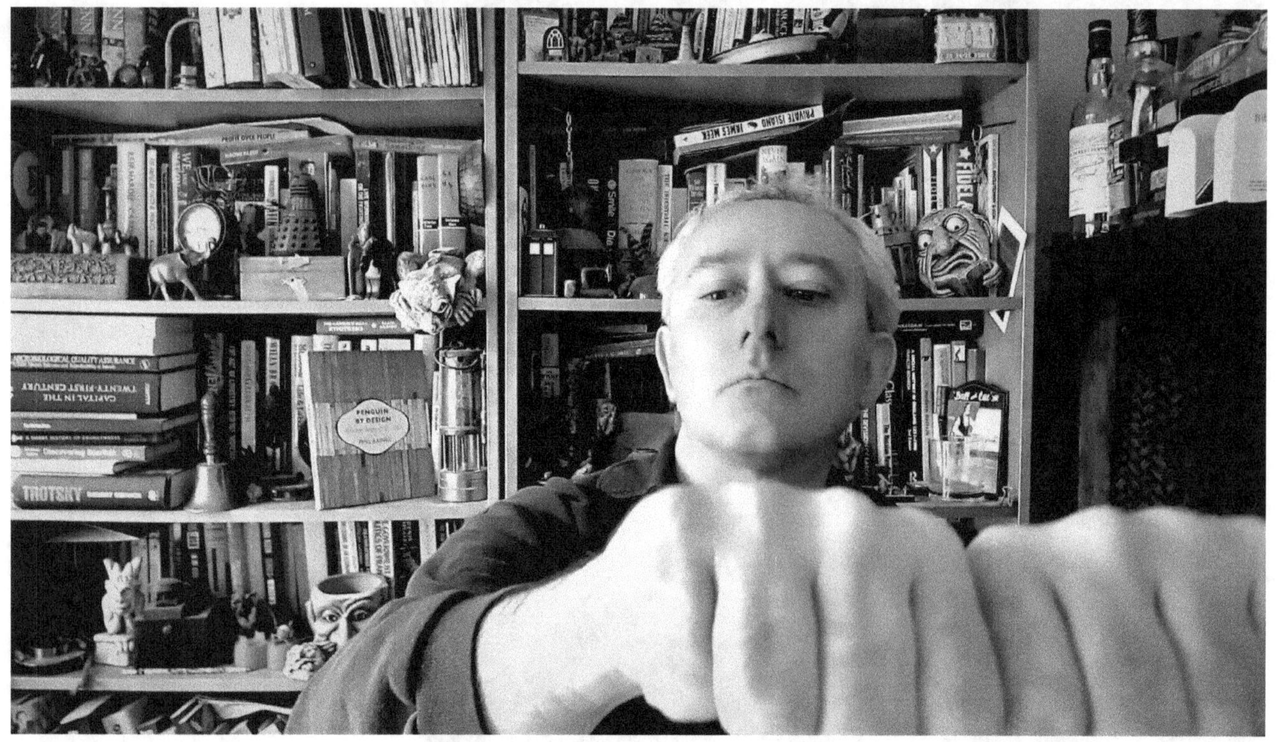

www.timsandle.com